Conflict and Sustainability in a Changing Environment

Anthem Environment and Sustainability Initiative (AESI)

The Anthem Environment and Sustainability Initiative (AESI) seeks to push the frontiers of scholarship while simultaneously offering prescriptive and programmatic advice to policymakers and practitioners around the world. The programme publishes research monographs, professional and major reference works, upper-level textbooks and general interest titles. Professor Lawrence Susskind, as General Editor of AESI, oversees the below book series, each with its own series editor and an editorial board featuring scholars, practitioners and business experts keen to link theory and practice.

Anthem Strategies for Sustainable Development Series
Series Editor: Professor Lawrence Susskind (MIT)

Anthem Climate Change and Policy Series
Series Editor: Dr. Brooke Hemming (US EPA)

Anthem Diplomacy at the Food-Water-Energy Nexus Series
Series Editor: Professor Shafi qul Islam (Tufts University)

Anthem International Environmental Policy Series
Series Editor: Professor Saleem Ali (University of Delaware)

Anthem Big Data and Sustainable Cities Series
Series Editor: Sarah Williams (MIT)

Included within the AESI is the Anthem EnviroExperts Review. Through this online micro-review site, Anthem Press seeks to build a community of practice involving scientists, policy analysts and activists committed to creating a clearer and deeper understanding of how ecological systems – at every level – operate, and how they have been damaged by unsustainable development. This site publishes short reviews of important books or reports in the environmental field, broadly defined. Visit the site: www.anthemenviroexperts.com.

Conflict and Sustainability in a Changing Environment

Through the Eyes of Communities

Gwendolyn Smith

and

Elena P. Bastidas

ANTHEM PRESS

Anthem Press
An imprint of Wimbledon Publishing Company
www.anthempress.com

This edition first published in UK and USA 2019
by ANTHEM PRESS
75–76 Blackfriars Road, London SE1 8HA, UK
or PO Box 9779, London SW19 7ZG, UK
and
244 Madison Ave #116, New York, NY 10016, USA

First published in the UK and USA by Anthem Press 2017

British Library Cataloguing-in-Publication Data
A catalogue record for this book is available from the British Library.

Library of Congress Cataloging-in-Publication Data
A catalog record for this book has been requested.

ISBN-13: 978-1-78527-127-4 (Pbk)
ISBN-10: 1-78527-127-X (Pbk)

This title is also available as an e-book.

CONTENTS

List of Illustrations   vii

Preface   ix

Acknowledgments   xiii

1. Introduction: Local Communities and Sustainable Development   1
    Views of Sustainable Development   6
    Communities under New Pressure   18
    Contents of the Book   25

2. Researching Views in Community Development   27
    Researching Community Views: Existing Frameworks   27
    Researching Views through Conflict-Resolution Frameworks   37

3. New Framework for Researching Views in Community Development   47
    Construction of a Community View   47
    The Life Story: Values, Meanings and Sustainable Decisions   50
    The VIEW Framework   57

4. Social Polygraphy: An Approach to Obtaining Information
    through Mutual Learning   67
    What Is Social Polygraphy?   67
    Theoretical, Conceptual and Methodological Basis of Social Polygraphy 68
    The "How-to" of Social Polygraphy   71
    Limitations of the Social Polygraphy Approach   80
    Alternative Forms of Communication and Mutual Learning   81

5. Exploring the Underlying Values   85
    The Trio Indigenous People   85
    Values Related to the Collective   88
    Values Related to Social Behavior   92
    Values Related to the Environment   95
    Values Related to Development   99
    Applying the VIEW Framework   104

6. Making Sense of the World 109
The Trios' Interests 110
The Rules for Survival 124
The Strategies for Adaptation 126
The Real Attitude 126
Applying the VIEW Framework 129

7. Sustainable Decisions 135
Conflicting Views 135
Decision Making under Uncertainty 142
Applying the VIEW Framework 145

8. Working with Community Views 149
Promoting Sustainability under Uncertainty 149
Bridging Differences in Views 152
Principles for Researchers and Practitioners 159
A Message for Policy Makers 168

References 171

Index 185

ILLUSTRATIONS

Figures

1.1 Countries with high forest cover (>50%) and low deforestation rates (<0.22%/year)   24
2.1 The system for nature-dependent communities   34
3.1 The community view during climate change   49
3.2 Bottom-up and top-down processes for analyzing a community's view   56
3.3 VIEW framework: The process for view construction under social and environmental change   58
4.1 People from the community of Robles drawing maps   74
4.2 A young Afro-Colombian woman presenting the map constructed by her group   75
4.3 Map showing what things, relations and processes the community would like to make disappear, conserve and make appear in the future   77
5.1 The Amazon rain forest and its boundaries   86
5.2 Local place names in the Trio territory near the village of Kwamalasamutu   88
5.3 The Trio indigenous peoples   90
5.4 The village of Kwamalasamutu   97
5.5 A typical indigenous family from South Suriname   99
5.6 Indigenous ranger post in the village of Kwamalasamutu   100
5.7 Values held by the Trio indigenous peoples across the dimensions of sustainable development   107
6.1 The predictor Poko Poko   115
6.2 The predictor Ëkui aki   116
6.3 The nuance indicator Akanopatoro   117
6.4 The nuance indicator Marakau   118
6.5 The soil health indicator Karau Alawata   119
6.6 The forest health indicator Tamo   120
6.7 The sensitivity indicator Kuweimë   121

6.8   Subsistence plots on hillsides as an adaptation strategy   127
6.9   A Trio man and woman working on cognitive maps   130
6.10 Meaning of climate change generated by the Trio
      indigenous peoples   133
7.1   Trio leader participating in the national negotiations   144
7.2   View of the Trio indigenous peoples on climate change
      analyzed with the VIEW framework   147
8.1   Model for collaboration of Trio indigenous peoples
      in REDD+ projects based on view differences   158

Tables

3.1   Information and tools required for analysis with
      the VIEW framework   59
6.1   Organization of information for understanding the process
      of meaning making using the VIEW framework. A case
      study of the Trio indigenous peoples   110
6.2   Names of seasonal indicators used by the Trio indigenous
      peoples to detect local climate change   112
7.1   Overview of the conflicting goals and issues between
      the Trio indigenous peoples and development organization
      in REDD+ projects   137

PREFACE

The green blanket of rain forest seemed never ending until our small, five-person airplane landed in the middle of nowhere, a place full of stilted wooden huts, covered with thatch leaves, playfully situated. The place was called Kwamalasamutu, an indigenous village named after the many bamboo bushes and sandy heaps near an elegantly flowing river. It was my first time so deep in the Amazon rain forest. My mission was to prepare medicines from forest plants together with the nature-dependent group of indigenous peoples called the Trio. After learning a few words of the local language, discussions about my sustainable development project started—with goals, activities, outcomes and indicators. When I explained that they had to collect plants from the forest and cook them into a bottled end product, the Trios were sitting around me, listening attentively and nodding their heads without saying too much.

Trading bottles of herbal medicine to markets outside the village suggested that the Trios could enjoy a steady income, which would also provide precious jobs for the next generation of Trios. A few weeks after my initial explanation about the project, I noticed the Trios hesitating to collect any medicinal plants. I tried to explain the goal and activities once more in my attempt to be clearer than before in my communication with them. Untiringly I kept explaining without receiving a positive response, until I realized there was a discrepancy between my view of sustainability and that of the Trios. And then it struck me: what was I going to teach these people about sustainability in their own journey? The truth was that I could only learn from them.

The Trios have been living in the Amazonian rain forest for an estimated period of 4,900 years. Generations of Trios have been known for their ingenuity in adaptation to and caretaking of their surrounding environment. Resource strategies have always been developed out of past experiences. Failure dictates which strategies these indigenous peoples will choose going forward. Their most important goal is to transfer the useful knowledge to future generations so they can nourish and sustain the forest that supplies their livelihood. Only trading herbal medicines does not fit within this Trio goal.

My quest to understand how indigenous peoples think about sustainability had started. During my observations and interactions with indigenous groups I have seen that the complexity of the view comes alive when an indigenous community experiences an incompatibility with its surroundings. The community seems to exist in a conflict. The conflict with small-scale gold miners, animal traders or other (illegal) groups that are likely to compete with indigenous peoples for resources is well known. The conflict caused by uncertainty in services generated by the environment, for example, when indigenous groups experience food scarcity because of climate change, is less obvious. Community members become tense and are clueless about what to decide for the future because they have never encountered environmental phenomena before. In this state of panic, communities are more likely to show and say what they really think or want. Soon they convey their underlying interest, their *real view*. Understanding how they deal with conflict is, thus, a necessary part of understanding the community's view for a sustainable future in a changing environment.

This book builds on theories of conflict resolution to lay the groundwork for a different understanding of the community's view. With this new approach I seek to gain insight into their decision making and how they delicately craft a path toward development while experiencing climate change. The information in this book is the result of more than twenty years of experience of working closely with several indigenous tribes in South America. The mutual trust and respect gained over the years offered an uncommon and unique insight for a Western-trained researcher like me. My understanding of the view of organizations that initiate development was obtained from leading a not-for-profit organization since 2004. Operating within this realm taught me valuable lessons on how communities are viewed as partners in development. It is from this experience that many of my comments and reflections are being shared in this book. Numerous ideas were complemented by my coauthor, Elena Bastidas, who relies on more than a decade of experience partnering with Afro-Colombian communities in their journey toward sustainable development. Elena has shared her valuable insights on research practice in the chapter titled "Social Polygraphy: An Approach to Obtaining Information through Mutual Learning" in this book.

Examination of research over the last five years demonstrates an increasing interest in looking at development through the eyes of communities that have lived in serenity and harmony with forests for hundreds of years. Such noteworthy research focuses on finding novel ways to collaborate with these communities particularly at the local level (Ife 2013; Lejano et al. 2011; Petheram et al. 2012; Sheppard et al. 2011). Independent researchers soon noticed that, however, community views are routinely fit into the scope of the modern development paradigm (Hulme 2010; Hall 2012), which leads to unsustainable outcomes and increasingly to unsuccessful development projects.

Sustainable development seems to proceed along an array of multiple drivers and stressors. To manage this enormous complexity, the book presents a systematic process to *analyze the view* of a community when progressing through the different stages of development under changing environmental conditions. My motivation in writing this book is to present a methodology for researchers and practitioners to break away from a positivist stance into one that involves working alongside communities as equal partners. The analytical framework discussed in this book can serve as a guide for scholars and practitioners to understand the divergent and unique local context in which communities make decisions. The readers can choose from a set of experience-based tools that they can use in helping communities succeed in sustainable development initiatives after obtaining a greater understanding of the dynamics occurring at the local level.

ACKNOWLEDGMENTS

This book is the result of my many journeys with knowledgeable indigenous groups and local communities living in the tropical rain forests in South America. It is only after years of dwelling among these "primitive" societies that my full learning cycle was fulfilled, and after reading this book you will understand what I mean. I could not have completed this life-changing experience without the continuous support of my Trio and other indigenous teachers, university professors and colleagues as well as family and friends who have guided me with their wisdom.

Sometime during my journey, I crossed paths with Elena Bastidas. It was then that my perspective on conflict and development matured and the journey started to have a different meaning. Our lengthy and inspiring conversations about the integration of research in community development, conflict and environment are the source from which this book sprouted. I sincerely want to thank Elena for her significant contribution to this book as an author and reviewer. It is not only her friendship that added to my journey but also the fact that she is one of the few people who deeply care about ethically sound research, the faith of local communities and the future of our planet.

In my journey of learning about the theory and practice of conflict analysis and resolution, I have had the privilege of participating in excellent lectures and receiving guidance from the teachers and mentors at Nova Southeastern University. They have given me insights and tools to conduct this research. It might be surprising to the reader that, in fact, most of my lessons on conflict resolution were given by the Trio indigenous peoples. They have taught me to look at life with different eyes, filled with faith, peace and sustainability. My gratitude goes out to the Trio chief, Ashongo Alalaparoe, for accepting me into the Trio family and treating me with wise, often metaphoric, words in our private conversations.

This book would not be possible without Trio rangers, with whom I closely worked in the gathering and processing of data on climate change and forests. My Western understanding of climate change gradually transformed after walking in the forest and having numerous conversations with them about traditional knowledge. My gratitude goes out to Tedde Shikoei, Siesikia Ashikawara, Ketrin Jami, Napoti Pantodina, Sheina Odeppe, Aritakose Asheja and Jonathan Sapa for their persistence during three years of data gathering and processing. I also want to express my appreciation for my dear indigenous friends Wuta Wajimnu, Puuru "Korotai" Puumona, Mohapi Koeki, Amashina Oedemmaloe and Taita Luciano for sharing their valuable knowledge and taking care of me physically and spiritually. Thanks to Nuta Toetsi for translating the languages spoken by the subtribes in Kwamalasamutu. I give special thanks to Japoma, the founder of the village of Kwamalasamutu, who, regrettably, left us in October 2011.

I want to express my gratitude to the Amazon Conservation Team (ACT), which supported my research with logistical support in the field, particularly my being able to stay at the field camp and using the dugout to pass through the forest. The case study research described in this book was supported with financial assistance provided by the African, Caribbean and Pacific Group of States (ACP) and the European Union (EU) under the EU-ACP project "Establishment of a Forestry Research Network for ACP Countries" (9 ACP RPR 91#1- FORENET).

Special thanks to my colleagues who have provided valuable support to the research: Mark Plotkin for determination of scientific plant names; Melvin Uiterloo for support in GIS mapmaking; Jupta Itoewaki and Natasha Kromokarijo for helping with the entry of interview data; Karin Lachmising for inspiring talks about combining study, work and motherhood; Katia Delvoye and Rachelle Bong A Jan for reviewing the climate change indicator descriptions; Rashida Alibux for transcribing part of the interviews; Santusha Pengel for managing my dissertation grant; Eric Sosrojoedo for field logistics; Sahieda Joemratie for helping in the climate change field mapping; the National Zoological Collection and the National Herbarium of Suriname for identifying animal and plant species; and last but not least Kenneth "Skapie" Wongsonadi for gathering the geographical positions of the climate change indicators. Also a sincere word of gratitude to other experts who have aided in the formatting and editing of this book: Pam Okosun, Nigel Sanitt, David Stone and Marlies Koorndijk.

My particular gratitude goes to my family. Their support started in 1993 when my grandmother, Esseline Ligeon, gave me financial resources, crucial for starting my academic career. A special thanks to my father, Sierd Smith, mother, Ellen Naarendorp, who taught me many valuable things, of which conceptual thinking, justice and ethics became the leading concepts in my research. Thanks to my brother, Oliver Smith, for always having a listening ear and giving subtle, but positive, remarks on my journey. His spouse, Edme Smith—thank you for mastering the graphic design for this book. Most importantly, a sincere thanks to my supportive daughter, Charmaine Emanuels. Many days away from home for letting me live my dream would not have been possible without her trust and unconditional love.

Chapter 1

INTRODUCTION: LOCAL COMMUNITIES AND SUSTAINABLE DEVELOPMENT

The concept of sustainable development has been debated for decades now. Although the definition of development has been a major area of controversy, certain characteristics were evident early on. After World War II, when the world was struggling with extreme poverty, food scarcity and chronic diseases, development initiatives were commonly defined in terms of socioeconomic structural transformation in pursuit of economic growth, and the objective was to create improved conditions for people existing in a precarious state and to provide better health care, education and job opportunities. This typical model of development was well accepted during the mid- to late 1940s because people were looking for a way to move out of the deplorable conditions in which they existed. The promise was Émile Durkheim's concept of a scenically modern, technologically advanced society (Ritzer 2008). In this sense, development implies a clean transformation from a starting point, a state that is not preferred, to an end point or a desired state. The 1940s change process was accompanied by the establishment of the now leading development agencies such as the World Bank, United Nations Development Program and many others (Hulse 2007). Such multilateral institutions developed a variety of global programs and worked intensely with governments to implement them at the national and local levels.

By 1972, the concept of sustainability was formally introduced, as it pertained to development at the United Nations Conference on the Human Environment held in Stockholm, Sweden. The question of maintaining sustainability in the wider context of economic growth and development was being contested: how can the rate of economic growth be maintained with earth's finite resources? Although the discussion commenced, however, it didn't gain momentum for the course to change. The development strategies employed at that time continued until the well-known environmental conventions were adopted by the world's nations in Rio de Janeiro in 1992. The undivided motivation for this agreement was the massive pollution coming from factories that contaminated water sources and soils—yes, ironically, the same factories that had provided advancement in jobs and income after World War II. The pollution was soon perceived as an invisible killer surrounding and affecting everyone. Yet instead of tackling the source of the problem, that of growing industrialization and human consumption, the world decided to draw a new portrait of sustainable development.

The most common definition of sustainable development is the one coined by the Brundtland Commission in 1987: "sustainable development is development that meets the needs of the present without compromising the ability of future generations to meet their own needs" (Brundtland 1987, 41). In the general sense, sustainable development is a process of progressing toward a combination of economic, social and environmental goals that at the same time seeks to eliminate poverty, strengthens local governance and protects the environment from overuse of resources by humans.

The new global goal was to take good care of our environment. The Rio conventions were the first essential step toward lessening the use of fossil fuels and the corresponding global warming (United Nations Framework Convention on Climate Change), toward protecting our ecosystems that provide us with food and many other goods and services (United Nations Convention on Biological Diversity) and toward preventing massive deforestation and alterations of landscapes (United Nations Convention on Combat Desertification). After this time, sustainable development was generally understood to have three dimensions. The first two, social and economic, were inherited from the post–World War II era, while the third dimension—environment—was a new reality. The three dimensions made up the new desired state: economic and social advancement without the overexploitation of resources that would cause future environmental problems.

So where do we stand with sustainable development in current times? To answer this question, I try to identify the change process, and how people are proceeding from the so-called undesired state into the desired state. Compared to the situation in the 1940s, more than 80 percent of the world's estimated seven billion people possess a certain comfort level by living on more than $10 a day and, thus, there is a lack of a specific or well-defined, confined state from which people want to escape (Rahim et al. 2014).

An essential question is to understand what the desired state has become. Sovereign countries seem to be in a race to expand the economy as fast as possible so they can keep up with the swiftly growing demand of citizens for energy, jobs, health care, education and, let us not forget, luxury. The majority of the world's citizens wish to encourage the use of technology not only to achieve significant wealth but also to easily solve environmental problems. Yet these advanced technological solutions, such as wind and solar power generators, only seem to address environmental problems for the short term in times of growing human consumption patterns (Ife 2013). For now, such technologies are just a quick fix and dubiously contribute to global sustainability, mainly because the root cause of excessive human consumption remains unaddressed.

Today, people also tend to feel less accountable for global development. They are more and more comfortable in delegating their human and environmental responsibility to their respective governments and locally operating development organizations. And these bodies, in turn, appear increasingly to hand over their tasks to global forums and networks (Habermas n.d.). What makes the issue much more complicated is that dialogues on a global level have become quite inflexible so that they no longer deliver the expected results. In the negotiations on climate change, for example, the participating countries deliberated six more years, following the meeting held in Copenhagen in 2009, to approve an agreement on greenhouse gas pollution in Paris (Smith 2010b).

Putting sustainable development into a so-called paradigm of economic growth also led to a change in its definition. This means that the formerly agreed-upon understanding of sustainable development has scattered into different fields and disciplines. Novel and rising concepts such as "sustainable mining" have suddenly emerged. This type of mining employs practices to reduce the use of pollutants, reduce water and energy consumption and minimize land change and waste generation (Fraser Institute 2012). It means reducing the environmental impact, while extractive mining is known as being a priori one of the most devastating practices to the environment. Another example is the concept of climate-compatible development, which means a type of "development that minimises the harm caused by climate impacts, while maximising the many human development opportunities presented by a low emissions, more resilient, future" (Mitchell and Maxwell 2010, 1). The designers of this concept apparently made, hopefully subconsciously, the environmental goal subordinate to the economic goal.

Thus, as demonstrated here, it is very difficult to understand what sustainable development means today. It seems to be operating on two distinct levels. On the global level, there are intense negotiations over global policies for mitigating all sorts of pressing economic, social and environmental problems. Here governments are, somewhat paternalistically, deciding what sustainable development should include and how it should be implemented by all the nations in the world. The second level of sustainable development operates locally and is more directed toward the one billion poor people living on less than $1 a day (Rahim et al. 2014). It aims to structurally align these less fortunate people with the system created and supported by global policies. But this goal may be far-fetched. Pessimists say that greater social and economic inequality is now seen as compared to 20 years ago, while optimists observe a gradual but steady improvement in poverty levels (Rahim et al. 2014). Although there is no explicit consensus on the causes and magnitude of inequality, there are still many people without food, water, housing and sufficient health care in this world. And the environmental problems have notably expanded, especially global warming, which is now the biggest threat to life on earth.

It is not surprising that there has been a strong and urgent call for new approaches to sustainable development since the Rio+20 world conference held in 2012.[1] The call comes from indigenous peoples who are seeking development opportunities at the local level. These groups, currently living in 22 percent of the global land area, successfully protect more than 80 percent of the world's plants and animals (Nakashima et al. 2012). They have noticed an immense intensification of resource use leading to overexploitation of the world's ecosystems, and are worried that this will cause problems with sustaining life on earth (see the Kari-Oca2 Declaration, United Nations 2011).

Indigenous peoples argue for a more holistic approach to development. Instead of implementing a development process from the modern economic perspective, they propose using more cultural-appropriate methodologies that have the right values and ethics to take care of the environment (Tebtebba 2012). These distinguished peoples promote a development model that goes hand in hand with the conservation of nature and its resources. With this ambitious model of "development with conservation," they foresee a more organic practice of social change characterized by a slow process along a broad set of social structures in society.

Indigenous peoples have often been thought of as natural conservationists because they seem to protect the forest more effectively than any other group in the world.[2] A tight connection with nature is generally perceived by indigenous peoples as a part of their existence, and animals, plants and other elements in the system are seen as equals (Pierotti 2011). Each indigenous group

---

1 United Nations Conference on Sustainable Development.
2 No common definition of indigenous peoples exists. The definition of indigenous peoples is derived from the ILO 169 convention, the United Nations, and other studies. In this definition, indigenous peoples are peoples who identify themselves as indigenous peoples and are, at the individual level, accepted as members of their community. They have a historical continuity or association with a given region or port of a given region prior to colonization; they have strong links to territories and surrounding natural processes; they maintain, at least in part, distinct social and political systems; they maintain, at least in part, distinct languages, cultures, beliefs and knowledge systems; they are resolved to maintain and further develop their identity and distinct social, economic, cultural and political institutions as distinct peoples and communities; and they form nondominant sectors of society (United Nations 2004).

has a traditional knowledge system, some more extensive than others, which allows them to survive in the forest and exist independently from mainstream society. Their all-embracing knowledge system is direct evidence of hundreds of years of interaction with the environment, amid influences coming from modern cultures.

There also is evidence that indigenous groups have substantially destroyed the environment they once inhabited. Because each group faces challenges specific to its home environment, these groups must make livelihood choices by constantly trading off between different needs (Berkes 2008). An indigenous group that has to choose between income-earning jobs and volunteer conservation programs will likely choose the first option. Even though conservation is an intrinsic part of the indigenous life script, it will not provide the money necessary for buying popular goods such as clothes, toiletries and electronics. It is thus true that, with increasing acculturation and the introduction of technology and markets, indigenous peoples are every so often regarded as having become less harmonious with nature.

Practitioners are still learning how to align the conservation interests of indigenous peoples with development. The way indigenous peoples operate conflicts with the heavily structured cause-and-effect analysis promoted in standard development efforts. Even up until today, practitioners witness sustainable development projects that seem to lack in optimally recognizing the needs and rights of these communities. Evidence comes from projects that undermined their human rights and livelihoods through displacement and the denial of access to valuable resources (Smith 2010a). Disappointing outcomes of projects ultimately pushed some practitioners to further examine the lifestyle and the needs of indigenous communities, and so they adopted a new approach known as community-based conservation.

Community-based conservation is a strategy that became popular in the 1990s. It seeks to achieve two things simultaneously: the protection of biodiversity and the improvement of the livelihoods of indigenous communities. Throughout the years, community-based conservation has run into difficulties in the actual implementation of projects. One widely used argument is that development organizations are unwilling to share power and authority with the local community, which, in turn, results in communities with hardly any responsibilities and little accountability (Berkes 2004). The other argument is that the primary goals of development and conservation are very difficult to link at the local level because people living in nature will always have a choice between protecting the environment and deliberately using it for their livelihood. This healthy tension has hindered community-based conservation from ever taking off as a large-scale conservation or development approach.

Conservationists went one step further by trying to create mechanisms in which indigenous peoples would help in the management and decision making of conservation areas. This approach is called comanagement (De Beer 2013). The principal objective of comanagement is to have indigenous peoples share management responsibility and be involved in a continuous process of negotiation over a resource targeted for protection (Armitage et al. 2007). In fact, in working with indigenous peoples, comanagement projects tend to be more successful than community-based conservation.

Comanagement projects usually entail a knowledge partnership where indigenous peoples and a government reach an arrangement for joint decision making regarding a natural resource (Berkes 2009). These projects typically build on the indigenous knowledge system and then skillfully bridge some useful parts with Western concepts to support a future protection effort. Although the projects envisage power sharing, they do not necessarily ensure that indigenous peoples will share power equally with the other partners. Sometimes comanagement arrangements can become very bureaucratic and then jeopardize the equity and fair distribution of assets, and the partners with more power suppress the less powerful (Armitage et al. 2007).

Views of Sustainable Development

From the view of the development organization

Lining up indigenous communities with development initiatives still seems a tricky task today. In this section I review the main reasons why projects may not be as successful as expected. A pragmatic review starts by looking at the perspective of the organization that has initiated and generated development, such as governments, aid institutions and nongovernmental organizations (NGOs). These institutions often believe that when communities share their local knowledge, they potentially have a greater stake in and better ownership over the project (Mansuri and Roa 2004). The underlying assumption is that increased participation facilitates the success of a project (Corbera et al. 2007; Walker 2011).

A genuine discussion on participation started when disenfranchised populations began advocating strongly for equity in development projects in the 1970s. Participation was then understood as "telling groups what is going to happen" (Erni 2011, 18). Although some organizations still adhere to these paternalistic practices (Box 1.1), today the concept of collaboration with local communities has evolved into a much more inclusive process. The call for improving participation came from Robert Chambers (1983), a leading scholar on participation from the development field. Chambers writes that

Box 1.1
The Two-Way Radio

A development organization had been working with an indigenous community for some time. As a gesture of support, the organization planned to donate a two-way radio so the community could communicate among its members and with the outside world. So, the organization's field coordinator placed the equipment on a small airplane and took off for a one-hour flight to the village located deep in the forest. After the airplane landed, the field coordinator met with the indigenous leader and enthusiastically told him about the two-way radio the community would receive. The leader reacted with astonishment and said, "We have six radios in the village. It is sufficient. The next thing we want is telephone communication." It was clear that the indigenous community had never asked for the radio, nor did its members have a conversation about it with the organization. They envisaged a more sophisticated means of communication with mobile phones and would have liked to see the construction and placement of a mobile tower. The field coordinator replied as follows, "We will take the radio back and keep it for you in case you need it." The radio was put back on the airplane and returned to the organization.

development organizations use power to impose their reality on others by using "top-down, north-south, centre-outwards patterns of administration and control give personal and financial reasons for conforming to professional and bureaucratic norms, and imposing these on others. This gives rise to a spectrum of distortion" (1997, 85). Chambers earnestly argues for communication that is visual and group oriented and discusses issues based on comparison rather than measurement. His valuable work has led to a movement for local communities to have an acknowledged stake in the planning (not design) and implementation of projects.

The discussion on participation has also emphasized a concept called social capital. This is the sum of all the social assets the community has to function, such as social organizations, social responsibility and cohesion among its members. Communities that possess lots of social capital are believed to be better equipped to strategically participate in development initiatives (Putnam 1993). Quite often this is true. However, there is evidence that some important elements necessary for development fall outside the realm of social capital (Mansuri and Roa 2004). The ability to trust, for example, is crucial for project success. I have learned that even communities that have excellent leadership, well-functioning social organizations and strong cohesion among the members may hesitate to bridge with other groups because of a lack of trust. Often such a breach of trust originates from previous bad experiences with other groups.

Today, participation is understood as the inclusion of the views and concerns of local actors into the dialogue and the process of decision making. For example, climate-change-mitigation projects such as REDD+ envision the inclusion of indigenous communities in reducing deforestation and promoting forest conservation and management (Stone and Chacón León 2010). Here participation is broadly defined to capture the rights and well-being of an indigenous community (Erni 2011), and enables a forum for information sharing, dialogues and sometimes even joint decision making.

Even while holding a wide concept of participation, community development remains a complex undertaking, and until today, there have been meager outcomes. You may ask how we know the outcomes are meager. How are these outcomes measured? One way development organizations have measured their project outcomes is by case studies. These studies are a means of critical analysis (Yin 2009) by which their products create a simple contextual picture of the community and its development undertakings. Besides case studies, development organizations have also tried to quantitatively measure project outcomes against a number of set goals, the so-called metrical evaluation (Mansuri and Roa 2004). Both these types of evaluation can reveal that projects seem to have limited success because of certain problems related to communities' social organization, technical capacity and scientific capacity.

Poor social organization

The general perception is that local communities may have a structural inability to participate in development due to a fundamental lack of effective social structures. Development organizations may explain, for example, that indigenous peoples have institutions too weak to facilitate development, and this assessment of weakness usually refers to the indigenous leadership that must control and manage the actions of tribal members (Hajek et al. 2011; Larson 2011). These tribes are often collective entities that consist of a number of families that willingly depend on each other for food and other living necessities. It seems almost impossible for them to control actions when power relations are horizontal, as is the case in such collective societies.

Development organizations also report that projects may fail because the majority of benefits are captured by the community leaders, a social phenomenon better known as elite capture. Development organizations reach the conclusion of elite capture because they view the community as a homogenous unit. It is inevitable that leaders will be on the forefront because they are usually one of the few who can read and write, and can ensure proper inclusion of the tribe's historical and cultural values (Mansuri and Rao 2004). In this elite position, as I have witnessed, it is very easy and common for leaders to receive incentives for their efforts or advance their own families more than others. I have encountered sons and daughters of community leaders receiving the best-paying jobs in the village, such as health worker, teacher, forest ranger or translator.

Another assumption I have seen development organizations make is that the community may have a capacity too low for decision making in a project. The organization expects that community leaders employ the Western mode of decision making. This includes having set time lines and taking decisions on single topics rather than considering a more holistic approach traditionally used by communities. Once community leaders cannot fully accommodate Western decision making, they may be labeled as weak in the eyes of development organizations. The foreseeable result is that organizations prefer to work with certain community leaders because of the high success rate of projects. In my premature career, as I like to call my time before I effectively engaged with communities, I also favored choosing certain project sites over others to make sure I could reach the project's objectives and requirements (and continued funding opportunities). After seeing how little impact "my" projects were making at the local level, however, I changed my strategy and intentionally put the community's needs first.

Limited technical capacity

Projects are typically put together by project experts. It is assumed that they are knowledgeable about the community and take into account the community dynamics in the project design. With regard to the understanding of project details, communities are expected to work from the same view as the project managers from development organizations. The stark reality is that communities may struggle in formulating detailed objectives and activities, and developing success indicators in the Western framework. Quite often, they also have trouble keeping to the time lines set by the project design team, which are usually too tight for them to adhere to.

This "projectism" asserts that it can introduce a strong change at the local level (Little 2005). A problem associated with this theory is that the project often overshadows the interests and goals of the indigenous community. When this so-called "dominant ignoring" occurs, local communities are likely to organically develop mechanisms to defend themselves and will place such peaceful defense above project objectives (Colfer 2011). One technique I observed time and again was when indigenous communities guarded themselves by participating opportunistically, which means participating only for their own benefit. An example is that of a community that participates in learning about the Western way of cooking meats, but essentially does not like eating such meat because the members prefer traditionally prepared meat or fish. They participated in the project to receive a small payment for the time allocated to cooking the meats. In cases like this, participation can then become superficial because it accommodates the project's requirements rather than fulfilling a community's real goals.

Development organizations propose to work with third parties as intermediaries to bridge the divide between their own and the community's view. Such middle persons can also be very helpful in informing community members about the project, lobbying and dealing with conflict (Kritsnaphan and Sajor 2011). Although this seems like a great solution for solving the discrepancy between community and development organization, this arrangement can become a flop in practice. The reality is that there is always a margin of distrust, caused by the power difference between the community and the development organization. Middle persons can make this margin grow even bigger. Especially in a situation of conflict, the distrust comes alive (Box 1.2).

Box 1.2
Trust in Selling Forest Nuts

A community was engaged in a project selling forest nuts with the help of an organization. The organization evidently acted as an intermediary, bringing the products from the village, remotely located deep in the rain forest, to the markets in the capital city. During the high-cost transportation in a small airplane, the products would dry out and lose a small amount of weight. The "poorly" educated community had no previous knowledge about this potential weight loss that occurred when the product was flown through drier air. When the product arrived in the city, the serving organization would immediately bring it to a local store, sell it and collect the money. Problems of distrust soon started after the community discovered that they received less money than expected because of the product's loss of weight. Such trust issues usually arise when money is involved, especially if there is uneven power and limited room for negotiation (Corbera et al. 2007).

Limited scientific capacity

Indigenous peoples use sight, sound, taste, touch and smell to assess and detect changes in the environment. For example, shamans identify a tree's medicinal capacity based on the structure of the leaves, the texture of the soil in which it grows, the average exposure to sun or rain and the smell of the leaves and bark. Scientists, in contrast, collect data based on documentary methods rather than through the use of their sensatory apparatus. This well-known scientific methodology follows Aristotle's reductionist approach, which typically excludes emotions and senses from human observations (Pierotti 2011). It breaks down the observed data, isolates and analyzes it without the social and environmental context and then organizes it in a way that only makes sense to the discourse held by the industrialized world (Agrawal 1995).

Nature-dependent communities are known for their traditional views and knowledge system, which are rather different from this modern view. Such traditional knowledge consists of a comprehensive body of knowledge and practice that comes from looking at the world as a system of interconnected relationships, and is thus directly linked with subsistence livelihood and spiritual beliefs (Berkes 2008). Indigenous peoples may have only a narrow understanding of knowledge types other than traditional knowledge they have gathered through experience. Most indigenous peoples lack a basis for comprehending scientific knowledge because they are not actively connected to that reality of the Western world. For example, even today, with small airplanes flying in and out of remote indigenous villages in the forest, the majority of elder women have never seen a street or car. Their reality is the forest with its seemingly irregular arrangement of trees, which they see as a form of order. The urban city with aligned streets and houses is probably a form of disorder for these women.

Numerous times I have observed that development researchers claim to respect indigenous knowledge when, in fact, they act differently. Decisions are made beforehand, and then the outcome is presented by highly educated scientists in such a way that it looks as though the indigenous community took the decision. It seems to me that scientists struggle in understanding how the indigenous knowledge system works (Chan et al. 2007). Solving this problem would imply that scientists must expand their contemporary frame of thinking and, for example, study not only biology or climate science but also social theories and practices for a better understanding of the communities.

From the view of the indigenous communities

Sustainable development researchers and practitioners are still learning how to support a community process of real social change. This transformative process improves the situation and conditions of indigenous communities according to their goals and aspirations. The big challenge for researchers and practitioners is to get a better understanding of these self-defined goals and aspirations. Once these priorities are exposed and clear to the researcher, there is an opportunity to strategically align the community's interests with the development project.

The effectiveness of a development project should thus be assessed by the difference it makes in the individual lives of community members and for the indigenous community as a whole. Communities themselves have to evaluate the long-term success of the project because they are the only ones who can feel the real impact it makes. This appears to be an extremely difficult process. Sometimes, as I have experienced, communities remain unresponsive or have an accommodating response when development organizations ask about the effectiveness of a project. Communities also may hold back because they certainly take into consideration the potential benefits they could receive if they intentionally continued working with the development organization in the future. The answer the communities then give is not at all specific. They may talk about the project in the story of their life, starting from historical events until the experience of today. This narrative, often lengthy, unfolds key information on how they actually feel but is incongruent with the scientifically founded evaluation mechanisms used by development organizations. After a number of years, researchers may hear communities' real thoughts about the project, which also suddenly reveal the reasons for the project's failure. Projects are impeded due to several reasons, here grouped into six broad categories.

The project is too general

Projects are normally formulated by development organizations because they are familiar with the complicated formats, language and process that are needed to get the project approved. The development organization thus exists in a better position than the community for crafting the project. If a development organization is not (fully) aware of the urgent and long-term needs at the local level, the project may end up as too general. It is then that project goals and activities may not be specific enough to address these needs. The inevitable result is that, once executed, the community is unmotivated to fully participate or take any ownership over the project. To illustrate, I observed this in a project on the mapping of ecosystem services executed with indigenous peoples (Box 1.3).

The project is too short

Researchers struggle with finding ways to make a significant social change locally with the short project life that is often dictated by the global

Box 1.3
An Ecosystem Services Map

A development organization designed a project to map the forest's ecosystem services in five indigenous villages in South America. The intention was to make a full inventory of a community's values, needs and activities within a piece of tropical rain forest, in and surrounding their village (Ramirez-Gomez et al. 2013). Researchers from the development organization were predominantly intrigued by the methodology for effectively communicating with indigenous peoples about their conservation priorities, thus, a scientific goal.

The project started out briskly with the indigenous peoples mapping out their dependence on the forest, including the way the forest provides for food, shelter and water; for cultural aspects such as recreation, aesthetics, place and sacred sites; and for income generation from tourism. Several women and men drew circles around places they use frequently and thought were absolutely necessary for sustaining life in the forest. The sketches were then processed into computerized maps with colors: darker colors showed high intensity of use, while lighter colors resembled use by a smaller number of peoples. Just as expected, the project provided very few benefits to the community, which also explained the low rate of participation of 191 persons from five villages with a total population exceeding 1,500. When there is a serious conversation about maps, the community seldom talks about these ecosystem maps, and when I ask, they say that the maps make no real sense to them. Community interest might have been boosted in this case by including their goals in the project, for example, using the maps for threat analysis. Yet the ultimate benefit was for the scientists, who could thoroughly study the mapping method and learn about its application.

development agenda. Projects are usually short lived, with execution times within two years. It is crucial that the community has sufficient time to fully assess the risks and opportunities the project brings forward. In this internal process, individuals in the community come together to thoroughly discuss the project among themselves and subsequently develop local strategies for its implementation. If the community has limited room to do this, it is likely that they cannot participate efficiently in the project. Especially when a community has to make a drastic shift to a new situation, time is of the essence (Box 1.4).

Box 1.4
A Relocated Tourism Project

I have seen a development organization decide to relocate a project from one place to another place in the forest. In the original location was an itinerant community with fewer than 50 members, who were partnering with the development organization in eco-tourism activities. The new location, in contrast, was crowded and populated with a community of approximately 1,000 people, who took relatively more ownership of their own development activities than did the community living in the original location.

The organization worked alongside this larger community to establish a number of luxurious lodges for high-end tourists in the middle of the dense tropical rain forest. Local men helped cut trees, carry them over water rapids and build the cabins close together with an outside contractor. The women learned how to improve and upgrade their traditional handicraft to Northern standards, and some of them were even selected to become skilled at cooking modern food. Not long after the tourists began coming, the problems began. Members of the local community-based organization (CBO), who were trained to run the site financially and logistically, started quarrelling about the division of monies, which resulted in a total collapse of the operations. The disappointed community explained that it needed much more time to fully understand the new payment structure and corresponding responsibilities because it wasn't used to it. This example shows how it is imperative for a community to engage in a project long enough so that it can provide some guidance and support to the complex social change process. If this is not made available, as is the case with the tourism project, the social change process may abruptly halt or sometimes even completely terminate.

The project is too narrow

When a project is too narrowly formulated, the community may have difficulty grasping it. What I have seen happen in this case is that the goals of the project are just too specialized to be comprehended by the community. The community starts participating in the project and hopes to gradually grasp the gist as the project evolves. But as time passes, two things can happen. The community is able to catch up with the project after its members educate themselves about its core function and activities. Or the discrepancy

Box 1.5
A Link between Food Security and Climate Change

I recall an organization that was working with an indigenous group to improve food security, especially in light of the constantly changing weather that was posing a threat. With much heavier rains and longer dry periods, the community was seeing an increase in food rot and plant-eating ants (Bynoe and Liddell 2013).

The organization enthusiastically started teaching the community about agricultural techniques to cultivate green-leaf vegetables in small gardens next to the members' houses in addition to the larger plots they employed in the forest. It was meant to be a classical agricultural project, with the noble goal of making the community more resilient against climate change. A year later, after the community stopped participating in the project, the gardens were completely taken over by nature. It was clear that the development organization assumed a (Western) causal link between climate change and food security: the influences from climate change had posed a threat to food security. The community, in contrast, firmly believed that the change in weather occurred because they neglected taking care of the forest, for which they were being punished.

between the community and the project may widen, and this usually comes to the forefront, when the project already is far into the execution phase (Box 1.5).

Particularly when a project is executed with indigenous communities who think holistically and connect several aspects from life together, it should have wide goals. The example in Box 1.5 shows a project that was too far off target to make a structural change. The narrowly formulated project should have included the agricultural plots the community used in the forest for growing cassava, bananas and other staple crops. Only then would the community actually be able to exercise the agricultural techniques and improve the care-taking of its own plots and, most importantly, the forest as a whole.

The project is too acultural

Sometimes a project is not entirely aligned with the cultural values of a community. The cultural values can be seen as the glue that holds the community together (Berkes 2008). When challenging the community on these values, I have seen two distinctive actions: they completely withdraw from

---

Box 1.6
A Mismatched Chicken Project

One profound example of cultural mismatch is the introduction of chickens in an indigenous community that was unfamiliar with raising chickens for either the production of eggs or meat. Small chickens were flown into the village, after which the development organization trained the community to self-build chicken pens. A tiny part of the village was excited about this plan and immediately started raising the small chicks. Eight weeks later, the chickens were full grown and the organization encouraged the slaughter of the chickens as a source of meat for the community members; however, because indigenous peoples do not believe in killing the animals they raise, to this day the chickens are still lively running around in the village. The project never seemed to make a real impact on the lives of the community members.

---

the development project because of the mismatch with their own values (Box 1.6), or they recognize and accept the new project and (partly) incorporate it into the existing cultural system. This means that the indigenous peoples uptake some of the project's Western values. It is understandable that indigenous peoples are here placed in a dilemma, and must choose between being traditional—maintaining their forest-dependent culture, and living with limited technology and production capacity—or becoming part of the market economy (Lu Holt 2005).

The project is too dominant

Dominance in projects is more often the case with science-driven projects that operate on the basis of a positivist paradigm that typically dictates a well-controlled environment in the collection and analysis of information. Factual data are then processed through complicated models or theories, and there is just no room for more traditional ways of knowledge generation, which are usually promoted by trial and error. The most striking experience with dominance I have seen was in a climate-change project called REDD+. The REDD+ project's primary objective is to maintain or lower the carbon emissions of forests and contribute to combating the global process of climate change. Forest-dependent communities are then encouraged and motivated to reduce forest deforestation and degradation as well as promote forest conservation and sustainable use.

Every REDD+ project must have factual information on the drivers of deforestation, more specifically, the exact measures on the amount of standing forest and the annual rate of deforestation or degradation. These data are required for calculating the tradable carbon credits, are subject to peer review and must be academically or nationally published for consideration in the analysis (UNU 2012). Before approval of any given REDD+ project, scientists from the development organization normally evaluate the presented data on their academic merit. The globally operating concept leaves few possibilities for including the interests and aspirations of the local community, leading to a structural unevenness in power between the development organization and the community. The community then can become easily overpowered, may face dilemmas between individual and societal goals and can start trading off goals to each other (Robards et al. 2011). One community member explained this huge power disparity to me as being "voluntarily obliged" to participate in REDD+. This means that they are only slightly convinced to participate, but if they refrain from participating, they would lose an important development opportunity.

The project is too fuzzy

Most organizations are true to the communities with which they partner and convey all the reasons for doing a project together with them. But sometimes a development organization purposely withholds information from the communities with which they implement projects. Organizations may only communicate part of the project's rationale, especially those elements that potentially benefit the community, but withhold the real interest they have in participating in and pursuing the project.

To illustrate, development organizations like to help indigenous peoples with demarcating and mapping their use of inhabited lands. Mapping entails working with the women and men, old and young, so they can precisely position on a map where they hunt, collect food, find medicinal plants and construction materials and use important cultural places. This intensive exercise can result in a land-use map, a sort of pictorial overview of the tribe's livelihood activities. Once I saw an NGO explain to the community with which it mapped that the land-use map would be a key negotiation tool for obtaining rights to land. Yet the organization seemed more interested in learning about the exact locations of local biodiversity than locations that would support the tribe's fight for land rights. When the community sensed this vagueness, it felt uncertain and lost interest in joining the project.

It is not surprising that the concept of Free and Prior Informed Consent (FPIC) was globally introduced for working with indigenous peoples on their lands. FPIC requires development organizations to inform the communities about development plans, and then these communities can autonomously decide if they want the development activity to proceed and under what conditions. Usually this process has a duration of one year. FPIC is now standard practice in many countries where indigenous peoples live, even when it requires development organizations to bring in significant amounts of money to execute the full one-year process.

Thus, as demonstrated in the previous examples, there are divergent views on why few development projects have success. The views of development organizations and indigenous communities are fairly distinct because of different expectations of development. Development organizations uphold strict deadlines for reaching set outcomes. Rather than checking off project outcomes, indigenous peoples may envisage a slower process in which change is expected to be organic. The difference in approach stems from researchers and practitioners (coming from development organizations) studying communities with their own Western assumptions, which are a result of many years of scientific training.

Communities under New Pressure

Indigenous communities always feel pressure when they are facing development activities. Local realities in developing countries find indigenous peoples living in lands that are hunted for mineral or forest resources. Competition from small-scale gold miners and loggers is increasingly leading to conflicts with indigenous peoples, especially in the Amazon rain forest (Bavinck et al. 2014). Here, even national governments can be in conflict with indigenous peoples as they have divergent views on how to develop the forest. Disputes typically arise when governments want to construct megaprojects, such as roads and dams, large-scale agricultural projects or mineral extraction factories (RAISG 2012). The weight put on the shoulders of indigenous peoples to deal with these new, usually unknown, technology-driven projects appears underestimated, and may lead to the complete disruption of their social structure.

Furthermore, on a global level, a major pressure faced by indigenous peoples today in their path to development is human-induced climate change generated by excessive use of natural resources combined with human consumption patterns. Climate change is seen as a modification of the weather caused by the release of greenhouse gases into the atmosphere. This release changes the makeup of the atmosphere, which marks a change in daily weather and a higher occurrence of hurricanes, floods and tsunamis. The impact of climate change is expected to affect all people living on earth, either by extreme weather or its consequences, such as an increase in contagious diseases or a decrease in the availability of food and water (Parry et al. 2007).

In response to climate change, nations have expressed their concern by entering into a debate. This debate, carried out under the rubric of the United Nations Framework Convention on Climate Change (UNFCCC), commenced in 1992 with the ambitious commitment of almost all of the world's nations. The fundamental purpose of this debate is to give each sovereign nation a fair opportunity to participate in a discussion on setting global policies for lowering the release of human-induced greenhouse gases and simultaneously safeguarding economic growth and the availability of food.

The UNFCCC structure was crafted during a time when the world was trying to balance equality between developed and developing nations. Postcolonial issues such as the violation of human rights and the massive extraction of raw natural resources were still in the forefront of international discussions (Mejía 2010). Developing countries were seeking attention concerning the unequal distribution of wealth and pursuing donor assistance from the developed world while struggling with securing basic human needs—water, food and housing—for their citizens (Roberts and Parks 2007). In the meantime, they were desperately trying to get their countries into gear with sustainable development.

The sharp division between the two worlds has resulted in polarized perspectives on the way forward in addressing the climate change problem: by convention, the industrialized nations of North America, Western Europe, Australia and New Zealand are referred to as the countries holding a "Northern view," while the developing nations of South America, Asia, Africa and the Pacific are referred to as the countries with a "Southern view." Nations holding a Southern view typically advocate for environmental justice. The environmental justice movement originated in the early 1990s and affirms "the sacredness of Mother Earth, the ecological unity and the interdependence of all species, and the right to be free from ecological destruction" (Barry 2007, 163). Countries with a Southern view strongly feel that wealthier nations should compensate them for the release of pollution in the past, which is associated with the rapid development of industrialized nations. They seek a sense of equality, in particular because the nations holding a Northern view enjoy a relatively superior standard of living (Ikeme 2003).

Although it looks like an oversimplified dichotomy, these views give a good representation of the opposing ends of a spectrum of views held in the debate. Since the Copenhagen negotiation in 2009, the two opposing blocks came closer after the positions of individual developing nations became more individualized, leading to the formation of new coalitions such as the BASIC countries (emerging large economies such as Brazil, South Africa,

India, China) and the LDC (least developed countries, consisting of 48 countries from Africa and Asia that are extremely vulnerable to climate change), among others (Gogus 2014). Six years later, in the Paris negotiations, softened positions eventually led countries to agree to keeping the earth's warming below two degrees Celsius through a system of commitments to voluntary contributions.

The North-South differences in viewpoint are also structured along dimensions other than positions in the debate alone. The nations holding a Northern view just seem indifferent to replacing their luxurious lifestyle with a simpler one that entails significantly reduced emissions (Ikeme 2003). More explicitly, a change in behavior is not their preferred way of handling climate change. The nations holding a Southern view, meanwhile, operate in a very different reality. Approximately 1.4 billion people (IFAD 2011), the wide majority in the South, live in extreme poverty and are uncertain about obtaining basic human requirements such as food, water and housing. One billion of these people are small farmers, peasants and members of other landed communities, highly dependent on their local environment and at the same time potentially vulnerable to the effects of climate change. The average income of each of these poor people is approximately 60 times smaller than that of people living in the 31 countries of Western Europe, the United States and Canada, clustered under the Organization for Economic Cooperation and Development (Mejía, 2010).

Besides economic implications, the strongest effects of climate change are expected to take place in low- and middle-income countries located in Africa, Asia and South America (Parry et al. 2007; Thomas and Twyman 2005). The World Bank reports that "low and middle income countries have the least capacity to cope, and in general, suffer the highest human toll, accounting to 85% of all disaster fatalities" (World Bank 2013, 6). Even when greenhouse gas emissions were reduced significantly now, the effect on poverty would still be felt beyond 2100 because of the long permanence of greenhouse gases in the atmosphere (IPCC 2013). As the data suggests, uneven geographical distribution of climate change risk seems to reinforce the already existing inequality between nations.

A powerful conclusion of the UNFCCC conferences is that the industrialized nations are obliged to decrease their emissions. The most obvious way to achieve this is by using sources of energy that are cleaner than the frequently used oil, coal or natural gas. Emissions from these sources contain greenhouse gases that gradually heat up our earth, causing the climate to change. Another way to compensate for emissions is by planting trees—tree leaves absorb gases. The gases that plants absorb are naturally transformed into water and oxygen, two things that humans need to live. The use of clean energy and the planting of trees are both strategies that fall under the umbrella of climate-change mitigation (Parry et al. 2007).

Besides these mitigation strategies, nations also can try to gradually adjust to the new circumstances that emerge with climate change. This approach is called adaptation and refers to "initiatives and measures to reduce the vulnerability of natural and human systems against actual or expected climate change effects" (Parry et al. 2007, 809). The adaptation approach assumes that humans are innovative and will organically find ways to adapt to new circumstances because they have the instinct to survive. Although sometimes disparaged as a "do-nothing" strategy, adaptation is more appealing to the Southern nations because of their limited technical capacity to tackle climate change.

Science as a primary source of power

The debate on climate change promotes discussions about scientific research, in particular regarding systematic observations and climate analysis. This stems from the tradition of a separate but influential body called the Intergovernmental Panel on Climate Change (IPCC). The IPCC was established in 1988 "to provide the world with a clear scientific view on the current state of knowledge in climate change and its potential environmental and socio-economic impacts" (IPCC, n.d.). This scientific body consists of knowledgeable and recognized experts from all over the world, carefully selected based on their relevant experience and academic credentials from a list compiled by individual nations, academia and observer organizations (UNU 2012). With plenty of expert power, the IPCC scientists seem to mold knowledge so that policy makers can make ostensibly correct decisions: solutions based on technology that fit within the framework of modern science (Aitken 2012).

In 1995, the second IPCC report was released. The 588-page report suggested that 1.6 billion tons of greenhouse gases were released through deforestation equal to 20 percent of global emissions (Parker et al. 2009). According to the nations with a Northern view, actual deforestation of forests mostly occurs in the developing world. They argued that the ongoing deforestation in Asia, South America and Africa would significantly reduce the global standing forests. However, to date insufficient data exist to support this argument (Bäckstrand and Lövbrand 2006; Fogel 2002).

The spark that set off a fire was a proposal set forth by the United States in 1997 calling for a free-market mechanism on emissions. The United States suggested that nations wouldn't necessarily have to reduce emissions but could compensate by saving trees. This model has been popularly termed emissions trading or carbon trading. At that time, no nation engaged in the debate was prepared to think about emissions outside its own territory, and the proposal was collectively declined. But the idea of a global trading scheme seems to have been tactfully placed on the negotiation table. It was the alternative route to emissions reduction that the nations holding a Northern view were seeking.

Scientists supporting the Northern view began to skillfully direct their research to the topic of global emissions trading. They had to figure out how to quantify deforestation, in other words, how to create a single unit of measurement needed for trade. Research on forest calculation was supported and advocated by universities and research institutions as the novel trend in climate-change science. Two other activities appeared crucial in preparing for the emissions market: large businesses such as oil companies were campaigning together with the Northern view holders to promote emissions trading in the debate (Meckling 2011), and the Northern view holders were heavily investing in experimental reforestation and afforestation projects (Bäckstrand and Lövbrand 2006).

By the time the third IPCC report was published in 2001, the focus of discussions had fully shifted to emissions trading (IPCC 2001). The reframing effort apparently had been successful, permitting the Northern view to become dominant in the discourse. In the meantime, by 2001 the wealthy nations already boasted 157 registered emissions projects worldwide (Bäckstrand and Lövbrand 2006). There was no turning back: emissions trading was accepted in the official debate and became the most important mitigation route in 2004.

Institutionalization of mitigation: REDD+

With the foundation in place, the nations with a Northern view moved to further institutionalize the emissions-trading scheme. The obligation of these nations to begin reducing emissions would be enforced in the debate for 2005, and it looked like they were running out of time. How would it be possible for the wealthy nations to maintain a fast-growing capitalistic system, keep their citizens in high spirits and at the same time reduce emissions?

Once the frame of thought on climate change was changed to one that supported economic growth, then the Northern view holders could connect their interests to the negotiations. The clever reframing started with a report on the economic impacts of climate change prepared by the British economist Nicholas Stern for his government. The report sought to provide a broad overview of the potential effects of climate change on water resources, food and health care needed for the citizens of the United Kingdom. In his 700-page review, Stern (2007) suggested that the overall cost of climate change would be the same as losing between 5 and 20 percent of the nation's economic growth, while the targeted expenditure of only 1 percent of revenues would be required to combat climate change each year. Stern pointed to the seriousness of climate change and proposed immediate action for all nations, emphasizing the reduction of deforestation in the developing world (Stern 2007).

The *Stern Review* is a popular report in the history of climate change, and it was referred to in the generation of the fourth assessment report of the IPCC in 2007. Besides the finding that humans were the main cause of global climate change, the IPCC report reached another conclusion that changed the course of action in mitigation: "reducing deforestation is the mitigation option with the largest and most immediate carbon stock impact in the short term per hectare per year globally" (Metz et al. 2007, 550). Forest was now seen as a common good that needed to be saved, and the indigenous peoples living in it should be included.

The deforestation paradigm permitted the wealthy countries to hold the developing nations responsible for the majority of clearing forests. At that time the scientific discourse opportunely revealed that ongoing deforestation in the Amazon and forests in Africa and Asia could account for up to 25 percent of global greenhouse gas emissions (Hall 2012). And compared with other mitigation options, such as reducing consumption and generating clean energy, lowering deforestation rates was deemed more efficient in terms of cost (Stephan 2012). Anticipating such economic efficiency, the debate commenced discussions about options for reducing emissions from deforestation and forest degradation, abbreviated as REDD. This frame of thinking then became the core foundation to build on plans for the future. The Bali Action Plan was adopted to institutionalize REDD in 2007. A year later, the UNREDD program was launched, and is currently helping more than 40 developing countries in their national REDD efforts by using common approaches and best (scientific) practices in project design and implementation (UN-REDD Programme 2009).

The Stern reframing diverted focus from finding solutions that could genuinely promote equality among nations. In effect, the Northern view holders promote a discourse that REDD projects must be implemented in a way that the forest-rich countries can choose to "buy in" to the conservation of forests (Von Stein 2008). The meaning of forests has notably changed in the REDD framework. Forests were first considered a tool for providing humans with wood, food and other necessary materials. Now, the debate sees forests as a tool for absorbing carbon. As such, in decreasing order, Suriname, French Guiana, Gabon, Guyana, Belize, Bhutan, Congo, Colombia, Zambia, Panama and Peru possess the highest forest cover and the lowest deforestation rates (Figure 1.1), and with that these countries own the highest estimated carbon sequestration potential globally (da Fonseca et al. 2007).

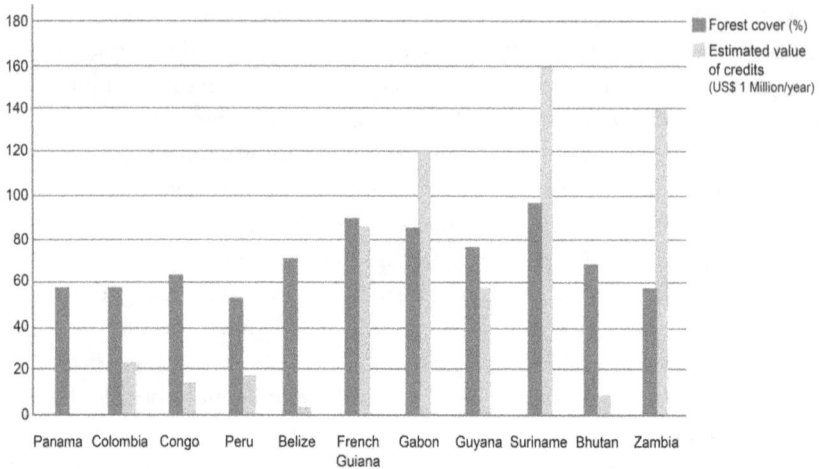

Figure 1.1 Countries with high forest cover (>50%) and low deforestation rates (<0.22%/year). *Source*: Data from da Fonseca et al. (2007).

The REDD framework envisages direct payment to indigenous peoples for preventing deforestation and forest degradation. To include the standing forests that are protected by these indigenous peoples, the REDD framework was expanded into REDD+. REDD+ creates financial incentives not only for decreasing deforestation and degradation but also for promoting sustainable forest conservation and management (Parker et al. 2009).

The reality in which indigenous communities live seems very different from the reality in which REDD+ operates. The relationship between indigenous peoples and their local ecosystem is usually based on thousands of years of experience, thoroughly tested and embedded in a system of cultural identity and livelihood (Pennesi 2007; Pierotti and Wildcat 2000; Turner and Clifton 2009). Indigenous communities hold on to views that are holistic and largely based on a spatial concept. Their "truth" comes from cultural traditions that promote a connection with the natural and the spiritual world around them (Pierotti 2011). Contrastingly, the social system from which development organizations operate appears temporal, meaning that the world is divided into separate events that are aligned in chronological order. It is unfortunate that this view seems to exclude emotions and mainly centers on finding the truth through validation in peer-reviewed publications, conferences and other academic instruments (Pierotti 2011).

The structure of REDD+ projects may exclude consideration of the life goals of indigenous peoples, prioritizing the efficient management of projects over local issues such as the struggle to obtain food and other human necessities

(Hajek et al. 2011). It looks like the views and interests of indigenous peoples are not given weight in global negotiations because it is unaligned with the science-based paradigm (Lejano et al. 2011). Thus, the REDD+ framework bears inequality through its structure to overpower the views and interests of indigenous peoples. It is an extra pressure created in the realm of climate-related development.

Contents of the Book

In this book I further explore the indigenous view and seek to answer the following questions: How does the community view sustainable development under conditions of climate change? How does this view conflict with the view held by the development organizations responsible for implementing projects to mitigate climate change? How can we best analyze these views? The book is organized in two parts: the first part explores theory and the second part practice.

The first part introduces a new framework for analyzing the views of local communities for sustainable development. This feature comprises chapters 2 to 4. Chapter 2 discusses the variety of theoretical frameworks that are currently used by researchers for the analysis of community views. This chapter introduces the theories and frameworks of conflict resolution and how they compare to conventional frameworks used in the social and environmental sciences. The main argument described here is that these conflict frameworks can be a new and improved way of understanding community views in sustainable development initiatives.

Chapter 3 thoroughly explores the internal transformation process a community undergoes when progressing in development. It demonstrates that values are the point of departure and that these dictate the course of action the communities take when they are dealing with environmental and/or social change. The chapter discloses that the community first creates meaning from the change encountered, after which it will enter into a complex process of decision making. The core of this chapter presents the VIEW framework for researching a community's view.

Chapter 4 describes the social polygraphy methodology used to assess conflicting views in practice. This chapter is authored by Elena Bastidas and reveals the importance of the territory as a space where humans and nature live together, with their traditions and practices engaging in constant change. Discrepancy in views is always bound by time and space, and social polygraphy addresses this characteristic by making maps of the past, present and future. It is a practical methodology where the researcher and the community can engage in a dialogue and collaboratively analyze, create meaning and gain empowerment through the process of drawing maps.

The second part of the book illustrates how to use the new framework by analyzing the view of the Trio indigenous community living in the Amazonian rain forest of Suriname in an era of climate-change projects. This part consists of chapters 5 through 7, and is founded on the case study presented in my doctoral dissertation. Chapter 5 contains a detailed discussion about values and how these can influence the social change processes in the Trio community. It shows that history shapes the Trio view, more specifically aspects of the tribe's ancestral primacy of togetherness, its religious conversion and its territorial stewardship.

Chapter 6 particularly addresses the way the Trio community constructs its views about climate change. In this chapter I illustrate this with an explicit description of the Trio view along five axes (Nudler 1993): the makeup of climate change (ontology), how climate change is detected (epistemology), how valuable climate change is (axiology), how climate change can be organized (logic) and how one should act on climate change (ethics). This chapter allows the reader to truly see climate change through the eyes of the community.

In chapter 7, the origin of sustainable decisions is broadly discussed. The case study is utilized to compare and contrast the Trio view with the view of development organizations. The chapter further explores how to find a sustainable solution for the Trios when engaging in a REDD+ project.

The book ends with a detailed conclusion on how to promote community sustainability under environmental uncertainty. In this final chapter I present ways to manage and transform a conflict of views, including a set of principles by which researchers and practitioners can work with communities fairly and ethically. The chapter also discusses the implications of the presented framework for policy making.

Chapter 2

RESEARCHING VIEWS
IN COMMUNITY DEVELOPMENT

So far, I have discussed the inequality that exists between an indigenous community and organizations working in nexus of climate change and development. To better understand this silent conflict, I am eager to find out how a typical community looks at development and how its members make fundamental decisions to plan for their own future. In my attempt to search for a practical framework that can help me comprehend this view, I have distinguished a number of theories and frameworks from the subject fields of environment, development and conflict resolution. Each of these progressive fields approaches a community differently. In this chapter, I try to look through the eyes of researchers from each of these specialties and visualize the way they would study an indigenous community that is dealing with environmental uncertainty. I further attempt to answer a key question for researchers, namely, are any of these frameworks applicable for studying the view of an indigenous community facing development while being influenced by climate change?

Researching Community Views: Existing Frameworks

When researchers are particularly interested in gaining insight into the behavior of an indigenous community, they travel to the site and try to answer a research question or address a specific need. This common practice gives them an opportunity to get to know the community and explain its behavior based on the information they gather on the historical, social, economic and political contexts. Quite frequently, however, researchers initiate a given project by approaching the indigenous community from a modernity paradigm, in which such a community is expected to move from being nature dependent and primitive into a more modern, urban society.

In my former research life, I confess, an indigenous community wearing little red cloths and full-feather headdresses would automatically be classified as traditional. It is no secret that indigenous peoples are accustomed to making fundamental decisions based on experience and custom (Inglehart and Baker 2000). This means that they depend on long-term strategies developed from stories of existence that spread over decades and sometimes even centuries. New combat strategies would only develop when this type of tranquil community was under some kind of pressure. My point is that they would rather hang around in their own customary world of "being" and that they have limited ambition to "progress further" and enter into the so-called modern world (Kluckhohn and Strodtbeck 1961). Therefore, I would have argued that this traditional direction is the most prominent reason for disagreement and conflict with the modern world. I was fortunate to learn that this anthropological paradigm is not always ample enough to fully clarify the behavior of an indigenous community in development (Box 2.1).

So the experience described in Box 2.1 taught me, among other experiences, that it is hard to obtain a clear picture of what a typical indigenous community thinks if one clarifies their behavior based only on an anthropological paradigm. It seemed to me that this approach lacked the room to obtain a good understanding of how a community deals with pressures and how it defines sustainability for the future. Anthropological approaches may emphasize the situation from the past until the present. And by applying ethnographical and observational research methods, a rich picture of this trajectory can be drawn. But important clues that lie on the boundary of the present

---

Box 2.1
A Researcher's Analysis

I had a memorable experience when I was working alongside an anthropologist on a quest to appreciate the choices indigenous women make when presented with a specific development opportunity: selling souvenirs. The anthropologist walked around in the village, intermingled with lots of women and carefully observed their behavior. After a couple of months, the anthropologist noticed that the indigenous women would rather swing in their hammocks most of the afternoon than assemble souvenirs. Indeed, the researcher concluded the women were uninterested in getting paid for selling souvenirs to tourists and simply categorized the community as very traditional. At that time I was in complete agreement with the researcher's analysis.

A few years later, working in the same community, it became clear to me that the indigenous women had made a well-thought-out and conscious choice to withdraw from the project because they would rather socialize with other women after customarily working hard in the morning. Later the women clarified that the project wouldn't make a difference in their lives because few tourists visited the village.

and future sometimes fall outside this paradigm, which made me search for other, more holistic, research methods.

Researching the community through the eyes of environmentalists

Another way of looking at a community in development is through the eyes of environmental scientists. These scientists typically integrate mathematics, physics, chemistry and biology to study the earth's ecosystems and find solutions to pressing environmental problems such as climate change. This "green" field is extremely large and consists of several disciplines, of which ecology, biology, soil science and geography are only a few. Environmental scientists interested in researching climate change are currently concentrating on the so-called risk theory. Risk theory is based on the assumption that all people now live in a society full of risk that comes from a range of environmental, social, health and economic pressures and threats (Barry 2007). Researchers who study risk theory are eager to know how people make choices when they are faced with climate change—for example, how they decide to act (or not) based upon changes in weather (Box 2.2).

Box 2.2
A Tsunami in Thailand

In my effort to explain how risk assessors research a community, I go back to the tsunami that struck Thailand in 2004. Along the coast lived an indigenous group known as the Moken, also called sea gypsies because they live for two-thirds of the year at sea and have been doing this for hundreds of years. A couple of days before the tsunami hit, they detected changes in their surroundings—indicated by the stillness of the water and the unusual behavior of animals—such as the absence of the usual bird calls, deep sea fish appearing at the surface of the water, large dolphins heading to deeper sea and crabs walking in the opposite direction—from the beach to the forest. The Moken leaders instructed their men and women to move away to a higher elevation (Budjeryn 2012). Risk researchers would be very interested in understanding what mechanism these Mokens possess to detect risk and how they collectively decided to run away, leaving behind their homes and belongings. Typically these researchers study how people select based on a mixture of habit, analyzing cost against benefit or by assessing potential constraints for livelihood in the future (Dietz and Stern 1995; Marx et al. 2007).

Risk researchers tend to rely on psychological choice models in trying to explain how people decide to take action (or not) when confronted with extreme risk. Such studies have been classically performed along a wide range of social variables in populations, such as gender, age, ethnicity, education, income, religious beliefs, political belief and group membership (Slimak and Dietz 2006). These studies demonstrate that people's decisions are almost always associated with feelings generated when they are experiencing a climate-related disaster. People's emotions are significantly reinforced when they see images related to climate change in real life or in the media (Leiserowitz 2006; Weber 2006).

Although psychological choice models have been quite successful in explaining the perceptions of individuals, I now direct attention to the next question: can this method be applied to indigenous communities? Keep in mind that indigenous peoples constantly walk in the vicinity of their village to assess the forest, and use their eyes and ears to compare and contrast situations from the past with current phenomena. Normally they make a decision on how to act collectively based on the levels that they define as acceptable (Weber 2006). In this functional and consistent process, the community creates an image of risk, and subsequently its members define which environmental behavior is tolerable. This image is directly linked to the way that the communities see the world and defines the organizing concept through which the community views local climate-related changes.

Every day each indigenous person makes a set of choices, for example, where to plant crops or which animals to shoot. Although it is normal that these choices are predescribed by the collective, individual members may adapt and change them constantly as they face new challenges. It seems that there exists an ongoing dynamic between the community and the outside environment that defines actions for the future, which makes individual choice models difficult to apply. For example, in a noteworthy study, the hypothesis that perception shaped coffee farmers' adaptive responses to climate change in Guatemala, Honduras and Mexico was tested. The hard-working farmers worried the most about the selling price of their coffee, leading the researchers to conclude that the farmers used a market analysis to make decisions regarding adaptive action (Tucker et al. 2010). This hallmark study showed the level at which the market economy can influence the collective perception.

Vulnerability and adaptation framework

Risk researchers came up with a clever idea to organize the risk-related information into a specific framework that would allow them to study a community. The point of departure of this vulnerability and adaptation framework is that communities have different levels of vulnerability to the risk posed by climate change and at some point they must adapt to prevent harm to themselves (Dodman and Mitlin 2013). When looking through the eyes of these researchers, four distinctive research tracks exist. The first track emphasizes modeling the impact of climate change on a community to simplify the real situation. Here the community itself tends to be diminished to a variable in a mathematical model. Such models seem to give little importance to the way a community interprets change and how its members make decisions in the place they exist (Smit and Wandel 2006). A more lively representation of a community is given in the second track where researchers look at the different measures taken when a community adapts—more specifically, how they choose between the different options presented to them when facing climate change (Adger et al. 2005; Smit and Wandel 2006).

Researchers adhering to the third track are inclined to compare communities by giving them a score for overall vulnerability against climate change. This is the most popular method used, and it is favored by most development organizations and also frequently referenced in the global climate policy debate (O'Brien et al. 2004). The difficulty I (and many other researchers) have with using this third track is that researchers tend to look at the community from the outside. Metaphorically, it is like watching a sports game from a seat in the top row of a stadium and looking down at the players. Spectators can see the players moving but cannot hear anything the players are saying to each other. It is therefore not surprising that such etic approaches are apt to exclude the community's interests and may eventually impair the success of the adaptation measures.

As a researcher I like to see a more insider (emic) view of the community. Studies following this route comply with the fourth track: researchers go to the field and like to work alongside the community to understand their respective actions for adapting to climate change (Petheram et al. 2010). They like to gain an understanding of a community's perception through participatory and culturally sensitive methods that, in turn, can identify development activities that will strengthen the community's capacity to adapt to climate change. It is unfortunate that hardly any studies in the literature come from an emic standpoint. As an illustration, even within a relatively extensive literature concerning the viewpoint of the Inuit indigenous community of Canada, the etic perspective is the "dominant" framework for studies of the peoples of the Arctic region (Cameron 2012). Only a few scholars have presented an emic viewpoint of the perception of that region's indigenous peoples (Ford et al. 2006; Laidler 2006).

Fairly recently there have been a number of attempts to study indigenous views from the inside. The studies of Wolf et al. (2013) and O'Brian and

Wolf (2010), after approximately twenty years of intense adaptation research, researched the values a community possessed to disclose their view. The researchers identified a wide range of values, both intangible (such as freedom, way of life) and tangible (such as wood collection, fishing). Intangible values supporting tradition, freedom, harmony, safety and unity, as demonstrated in the research, shape the total view of communities in Labrador, Canada.

Traditional ecological knowledge

Another way environmental scientists explore an indigenous community is by studying the traditional knowledge system it possesses to overcome the risk presented by climate change. Such traditional ecological knowledge (TEK) is better known as a "cumulative body of knowledge, practice and belief, evolving by adaptive processes and handed down through generations of cultural transmission, about the relationship of living beings (including humans) with one another and the environment" (Berkes 2008, 7). It is direct evidence of hundreds of years of seemingly inseparable interplay with the environment, among influences that come from adapting to modern culture.

The knowledge system of an indigenous community seems to represent their life's blueprint. For example, Byg and Salick (2009) examined the knowledge of the residents of six Tibetan villages with regard to changes in snow, rain, river level, temperature, storms and slides, planting and harvesting of crops, crop disease and the existence of wild plants. They discovered that the villagers possessed a detailed climate-change knowledge base that was linked to the moral and spiritual aspects of the communities. The tight link between knowledge, values and beliefs was further explored in a significant eight-year study on the climate-change viewpoint of the Gitga'at indigenous peoples of British Columbia in Canada (Turner and Clifton 2009). Over hundreds of years, the Gitga'at people have developed a large skill set to detect changes in fauna, flora, forests and weather. In the researchers' ethnography, they show how the Gitga'at's climate perspective is heavily linked to a cosmovision epitomizing an embedded and universal view, including aspects of sustainable resource use and well-being for the future.

An interesting study examines what happens in the case when an indigenous community is surrounded by both climate change and development activities. This is the case with the Miriwoong indigenous peoples living in East Kimberley, Northern Australia (Leonard et al. 2013). The researchers showed that for these nature-dependent peoples, climate change is the surprising result of three factors: development pressures (dams and irrigated agriculture), extreme events (floods) and spiritual punishment. Leonard and colleagues concluded that this community's view is not only dependent on the traditional ecological knowledge but also on the wide range of contextual factors that ultimately define their strategy in climate change.

With only a handful of studies, I believe the field of perception research is still in its infancy. A considerable obstacle is that such studies require researchers to stay for a long period of time under primitive conditions in the field. When I look at my own experience, the hardest part of my field research was living without electricity, running water, telephone and the Internet, and sleeping with the black, hairy tarantulas hanging above my hammock. But in the end, the time and effort I invested gained trust from the community not only to access their lives as well as share precious experiences and valuable knowledge, but also sufficient time to validate my research outcomes. So researchers have to keep in mind that giving up time (and much more) for doing this work should be a conscious choice. This means that it will interfere with pursuing a traditional academic career, because the reality is that field-based studies are not easily compatible with or typical for academic research careers in which each scholar needs to publish several papers, attend conferences and guide students through theses and dissertations each year.

Researching the community through the eyes of the development specialist

Researchers following this paradigm want to make sure a community undergoes a smooth change process that is part of a larger social, economic and political setting. This process typically encompasses understanding how each indigenous group depends on an intrinsic connection with the surrounding natural environment, seeing themselves as a part of a world full of animals, plants, water, soil and sky. Besides this human-environment relationship, indigenous communities also have functional interactions and links with other social groups. More significant to development researchers are the internal connections among the community's members themselves. The development paradigm allows further study of the structures and relationships a community possesses and how these (permanently) change when facing a serious threat from the outside.

Through the eyes of development researchers, an indigenous community possesses three fundamental elements: connections with the forest, connections among community members and connections with other social groups. These elements make up the community's system (Figure 2.1), which according to systems theory possesses two interesting properties. If one part of the system is removed, the whole system will be unable to function (Laszlo and Krippner 1998), for example, when one functional group, the customary hunters and

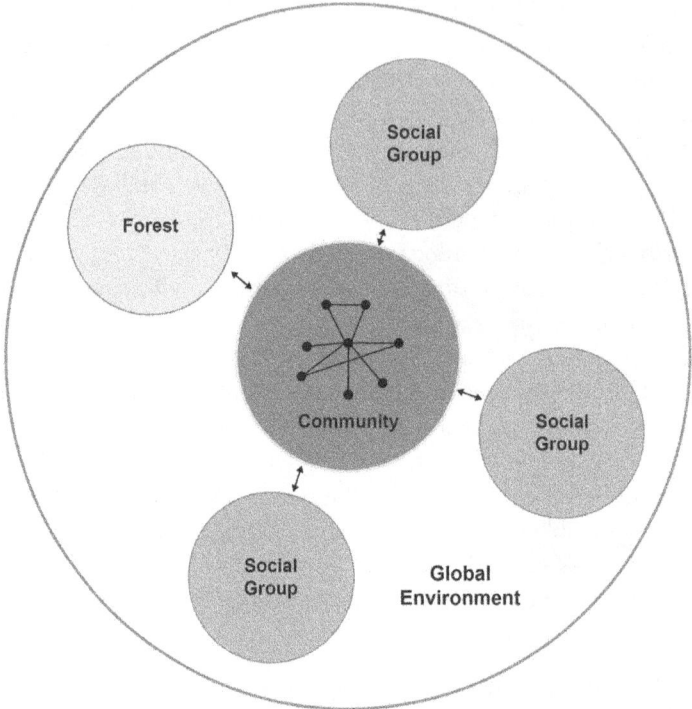

Figure 2.1 The system for nature-dependent communities.

fishers, leaves the community all at once. In the absence of this vital human resource, the community has no one with skills and expertise to catch animals and fish, resulting in a serious threat to food security. It is also true that if one component of the system is removed, it cannot function on its own (Laszlo and Krippner 1998). In the case in which the same indigenous hunters and fishers have no forest left, they may struggle to survive on their own because they lack the necessary traditional knowledge to simply move to another resource base, for example, a coastal ecosystem.

A system's approach permits a researcher to depart from comparing communities with each other based on their knowledge or adaptive capacity and to thoroughly study the nature of relationships that constitute the community's well-being. It seeks to understand the complexity of all the community's existing relationships, including those with nature, with other groups and with the global politics (Laszlo and Krippner 1998). System researchers are thus able to investigate the complexity of a community without getting caught up in abstract (causal) analysis that constitutes an absolute truth usually prescribed by the development paradigm (Laszlo and Krippner 1998).

I have learned that a systems approach particularly gives a rich understanding of how an indigenous community reacts when it is facing environmental pressures. When such pressure is easily cushioned, the system becomes resilient and moves back into the natural state. I find that in situations when the community has difficulty dealing with the rapid change, however, the system can become fragile and move into an unsteady state. It is then that intrinsic relationships will be tested and may become vulnerable. In communities that have trouble getting out of the chaos, as I have seen, there can (unexpectedly) emerge a situation of conflict among the members of the system or between the community and other systems (Li et al. 2012; Mayer 2004). Development researchers normally notice this conflict when internal shifts take place within communities, leading to a change in power relations and sometimes a transformation of the community structure or leadership (Agrawal and Gibson 2001; Brennan and Israel 2008; Giddens, 1984).

Sustainable livelihood framework

By far the most useful and popular framework for researching a community system is the sustainable livelihood framework. In 1997, the framework was developed by the Department for International Development of the United Kingdom during the time when development organizations were looking for a way to gain a better understanding of the livelihoods of poor communities living in natural habitats. The framework is widely used by researchers to determine the multifaceted capacity a community has in terms of its sustainable development.

Development specialists assess five main assets to get an inside view of the multifaceted processes that underlie decisions a community makes for its development. They assume that any community consistently shapes its livelihood based on social, natural, human, financial and physical capital (DFID 1999). Besides these assets, in the view of these practitioners, a typical community also can possess supporting structures that are necessary to define the livelihood direction, such as culture, internal rules, social institutions and governance structures (DFID 1999). A strong characteristic of this framework is that the community defines its own livelihood goals. Examples of end goals are typically human development oriented, such as improved income, increased well-being, reduced vulnerability, enhanced food security and sustainable use of the natural resource base. I was also lucky to have met communities that consistently favor peace and freedom above the classic economic goal of securing more income and other material needs.

Next, I try to look at indigenous communities facing climate change through the eyes of the researchers using this framework. These researchers would typically assess which livelihood assets the community uses and evaluate whether they would be vulnerable to trends, shocks and influences from seasonality. The livelihood analysis distinguishes shocks coming from conflict and human and animal health as well as economic and natural change. It considers trends arising from changes in population, economy, resources, technology and governance. Analysis of seasonality includes influences from varying prices, production, health and employment opportunities (DFID 1999). To illustrate this, I conveniently discuss my own research on getting more insight into the internal dynamics of a South American community livelihood system when it was facing climate change (Smith 2010a). My fieldwork revealed that besides the five known assets, two other assets are central in the indigenous community's decision making for livelihood under climate change: the community's history and internal values (historical capital), and its decision-making capacity and the degree to which it is susceptible to power exercised by outside actors (political capital).

The sustainable livelihood framework seems an excellent tool to picture how a community uses and depend on its specific livelihood assets when they are threatened. For example, when a community is facing pest intrusion due to climate change, it may want to adapt using its current natural assets (traditional farms) and depend on its financial assets (money) to purchase pest-resistant seeds that will stand up against the pest. Although the framework demonstrates the significance of assets in the choice of livelihood strategies, it reveals very little of the community's own view about how to act in situations of climate change.

Capability framework

Numerous researchers working with the capability framework support the work of Amartya Sen, a Nobel Prize-winning economist. Sen (1999) distinctively argues that people strive toward freedom as the main goal of progress and development. People can create and shape their own development goal, and this goal always embraces greater social, economic and political freedom than they had previously. Examples of such freedom are having social opportunities, social transparency, political freedom, protective security and economic facilities. For a discussion on climate change, this might mean finding ways to assess how indigenous communities would obtain more collective income, environmental security and a better political position than before.

Sen's line of thought has been a superb breakthrough from the economically driven view of development to a more holistic approach of individual well-being. There is a much broader definition of development than the one held in the Sustainable Livelihood Framework. I illustrate this point with one of my experiences in Box 2.3.

Box 2.3
Two Ways of Analyzing Communities in Development

An indigenous community proposes renovating a 30-meter-long bridge across a creek that divided its village in two parts. The community members started by organizing themselves, after which the leaders customarily allocated different tasks among them: younger men had to cut down the trees, older men had to saw the trees into planks, boatmen had to transport the planks from the forest to the village and the women had to make fermented beer as a reward for the men doing all the hard work. If a development researcher using the Sustainable Livelihood Framework looked at this practical scenario, he or she would typically study the way the community organized itself (social capital) and gathered natural resources (natural capital) to build the bridge. A development researcher following Sen's framework would study the reason why the bridge was built in the first place, which was to make sure the villagers living on both sides of the bridge would be able to socialize and thus attain more freedom.

Sen's theoretical framework opens up various possibilities for looking at community development in a more holistic way. I base this conclusion on the fact that Sen and his protégés look more specifically at the process by which people define goals, based on their personal, social and environmental arrangements (Frediani 2010). Examples of such personal arrangements are physical condition, sex, reading skills and intelligence; social arrangements are public policies, social norms, gender roles, discrimination, hierarchies and power relations; environmental arrangements are climate, infrastructure, institutions and the public good.

Although this framework is well thought out and described, there is an urgent need for practical guidelines so researchers can apply them to communities in the field. Several development researchers have attempted to make Sen's framework suitable for practical use, and are now trying out participatory methods to understand the different dimensions of how individuals define their own development goals (Biggeri et al. 2006; Frediani 2007).

Researching Views through Conflict-Resolution Frameworks

It is obvious that the frameworks discussed so far all have their limitation in explaining the view an indigenous community holds when facing climate change. In fact, I have encountered five fundamental problems in the discussion: (1) researchers look at the community from the outside rather than making an inside assessment; (2) researchers present a static representation of a community, which disallows focusing on the specific process by which a community view is constructed; (3) researchers approach the community from a donor-driven, economic-modernity paradigm rather than looking at what the community wants for itself; (4) researchers are unable to create a whole picture encompassing the past, present and future; and (5) some of the frameworks are just not practical enough for researchers to apply in a community setting in the field.

A discipline that is purposely set up for researching views is conflict resolution. It can be best described as a collective noun for a series of methods and processes involved in facilitating the peaceful ending of conflict. Stemming from social psychology in the 1930s, conflict resolution has evolved gradually into a full scientific discipline. This fairly young field is founded on the assumption that conflict is a result of perceived differences between two or more groups in social structure (Mitchell 1981; Kriesberg 2003; Bercovitch 1996), in social agency (Lederach 1995; Galtung 1996), in communication (Katz et al. 2011; Tannen 1986), in cultural values (Ting-Toomey 2001; Cohen 1997; Avruch 1998; Docherty 2001) and in needs or interests (Burton 1990).

Conflict resolution found its way into the development field in the 1970s. Multilateral and development organizations, such as the United Nations, the World Bank and others were very interested in resolving international conflict because at that time the Cold War between Russia and the United States was sparking. Conflict scholars put their heads together to resolve this type of conflict and to gradually help improve the poor relationship between these countries. At the same time, conflict researchers were trying to find new ways to end violent conflict in others parts of the world, especially Africa. Specific emphasis was then placed on the delivery of aid and the initiation of development activities in a postconflict situation (Anderson 1999).

Donors from developed countries like to see the end of violent conflict as a prerequisite for development to commence in the countries that they want to support. It is obvious that conflict is here explored as an internal failure of a poor country to have structures in place for reducing violence, promoting stability and preventing conflict. Through development organizations, developed countries can then provide the necessary assistance at the international level, from country to country. These organizations typically like to work with poor countries to improve their governance and democracy and strengthen civil society (ODI 1998). Peace tends to be seen as a precondition to human progress. And in situations of conflict, people will have trouble progressing in their individual well-being because they have to handle the existing conflict first.

A lesser-known area of interest in the development field is that of "pro-poor" participation. Conflict specialists working in this area argue that the civic participation of poor people in development is structurally hindered by social, physical and political factors beyond the control of these people (Jantzi and Jantzi 2009). Usually these barriers, which are often insurmountable, come from the more powerful organizations that want to implement projects at the local level. The gracious goal of these organizations is to design systems to ensure that local communities can effectively participate in negotiations. Conflict in this case, according to the experts, is caused by the structural inequality between the development organization and disadvantaged community. The root causes of conflict are the underlying issues of injustice, exploitation, threats to identity and security and people's sense of victimization (Jantzi and Jantzi 2009). The pro-poor research track is explored further in this book.

Scholars studying in the pro-poor track are increasingly interested in improving their understanding about the causes of conflicts related to inequality in development. Conflicts that deal with this issue generally fall within the pool of constructive conflicts. Such conflicts center on the process itself and have the potential to leaves parties with more benefit than costs. This is not the case with destructive conflicts, where parties are stuck in narrow and rigid paths to their goals and use threats and hostility to ultimately produce negative outcomes (Kriesberg 2003). In any kind of constructive conflict there is space for parties to improve communication, thoroughly discuss issues and then enhance mutual learning. Such "conflict management" strategies can result in parties developing new ideas and venues together. Managing conflict requires conflict specialists to rely on a set of quick techniques that can consist of general steps (Burton, Fisher and Ury 1981; Weeks 1992; Bolton 1979) or more complicated models that sometimes require intervention from a third party (Moore 2003; Bush and Folger 2005; Winslade and Monk 2001; Furlong 2005).

Conflict specialists like me believe that conflict in development can first be managed and then progressively transformed. Any kind of conflict transformation is key in pro-poor development where the parties engage in a relationship for a longer period of time, and this relationship develops in a dynamic social environment (Lederach 2003). The potential for such structural change is present when there are means to overcome the hefty power difference/inequality and at the same time improve communication, cooperation and social learning between the development organization and community (Odi 1998; Smith et al. 2014). In my further discussion of conflict, I primarily pay attention to methods applicable for making a long-term transformation between a community and development organization.

Characteristics of conflict frameworks

Scholars and practitioners in the pro-poor participation track have tried to comprehend the reason why numerous development initiatives with indigenous peoples are not as successful as expected. In chapter 1, I discussed how researchers from the development field address this inquiry by explicitly focusing on issues affecting communities, such as participation, power disparity/inequality and social agency. Now I try to look at this question through the eyes of conflict researchers. These researchers typically put emphasis on one party and systematically research how this party is in conflict with others. The focus here is on the conflict itself, such as analyzing complex and heated problems and improving the party's capacity to learn and cooperate. The frameworks used to assess conflicts have several characteristics that are very useful for research in the pro-poor development track, which is discussed below.

Characteristic 1: Conflict frameworks have a systems approach

Conflict scholars believe that there is a process of inseparable interaction between the different members in each community. Any of these functional members can be influenced from within the system, such as through family, or be affected by an external actor such as an alliance or the media. The goal is to study how each relationship within the community system is influenced, which, in turn, has an influence on the community's view. Conflict researchers normally use conflict-mapping tools, which aim to assess the whole system and seemingly assume that parties make crucial decisions based on the opportunities and threats that are presented to them (Wehr 1979; Byrne and Carter 1996).

Characteristic 2: Conflict frameworks are holistic

Conflict-resolution frameworks are developed by scholars who come from disciplines in the social sciences, humanities, business and abstract science. This multidisciplinary approach causes the frameworks to be holistic, so they can be applied to an array of situations such as in a setting of the family, an organization, a community and even a whole nation. Holism is also reinforced by a very broad definition of conflict that is active in the field: "conflicts arise when concerned parties hold competing claims to scarce status, power and/or resources or when parties have substantial or perceived divergence of beliefs, opinions or interests" (Li et al. 2012, 210). Such an extensive definition of conflict gives researchers like me an opportunity to thoroughly investigate the nexus between conflict, development and environment, necessary for getting a better understanding of the complex indigenous view in an era of climate change.

Characteristic 3: Conflict frameworks can be context specific

A conflict researcher can choose from a wide range of theories, models and tools to understand the interaction between parties in a conflict he or she is handling. Conflict theories are specialized on concepts of rational choice, exchange of assets and power disparity, among others (Folger et al. 2005; Pruitt and Kim 2004). These theories feed into models, purposely designed to understand the behavior of parties in conflict. More specific are the tools available for managing and resolving conflict. The field distinguishes the following important tools: communication techniques (Katz et al. 2011), problem-solving workshops (Burton 1990), mediation techniques (Bush and Folger 2005; Winslade and Monk 2001; Moore 2003) and negotiation techniques (Fisher and Ury 1981, Lewicky et al. 2007). It is from this large tool set that conflict researchers select based on the type and character of the conflict.

Characteristic 4: Conflict frameworks can address power disparities

A serious and structural problem in community development is the uneven power between a local community and a development organization. This inequality goes far back in history, in fact, to the divide between developed and developing countries that became visible with global industrialization in the 1950s. Researchers need to address this historic imbalance. Conflict-resolution frameworks like to normally concentrate on the present and future, but there are certain opportunities for researchers to address significant experiences and events from the past. Exclusive frameworks that work from the bottom up can reveal and address historic events, such as Lederach's (1995) elicit training model, in which involved parties undertake training as a unique opportunity to learn and discover so that they can easily bring forward past events (Sharoni 1996). Another bottom-up model, purposefully designed by my colleagues and me, named MAPCID[1], helps the researcher analyze the community's history, culture and goals and make strategic interventions to align these aspects with those from the development initiative (Smith et al. 2014).

---

1 Model for the Analysis of Potential Conflict in Development.

Characteristic 5: Conflict frameworks recognize each party as an actor

Conflict creates a situation of distress and unease, puts extra tension on each party and hampers them from thinking clearly, communicating effectively and making sound decisions. It is not at all surprising that every party soon wants to get out of a conflict situation in which they are engaged. A comparable situation is expected in our climate-change discussion. It is assumed that an indigenous community has a strong urge to escape the uncomfortable situation of environmental uncertainty and potentially conflict. The community then wants to act. The members can decide for themselves how to behave in situations of conflict.

Characteristic 6: Conflict frameworks can focus on differences rather than similarities

Conflict frameworks exclusively research the interaction between two or more parties rather than emphasizing the makeup of only one party (Mayer 2004). Conflict specialists can apply such frameworks to assess both the differences and similarities between those parties, and even capture differences in culture, interests and agency between communities and development organizations (Barron et al. 2007; Oishi 1995). The wide range of frameworks that are available to researchers allows them enough space to include the typical characteristics of each party to be studied.

Characteristic 7: Conflict frameworks can focus on the social-change process rather than the status quo

Conflict frameworks always seek to positively transform the relationship between the disputing parties (Sharoni 1996). The general idea is that a researcher should initiate this change process when working with the parties to define common goals (Parsons 2003; Kriesberg 2003; Smith et al. 2014). The researcher can do this after making a full assessment of the structure of the parties (history, culture, values, economy and politics), the interaction between parties (strategies, tactics, change, limiting factors and environment) and the issues of conflict (source, issue development) (Wehr 1997; Byrne and Carter 1996).

Characteristic 8: Conflict frameworks can address hidden values

Values are important drivers for conflict. Tribal groups may expose such values, sometimes accidentally, as they become upset and angry in conflict. Conflict frameworks can provide an inclusive structure for in-depth analysis of these values because it defines the lens through which people see the world.

Researchers like me would like to assess these values in indigenous groups when they are facing environmental pressure (Barr et al. 2011).

In summary, the field of conflict resolution can provide research frameworks that can be used for deep analysis of a community itself. Each type of these frameworks is founded on the assumption that conflict is rooted in differences in the parties' perception of reality. And this reality is linked to the system from which a community operates, which encompasses social, political, environmental and economic factors. A real advantage of working from such a reality perception is that the researchers explore the situation as is, without fitting it into any type of abstract (positivist) paradigm.

Conflict as a framework for researching views

The view is the lens through which the community sees the outside world. Every indigenous community crafts a view based on its own knowledge, values and beliefs obtained through its (usually lengthy) journey of existence. When such a community is challenged and confronted with a novel situation, such as from climate change, the initial view may be reconstructed to overcome the pressure. I like to compare this to a recognizable modern world example: a situation of a boy growing up with the values and traditions of the family. When the boy grows up and becomes a teenager, he makes new friends and is confronted with new values and norms. It is then that his initial views can face conflict, and he can do one of two things: he can completely ignore the new information and stick to his own views or he can uptake new information and change his original views. So, the point I want to make is, with environmental change, one's view is challenged—an interesting moment because this is when a community constructs a new view.

View conflict encompasses differences in knowledge, values and ideology. These structural but often invisible differences become apparent and are challenged through social interaction. When one party is unable to find elements and constructs in common between its view and that of another party, that party may try to negotiate its own reality (Docherty 2001). If we use the example discussed above, the teenage boy is confronted with a new house rule: he has to give up social time to study two more hours a day. Having lots of difficulty understanding this rule, the typical teenager starts arguing with his parents about the hardship of his life, for example, in school, in sports, in music and in the family. He apparently is negotiating about his own reality rather than trying to understand the reality of his parents. The teenager thus cannot participate in issue-specific negotiation and tactically avoids talking about the mechanics of the new house rules. Little overlap exists between the perspective of the teenager and the parents, signifying view conflict (Docherty 2001).

Conflict researchers like me study the discrepancy between the two views by using practical frameworks that can provide a wide enough analysis to incorporate the contextual factors and aspirations of both actors. In the case of the teenage boy, I can systematically describe the situation of the challenges he faces in the family and any other relevant social setting, and then make a careful but detailed reconstruction of the teenager's everyday reality using the framework. A similar exercise can be done for the parents. Only then would I be capable of diving deeply enough into reality to get a thorough understanding of the (hidden) values that are the anchor from which one makes a decision. Using the same example, I would be adept at revealing that the teenager highly values music and likes to spend his time practicing and attending concerts, while his parents want him to get educated in abstract science, for which he needs to study several hours a day.

There are two distinctive methods used in practice to study view conflict. The method most widely employed by researchers is narrative analysis, in which researchers emphasize identifying and categorizing the language each party uses when in conflict. A significant case study by Docherty (2001) provides a narrative analysis of the widely known conflict between a religious group in Waco, Texas, known as the Branch Davidians, and negotiators of the United States Federal Bureau of Investigation (FBI). Docherty cunningly illustrates how the parties in conflict operated from completely different realities: the Branch Davidians understood the conflict as a phase of a predicted apocalypse, while the FBI believed that they could use police tactics to make the Branch Davidians surrender individuals considered hostages. Docherty studied the words spoken to find differences and similarities in interpretations, values and communication style between groups. She specifically searched for the naming, framing and blaming language of each party and then proposed ways that the parties could effectively communicate with each other and possibly overcome the conflict. Docherty stresses the need for groups such as the FBI to consider their own view in negotiations and to adopt existing conflict-resolution methods to prevent escalation.

A second way researchers study view differences is through a model developed by Nudler (1993). This model seems useful in situations where language is less direct, as is the case with indigenous communities living in the forest. Their views define the organizing concept through which a community views local climate-related changes (Wolf and Moser 2011). Five questions are useful in obtaining an understanding of such a view:

1. Ontologically framed question: What is real or true? The question seeks to explain how a community understands climate change in its daily life. The community heavily relies on its traditional knowledge to make sense of the elements that interest its members in the surrounding environment.

2. Logically framed question: How is the "real" organized? This question seeks to understand the system a community has for understanding climate change. The traditional knowledge system is embedded in a community and includes the transfer of knowledge from older to younger generations. Answering the question will give more insight into the strength and breadth of this knowledge system.

3. Epistemologically framed question: How do we know what "is"? This question seeks to understand how a community knows it is dealing with climate change. The community uses the traditional knowledge system to detect change, and the question will disclose the elements that are categorized as risks and their potential thresholds.

4. Axiologically framed question: What is valuable or important? This question seeks to understand what is valuable or important when a community deals with climate change. The role of values in local climate change can then be defined.

5. Ethically framed question: How should I or we act? This question seeks to understand what attitude and strategies a community has in handling climate change.

These five questions enable a researcher to draw a good picture of the present view of a community. However, after applying Nudler's framework in practice several times, it was difficult for me to gather insight into how the community view is linked to its decision-making process.

So far, I have touched upon several methodologies in my quest to find a suitable method to research a community's view. The theoretical frameworks from the field of conflict resolution seem holistic enough to address power disparities and deep enough to unravel the values on which the community constructs a view. But I couldn't find a single framework to analyze in detail how an ingrained nature-dependent group, such as an indigenous community, forms its own development view and formulates its decisions. It would be very useful to have an overall methodology for obtaining a systematic understanding of how an indigenous community views its own future development, especially under environmental change.

Chapter 3

NEW FRAMEWORK FOR RESEARCHING VIEWS IN COMMUNITY DEVELOPMENT

Communities appear to be struggling with climate change. The views they hold have to change swiftly and, as a result, a researcher's understanding of a community's view becomes even more challenging. Countless times I have witnessed how a community's view defers and alters under circumstances I could have never predicted beforehand or, many times, not even slightly understood. At that moment, I wish to have the unique but unattainable ability to see through the eyes of a community to discover its thoughts and choices when it is combatting the changing climate. The closest I came to looking through the eyes of communities is with a practical framework I have gradually developed over a period of more than ten years. I was privileged to test this framework with the help of numerous colleagues in several indigenous (and other) communities spread over countries in South America. The new framework is presented in this chapter.

Construction of a Community View

Indigenous communities are entrenched societies made up of several functioning members who live collectively in a certain place. They are often called "natives" because they belong to a location close to or in nature, usually a great distance away from mainstream society. Every so often researchers even say indigenous peoples have their "own" society based on rules and norms that are politically and socially different from modern society. Any kind of economic involvement with modern society seems necessary to contribute to the community's basic need for clothes, personal hygiene and essential food items. Some indigenous groups may have more involvement in mainstream society than others, and many social science researchers refer to this difference as their level of acculturation. This term refers to the process of losing one's culture to new influences from the market economy in the Western world.

Living in serenity with the forest for generations to come is one essential goal of these extraordinary peoples. It is apparent that most indigenous groups generate a vigorous and robust view of their life based on the aspects they select as important in life based on previous experience (Docherty 2001). The construction of their views habitually takes place throughout their mutual existence with nature, and this interactive process can stretch over decades or sometimes hundreds or thousands of years. Transferred from old to new generations, such a traditional view is often reinforced through a series of selected stories, dances and music.

There is agreement among scientists that each member of an indigenous group possesses extensive knowledge of and experience with environmental change in their specific living place that has been accumulated over long periods of time. Possessing the distinctive capacity to identify changes, indigenous peoples can easily group forest change into short-term events or longer trends and anomalies. Special skills to foresee the unpredictable cycles of nature, of which tsunamis, floods and infestation of disease are embedded in many of these nature-dependent groups. The view constructed in this close relationship with the forest is difficult to understand when a researcher is closed off from understanding other types of knowledge than that learned in school. Apparently every researcher, including me, has a tendency to fall back on his or her own frame of thinking because it is the one that is safe and familiar (Box 3.1).

Box 3.1
A View of a Woman Shaman

To illustrate the classic ignorance of researchers in interpreting indigenous views, I recall a special moment when an old female shaman told me about an episode when the forest became extremely dry, leading large and robust trees to shed all of their leaves. By comparing this event to a rebirth, she explained to me how unusual and special this time was because the forest becomes highly fertile. Indeed, I looked very differently at the same event. As a typical researcher with roots in biology, I saw it as an abnormality since the full-bodied trees had never previously shown this behavior. I apparently relied on biological laws to suspect that the ecological equilibrium was challenged. At that juncture, unfortunately, I was still putting this woman's pragmatic view into my own positivist, at times even paternalistic, frame of thinking.

Views under climate change

Let us now look at an indigenous community facing a severe flood or other climate-change event it has never experienced before. A climate event is any weather episode that falls outside of the norm as experienced by the community over the years that it has lived in one place. Once there is no delineated recollection of a climate event in the traditional knowledge base, the community experiences the event as new (Figure 3.1, point A). This is the time when tribal men and women struggle in their effort to try to cope with the ongoing changes. What I have seen is that a rapid environmental change event may inflict a level of discomfort and confusion about how to act in the future, which in turn creates a situation of disorder within the community. Community members depart from daily activities and start engaging closely with each other to find ways to elucidate the problems associated with the climate event. The community is thus in a state of chaos (Figure 3.1, point B). To illustrate, an indigenous group I worked with suddenly discovered a pest attacking its cassava crop after a flood event. The extremely aggressive pest made the cassava root decay when planted in plots situated within the dense forest. The community members had never seen this kind of attack before and thus couldn't rely on their traditional knowledge base for an applicable resolution. The group had to rapidly develop one or more new coping strategies,

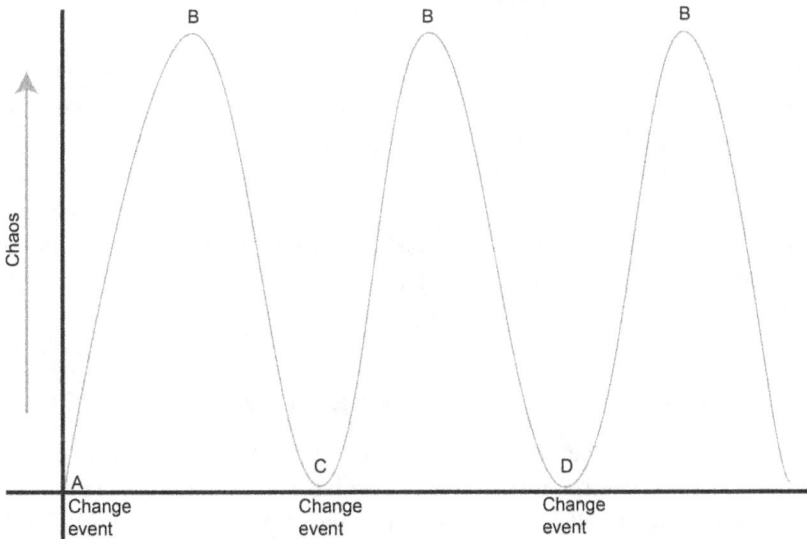

Figure 3.1 The community view during climate change.

now that they literally saw their food supply decreasing in front of their eyes. In their effort trying to find a solution fast, the community became restless and, during this time of confusion, used all their energy to discuss the pest problem as a collective.

The level of panic increased until the community members were able to find an acceptable solution to the emergency. The men and women came up with various strategies to handle the pest attack. One solution was to plant fast-growing crops as an addition to the main crop. Another alternative plan the community made was to begin harvesting cassava at an earlier time to temporally interfere with the pest's life cycle; however, this may have led to obtaining smaller-sized crops. Through devising all of these strategies, the community started the process of creating a new view.

The original story of the community was about planting and sharing abundant food among its members, only without any serious problems. But the life story changed soon after the flood experience. The community placed the "pest intrusion" event in the midst of the story, which had a beginning in the past (sharing food) and an end in the future (new strategies: planting fast-growing crops and early harvesting). Once the novel life story was compiled entirely, the community finished shaping a new view and then returned to its normal state of being (Figure 3.1, point C). The whole view-making process can repeat itself after the occurrence of a new event. For example, a climate-related drought may lead once more to an altered life story and an altered view.

Keep in mind that communities' strategies derive from a complex cognitive view-making process that normally takes place among most members. Yet I have seen situations in which some of the tribal men and women were unable to conceptualize a novel view. Members of more modern-oriented groups relate more to individual interest, which implies that some members may want to take a different route than others. What is imperative to understand is that even such modern communities possess some kind of life story, usually based on considerable common experience. Researchers like me are therefore interested in the life story of any type of community to better comprehend how it crafts a view for its future life.

The Life Story: Values, Meanings and Sustainable Decisions

A life story defines what is important in a community's life. It originates from the past through community members who have a set of shared experiences and subsequently develop values and norms that they live by (Docherty 2001). This inner script can be metaphorically compared to the skeleton of a human body: a skeleton gives overall strength and allows the body to stand firmly upright. Similarly, a life story strengthens a community's cognition about its

Box 3.2
The Life Story of the Surui Indigenous Peoples

A profound example is the life story of the Surui indigenous peoples of the Brazilian state of Rondônia, which is dominated by health and reproduction, because the Surui formerly were plagued with disease to the extent that their entire population decreased by nearly 90 percent following contact with modern people in 1969. Additionally, in modern times, the Surui have been completely surrounded by company-driven, large-scale logging activities. From that point forward, deforestation became another major theme in the life story of the Surui peoples. As a way to combat the deforestation pressure, the Surui participated in REDD+ projects (Carrero et al. 2012). They were proud to be the first community in the Amazon region to offer 120,000 carbon credits on the voluntary market, which were bought in 2013 by Latin America's largest cosmetics company, Natura Cosméticos.

own existence, and a comprehensive and well-accepted life story seems to feed into a strong view. Indigenous peoples tend to have such a durable view about the environment: they typically fall back on a life story that stretches into decades or sometimes even centuries (Box 3.2).

During my years in the field I have observed a wide variety of communities in different stages of development that taught me how a view is assembled from a life story. Every time, I have distinguished three distinctive but important processes: (1) judgement against values; (2) meaning making; and (3) decision making. I now further go into what each of these processes entails and clarify how they relate to the community's life story.

Values

The first process is when a community initially detects environmental changes and automatically starts making a judgment about these changes against their past values. Values are the "standards by which we judge events and the behavior of other people and by which we decide what is worthy of our support and what deserves our condemnation" (Carpenter and Kennedy 2001, 197). Values can be considered the anchor in the process of view making. Indigenous communities build on these anchors to judge incidents of climate change and decide which direction to go in the future. To illustrate the importance of values, I return to the previous example of climate-change-related pest infestation in the cassava crop. The destructive insect now spreads to two indigenous villages, A and B, situated in the same tropical forest ecoregion. The history of community A is dominated by repeated incidents of food scarcity and malnutrition among its members. Building just enough insurance so these incidents don't reoccur in the future is the essence of this community's life story. With a customary responsibility for growing and preparing food, the women in community A would like to pursue those activities that boost people's nutrition levels. Planting several types of crops that possess high nutrition levels is one of the women's remedies.

In community B, the life story is characterized by violence and war. For decades, the community has been continuously provoked, contested and targeted by others over food. The women in community B propose quite a different strategy from that in community A, although they face an identical pest problem and have a similar interest as the other women in safeguarding food. Here, the women collectively propose growing and nurturing crops in small planting beds near their houses rather than on subsistence plots many kilometers away. By being physically close to the plants, the women foresee having improved control over both pests and thieves. Women in both communities, in a strict sense, have a common interest in safeguarding their food but value different features from their life story. The women in community A, valuing food nutrition, craft important decisions because their life story particularly underscores prevention of malnutrition, while in community B, where food security is also valued, the women make principal choices based on a life story of protecting crops from nearby robbers. This example, indeed, shows development researchers how important it is to understand significant incidents from the past, especially because these incidents tend to stretch into present and future decision making.

Researchers in sustainable development would be interested in finding out specific details about the women in the example. They would be primarily study the activities these indigenous women employ to promote food security and how this actually contributes to their social and economic progress as well as their efforts in protecting the environment. This forward thinking tends to leave out the community's past experiences. What makes development researchers highly uncomfortable, as I have experienced, is to cross the disciplinary boundaries from environmental science into social science, which is needed for effectively studying the community's history.

Meanings

After an indigenous community has successfully judged a climate event against its historic values, it continues processing the new information it receives. Recognizing and selecting what information is useful and what is not is the next focal activity. This so-called meaning-making process encompasses a lively discussion among community members, and often divergent opinions are expressed by various functional groups in the community, such as men responsible for gathering meat and fish, women in charge of agriculture and rearing children, the youth or the visionary elders. Once there is a consensus about what information to discard and what to retain, the meaning making ends.

To illustrate the meaning-making action, I now return to the pest infestation example. The women from community A, who highly value food nutrition, will try to make sense of the new pest they see attacking their crops. Identifying the pest by looking at its appearance and following its behavior would be the women's first instinctive action. The women, exploratory and curious, might want to know what types of crops the pest attacks and during which part of the day or night this happens. The group might also try to map out the pest's life cycle and put a time stamp to its birth, upgrowth and death. Understanding what the caterpillar-like insect eats, where it lives and how much offspring it produces may be also essential for the women's understanding of the pest's behavior. During this course of identifying and characterizing, the women compare new information they gathered with what they already know. They try to see if the pest looks or behaves similarly to or differently from any other type of food destroyer encountered in the past. By finding some kind of similarity or difference, the women can connect the new pest to their life story.

Another conceivable part of the meaning-making process is when a community is trying to find an explanation for a new climate event. The women in the pest example are intrinsically connected to the environment, which teaches them to think in terms of universal cycles of birth, death and rebirth, a discourse shared with most indigenous peoples (Pierotti 2011). It would not be surprising to me that these nature-dependent women seek a spiritual reason for explaining the new pest infestation. One explanation could be that evil spirits are sending aggressive pests as a warning sign for the collectively unaccepted or immoral behavior of community members. Another keen explanation could be that good spirits are sending the community a message to move away from its current location, a typical practice for originally nomadically living indigenous peoples. Such explanations are key to fit the pest event into the women's life story.

The process of making sense of a new climate event is thus very much dependent on the reality in which the community lives. If researchers systematically study this reality, will they be embedded enough to identify a community's frame of reference. I think that for researchers to fully comprehend

Box 3.3
Understanding the Local Reality of Indigenous Peoples

In a life-changing moment I got the opportunity to really understand the local reality of indigenous peoples. My colleagues and I visited an indigenous village to implement a development project. When we landed our five-person airplane, everybody in the community seemed hungry because of the food problems this village had. Every day, on numerous occasions, we shared our brought-in food with villagers who would come by our hut to talk and share stories. When it came time to leave, we received a message that the airfield was closed due to excessive rain. We were stuck, with no food left. Desperately we started searching for food and could feel the same panic the community felt. The point I want to make with this example is that we, as researchers, should be extremely sensitive to a community's on-the-ground reality. We should try as much as possible to genuinely experience things similar to what a community undergoes in order to be able to truly understand the local reality.

a local reality is one of the most prominent problems in community development today. Researchers usually interact with a community for a couple of years and comfortably assume they understand the local reality. When I reflect on my own fieldwork, I would visit an indigenous community at least once every month for a few days. During this time of intense interaction, I would observe, study and engage with the community members, and after a few years, confidently thought I knew these people's reality. Yet, this was not the case (Box 3.3).

Sustainable decisions

As soon as an indigenous community makes sense of a specific climate event, it is ready to take one or more decisions on how to act. Because each group faces challenges specific to its home environment, it must make choices by constantly trading off between different needs (Berkes 2008). After this, the community is ready to set goals for the future. If a project researcher is unable to assess the community's readiness, a mismatch may emerge between the goals of this community and those of the project. Most of these projects either end up in a dispute or conclude with a recommendation that the community needs capacity building so it can "grasp" the project (Box 3.4).

Box 3.4
Defining Goals for Sustainable Development

If the indigenous women from community A, who value food security, must choose between conserving exotic birds and selling these birds for income needed to keep their children in school, I have seen them choose the second option. This option is probably the best for their future survival because this group does not traditionally use exotic birds for food. One elder explained to me that beautiful multicolored birds were given by God to earn some cash. When we look through the eyes of this community, the birds are sold for getting children educated, which ultimately improves their chances of participating in mainstream society, which is one of the community's principal life goals. This example teaches me that sustainability can only be considered in the context of the goals a community sets for itself (Sen 1999).

It is not always noticeable that community goals may be distinct from the goals set by a development organization. To demonstrate, using the same example of selling exotic birds, the indigenous community wanted their children to attend school and learn how to speak and write in the indigenous language so they could have better chances at finding a job. A development organization spoke with the bird-selling community, capturing the community's interest in better job opportunities. The scientists from this organization were convinced youngsters were unable to reach the job market because they struggled with transitioning from using the indigenous language to speaking and writing the main language. This organization, supporting programs in human development, proposed to initiate a project on bilingual education so the community's youngsters had an opportunity to simultaneously learn both the indigenous and the main language. Assuming that bilingual education would help the community in terms of lowering drop-out rates and increasing the number of graduates, the organization fell back on a typical global indicator for human development. The community, on the other hand, saw bilingual education as a setback.

This project, as it is defined by the development organization, will never lead to a sustainable outcome because it is unaligned with the goals of the community. It is a classic example of how a development organization comes in from the outside and analyzes a community from the top down. In such macroanalysis, researchers tend to only hear about a community's goals but cannot reach deeply enough to discover the reason it chooses these goals. Unaware of how important it was for the youth to learn about speaking and writing the main language, the development organization proceeded with the original project.

So what should the development organization in Box 3.4 have done differently for building a truly sustainable project? I think researchers coming from these organizations can study a community's view from the bottom up. Bottom-up analysis starts with examining the values held by the community. So, returning to the example in Box 3.4, if researchers had started from the bottom up, they would have had a unique opportunity to design a project by integrating both the goals and values of the community, rather than addressing only the goals. Having understood how important the main language value was for the community, the development organization would have never proposed for a bilingual project but rather a project to support youth education in the main language.

As I have learned—by making countless mistakes—a researcher should work alongside the community to consciously develop a set of shared goals that is built on the community's own values and goals (Smith et al. 2014). Reality teaches that projects designed in this bottom-up way belong to the pool of those that run for the long term because of a higher level of community ownership. Projects designed this way take a lot of time. Researchers from development organizations are usually bound to strict time lines, and designing bottom-up projects is often an incongruity with the organisation's operational system (Figure 3.2).

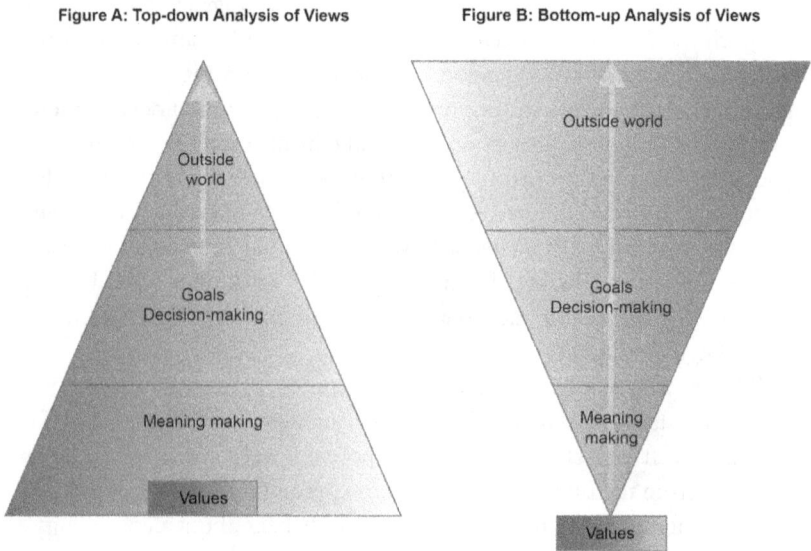

Figure 3.2 Bottom-up and top-down processes for analyzing a community's view.

The VIEW Framework

The bottom-up approach for researching a community view is presented in this section as a new framework called VIEW. The VIEW framework operates from a constructivist (postpositivist) paradigm, in which the reality of a community in its setting is considered as part of the current cultural, economic and political context of global climate-change-related development programs. The interesting part of this method is that a researcher studies the self-identified needs of a community rather than following the usually paternalistic position of a development organization.

Building on the principles of sustainable development and conflict resolution, the practical framework approaches a community as a system with functional connections to nature and other groups, such as the organization that wants to team up for implementing a development activity. Any functionally operating community within the system should be able to define its own development goals, I assume, which will ultimately lead to a greater amount of political, social and economic freedom. Thus, there is a strong focus in the VIEW framework on the values and interests of a community itself.

In this book I principally focus on environmental change events, but the VIEW framework can also be adopted for scenarios when a community (or any other actor) faces rapid change with the introduction of new technologies, exploration of new economic markets or implementation of new policies. Thus, this framework is holistically designed for use in several situations in the development field, such as in education, health, income and livelihood, infrastructure, natural resource extraction and the environment.

Following VIEW, in each situation of rapid change, the researcher can observe one or more of the following processes: after a community physically experiences a change process, it will mentally judge new information it receives against its values, which originate from its embedded historical knowledge. With the information that survives the judging process, the community is bound to make meaning by selecting the material that makes sense in the present reality in which it exists. After this internal cognitive process is entirely completed, the community appears ready to interact with others by disclosing a new discourse that conveys its decisions for the future (Figure 3.3). The following discussion clarifies each of these processes in further detail.

Judgment against values

The first process a community may undergo is to compare its own values with new information it receives from a change event. Then it makes a value

Change event

Judgment

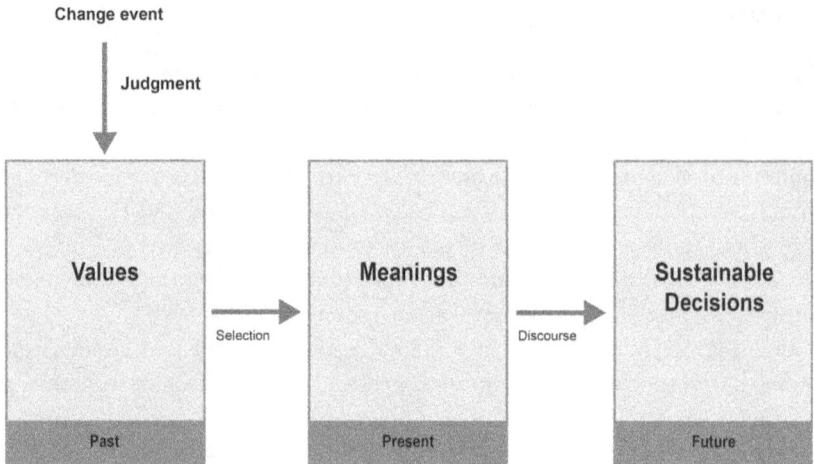

Figure 3.3 VIEW framework: The process for view construction under social and environmental change.

judgment by comparing the new information with the knowledge contained in the traditional knowledge base. Similarly, when implementing a development project under such rapid change, the community may compare the values embedded in the project against its own values. When there is a mismatch in values between the community and the project, I have seen the project often end up in a conflict. Values seem to be silent aspects that may become perceptible when a project passes into a stage of conflict, in which "trust and respect are threatened, and distorted perceptions and simplified stereotypes emerge" (Pruitt and Kim 2004, 255).

Selection of useful information

The next process in which a community can engage is the selection of information. The selection process, usually tiresome and tricky, includes an interactive process in which community members collectively pick material that is useful to and compatible with their life story. When unable to choose, for any reason, the community wants to keep its options open and may start to avoid, postpone or withdraw. Thus, a logical question to ask here is, under what circumstances will a community (purposely) interrupt the selection process?

Sometimes a community needs more time to get an accurate picture before deciding on a selection. Communities constantly seem to renegotiate relations and interests, making them generally insufficient at responding fast and efficiently (O'Riordan and Jordan 1999). So, giving fast responses to, for instance, development organizations may not always be in line with their culture, and communities need more time to select information.

At other times, as one community explained to me, the activity may be irrelevant to them. They may intentionally put up a barrier that is almost impossible to overturn. This happened in an indigenous community that saw relevance in advancing elementary education by setting up a middle school. Once a development organization came to the community to interest them in a species-conservation project, the community clarified the school as the highest priority as it was essential for providing education to the children. The community leaders purposely determined the school to be a prerequisite to the conservation project, being aware that establishing a school and finding teachers is a lengthy process that will take many years to accomplish. Postponing the conservation project gave the community extra time to engage in the selection process.

The sudden introduction of new information generated by change events places an invisible but weighty pressure on a community. Occasionally, a community has problems setting priorities because it is dealing with an internal power imbalance or conflict. I have observed a number of communities withdraw from a project because they felt they were victims of the development initiative and thus used withdrawal as a tool to demonstrate their power (ODI 1998). I think researchers certainly need to be aware of this level of pressure.

As a researcher I find it essential to recognize what information a community selects and what it discards. When having no clue about this, I am unable to understand and appreciate decisions the community takes. However, when I have some idea, I am able to provide support in the community's meaning-making process, for example, with clarifications or by supplying more information on the change event. Thus, the bottom line is that the community's selection capacity can be used by a researcher as an indicator for completing the meaning-making process in the VIEW framework (Table 3.1).

Table 3.1 Information and tools required for analysis with the VIEW framework.

Process Phase	Indicator	Information to Gather	Practical Tool
Values	Judgment	Historical values	Social polygraphy—Map of the past
Meanings	Selection	Reality description	Social polygraphy—Map of the present
Sustainable decisions	Discourse	Goals and aspirations	Social polygraphy—Map of the future

Discourse toward sustainable development

After meaning making takes place, the community can take selected information and then blend it into the life story. Based on my years of experience with nature-dependent groups, I assume that each community wants to have a better future for which it will create a discourse of its new life story. At some time the community will convey this novel discourse to people from outside the community, a process I call discoursing. Discoursing automatically follows after a community makes meaning of a new climate event.

Usually, discoursing is initiated by the leaders because they always have more information about the group's historic choices than does any other community member. These leaders tend to have a unique ability to craft new information into the community's life story, as I have repeatedly witnessed, which starts from the time it entered into existence to when it will end in the future. The other community members, out of respect and in compliance with rules, will build on the vision of seniors and add to it until the final discourse is completed.

In quite a few communities a twist can arise in the discoursing process. Sometimes a community is unable to create a discourse with the information it has selected, it may put some information to the side—meaning outside of the main discourse held in the community. Once this happens, the community may categorize the chosen information as less important than the main discourse, and eventually this information fades away and is forgotten. I have also observed situations when a community cooperatively decided to blame a development organization for aspects related to information they preferred to exclude from the discourse. Making the development organization the culprit of the community's own failures, for example, the inability to make decisions or internal conflict, is a profound example of a community's blaming tactic. In that way it consciously wants to create a negative image about the organization (Pruitt and Kim 2004).

Indeed, it is useful for researchers to study the discourse of a community because it is a crucial indicator to see how the final life story is created. During discoursing, valuable information is released by the community. Researchers can easily obtain information on how the new change event is interpreted, how it is linked with values and how it is integrated into new strategies and goals. Because the discourse occurs via interaction with others, it is an outside process and relatively easy to follow compared to the two internally occurring processes: judgment and meaning making.

Useful tool

In this section I explore what type of information researchers should obtain from the field to make the VIEW framework useful in practice. Before actually working with a community in the field, researchers normally start by gathering baseline information on the context in which the community lives. This general practice is well known. Baseline information normally consists of social and environmental studies that compile a full picture of the community in terms of its history, education, health, livelihood, income, employment, natural resource use and social and physical infrastructure.

The danger of such studies is that they contribute to a view construction that deters domination by Northern methods (Smith 1999). One problem I have seen is that many of these studies are conducted by researchers who are just not familiar enough with the context in which the community lives. They carefully design a questionnaire to gather baseline information, and because of limited knowledge of the real context in which the community operates, the questionnaire can be "off" and researchers may nondeliberately misinterpret the answers of the interviewees.

Therefore, I suggest that researchers gather information in a different way: through local knowledge and cultural interpretations, with minimal interference from the researcher. I recommend a truly interactive process between researcher and community in which the community itself can provide information, so the researcher is solely responsible for inserting this relevant information into the VIEW framework (Table 3.1).

The information needed for value judgment consists of a historical value analysis of a community. It is plausible that this type of information will permit a researcher to identify aspects of life that are important to the community as well as for their judgment of a new change event. For the meaning-making process, I suggest gathering information about the reality context in which a community presently lives. The five questions from Nudler's (1993) framework are wide enough to describe the reality context: the makeup of reality (ontology); how reality is detected (epistemology); how valuable a part of reality is (axiology); how reality is organized (logic); and how one should act on reality (ethics). For the decision-making process, I particularly propose to obtain information about the future goals and aspirations of a community.

The way a researcher can gather this information is through a comprehensive participatory process called social polygraphy. This includes a systematic process that "helps participants understand the complex interactions between context, structure, actors, and goals" (Bastidas and Gonzales 2008, 11) between these groups, in an effort to initiate dialogue and achieve mutual learning in dynamic systems. It is a methodology by which a researcher and community can engage in a thorough dialogue through a set of steps and collaboratively analyze, create meaning and draw this on a map. The maps of the past, present and future, and these are particular useful in obtaining the information necessary for the VIEW analysis (Table 3.1). My colleague Elena Bastidas, who has significant experience in using this social polygraphy methodology, explains it in more detail in the next chapter.

The VIEW framework in climate-change-related development

In this section I present two considerations for researchers when using the VIEW framework in the specific context of climate-change-development projects. The first consideration is that a community's view may get partially (or even fully) lost in the project design. I think this is crucial for researchers to know because it is often a source of (potential) conflict and sometimes even causes termination of a project. A second consideration is that a community's view, when completely constructed, can be in conflict with a view from any other actor in the system. Researchers should be aware of different actors who hold different views because they may exist and operate in different realities. In the following sections I discuss these two considerations in more detail, as well as how researchers can address these issues in practice.

Community view lost in development paradigm

A development organization links with a specific community for one or more, usually strategic, reasons. The main reason for undertaking projects in climate-change-related development is to eradicate the poverty of marginalized communities and create new opportunities in the global climate-change-mitigation scheme. Besides this noble goal, I have seen development organizations also select a community because of their charm, appearance or popularity in the national and international settings. A more appealing reason for choosing a certain community, however, is their willingness to participate in the project. It is obvious that in cases in which a community is willing to participate from the beginning, a development organization has to do little mobilization and engagement effort. And development organizations also like to favor specific locations that are prioritized by influential policy makers or funders. It is hard to imagine that a community may not be chosen because of its specific needs.

The proper way to start a community development project is for a researcher to begin with a needs assessment. Such a baseline analysis is usually performed by one or more researchers from a development organization in collaboration with the chosen community. The idea is to obtain information from the field context about the specific needs of the community. Sometimes researchers,

Box 3.4
A Story of Water

One community envisioned having running water in its remotely located village where everyone would use the river to bathe, drink, cook and wash clothes. The argument was that this would prevent an outbreak of diarrhea that affected children and elderly every year in the dry season. Regrettably, this idea ended up in a template soaked with technical details about the water supply, such as installation drawings and maintenance requirements. Having a better health situation compared to before (past) and safeguarding their survival (future) was the community's original objective. This life story—consisting of a description of the past, present and future—got lost in the project, however. The project was executed by constructing one water tap, in the middle of the village. The tap was only used by a small part of the community living in its vicinity, and the diarrhea outbreak still happened every year.

probably unconsciously, mold the community's view into a scientific template required by development organizations to move a project toward its execution. In plenty of these projects there appeared a significant loss of relevant information. What becomes lost is often the life story from which the community view originates (Box 3.4).

Once an appropriate needs assessment is completed, a development organization runs a project through a cycle of design, preparation, implementation and evaluation. The project is crafted by subject-area experts among different themes (for example, climate change, biodiversity, poverty eradication), or with a general theme among different locations (for example, climate mitigation in several countries in Latin America). Whatever the design is, in hundreds of projects I have seen, some community information gets lost. It can become very difficult to tackle the real needs of a community when filtering out information relevant to the community's life story. However, I have seen few communities object when development organizations remove these elements. The community might just continue with the project opportunistically because it provides some level of desperately needed support.

A similar situation of dominance is seen in the next step: the implementation phase. Projects are expected to be well thought out and implemented without any setbacks and delays. Communities should adjust and facilitate reaching project targets on time so they can be called "good implementers." The problem with this frame of thinking is a community is seen as static. A few years ago, I witnessed a development organization command the community members like they were soldiers. To execute the activities as prescribed, the community bravely followed orders given by the organization. Then I overheard community members talking about a new plan: complying with the requests of the development organization while at the same time trying as much as possible to get material goods out of the project. As this classic example shows, this community had a lively view about the activity in which it engaged.

Such views are not static in time either: they can frequently change during the project because of the internal transformation the community is undergoing. I have experienced that the view of a community in the middle or at the end is very different from the view held at the beginning of a project. It is also evident from practice that development organizations are normally unwilling to accommodate a community changing its views because it interferes with the project execution.

Thus, as a researcher, I am fully aware that in the majority of cases, a community's view gets (partially) lost somewhere in the design and execution of a development project. Project design and execution is more an affair of a development organization, and this fits in a paradigm of "communities for development." This paradigm implies that a community should adhere to projects as designed and executed by a development organization. What if researchers turned this around and worked along a paradigm of "development for communities"? Then they would have to design and build on the community ideas and facilitate them in their path to development. Throughout all phases of a project, indeed, researchers should have a clue as to what a community is interested in, and the community should have a clue as to what a development organization is interested in. For me, it is crucial to address the rooted difference in power from the beginning of work with a community. Especially because the VIEW framework presented here can be easily adapted to the dynamism of the community system, I suggest using the framework for assessing views during the different phases of the development project: before, during and after the project. In that way, power disparities can be assessed by looking at the way the view changes.

There is an opportunity to improve project design by using the VIEW framework. The framework allows a project designer to gather the necessary information and get a full understanding of the community's life story before designing the project. Also important is the information that is gathered on how the community interprets information and how it uses this information to negotiate its own development goals. By knowing this, project designers can get into a position to craft a project based on the values and goals of the community, rather than focusing solely on global goals. It is then that a project

Box 3.5
Facilitating through the Rigidity of the REDD+ Design

I was assigned as a facilitator in the REDD+ process to ensure adequate stakeholder engagement in drafting a country's project proposal for inclusion in the World Bank's Forest Carbon Partnership Facility. A supporting donor organization assigned four experts to help with writing the proposal. The experts wanted to solicit input from stakeholders to find answers to inquiries, and therefore they prepared presentations and matrices. They proposed having the representatives of the forest user groups—ranging from those of indigenous peoples to those of academia—fill in the matrices during an inception workshop.

As facilitator, I requested time to review the presentations and the matrices the night before the workshop. When opening the files, I immediately observed that the presentations were too difficult for the attendees. Even with sufficient scientific background, I had to review the slides full of text and sophisticated graphics, three times before I completely understood them. My proposal to the experts was to cut the presentations back to half the number of slides and eliminate the complex matrices. Upon these suggestions, the experts appeared uncomfortable and some even frustrated. After some hours of negotiation, the experts somewhat agreed on a simplified form for the presentations. We all concurred with having a facilitated discussion after each presentation to solicit the necessary input from the stakeholders.

On the day of the event, each expert gave a 15-minute presentation and posted some questions on REDD+ at the end so that I could initiate the discussion. In the middle of the last facilitated discussion, one of the experts stood up, took the microphone and requested that the participants fill out the matrices he posted on the screen. The attendees, however, had been simply tossing around ideas and weren't ready to make a commitment on filling in matrices. The consultant continued to insist on the need to fill out the matrices.

I followed the first rule of facilitation: listen to the group. I explained that the group decides how to move forward, and at that time the rigidity of the REDD+ design was broken, at least for this part of the project. This example shows how representatives of development organizations may safeguard the rigidity of the design, which eliminates the flexibility needed to capture the needs of stakeholders.

designer can make a true connection between local and global goals, generally leading to better and improved project outcomes for both the community and the development organization.

If researchers could build in more leeway in project design and execution, they could learn about new ways to maneuver alongside change experienced by a community. It is possible, I believe, that a community and development organization can then build mutual trust and create space to evaluate its alternatives before making joint decisions (Colfer 2011). Working this way would bring much more fulfillment for both the community and development organization, I think.

Conflicting views in climate-change projects

Researchers can improve their understanding of situations in which the view of the community and the development organization are so different that it leads to conflict in the execution of the climate-change project. Globally, more than 700 climate-change-development projects are being carried out with local communities under the REDD+ umbrella. The projections for REDD+ are to create a better life for 150 million low-income people worldwide by 2030 (Hall 2012). Developed from a scientific paradigm, REDD+ projects operate from a set of rigid guidelines that often are not well understood by indigenous peoples who have been living in forests for centuries. They have different perspectives from development organizations vis-à-vis the value of the forest. Indigenous views that are forest oriented, are one reason for these people's poor participation in the science-based, top-down approach to decision making often applied by development organizations (Hulme 2010). In fact, ineffective engagement of indigenous peoples is becoming a major cause of conflict in climate-change-related development (Barr et al. 2011; Barron et al. 2007; Oishi 1995; Rubin 2010). Such conflict arises from existing tensions between community members' "everyday" livelihood needs and the global interest of carbon sequestration (Barr et al. 2011). The VIEW framework is one possibility for studying both parties' views and finding ways to overcome the view conflict (Box 3.5).

Chapter 4

SOCIAL POLYGRAPHY: AN APPROACH TO OBTAINING INFORMATION THROUGH MUTUAL LEARNING

This chapter is a part of a practical framework for analyzing the view of local communities on sustainable development. It introduces a participatory approach called social polygraphy that I believe has the potential to put into practice the VIEW framework discussed in chapter 3. The present chapter highlights the characteristics that make social polygraphy a promising approach to reaching a better understanding of the self-defined goals and aspirations of local communities, and at the same time, fostering mutual learning. The previous chapters revealed the challenges of studying indigenous peoples' systems in a holistic manner. Finding appropriate ways to interact, initiate dialogue and learn together becomes crucial, especially in situations dealing with projects tinted by political interests, such as in the case of climate-change programs. Social polygraphy presents a promising approach for engaging with local communities and discovering diverse ways of reaching a mutual understanding among community members and outsiders about their complex and dynamic systems.

The present chapter is written based upon my experiences working for more than eleven years with an Afro-Colombian community that started a long-term process of reawakening, empowerment and self-determination through social polygraphy, which was called social cartography at the time. The chapter also incorporates examples from the literature that capture the same type of experiences as a product of engaging in this type of participatory process.

What Is Social Polygraphy?

Social polygraphy has its origins in participatory mapping. Participatory mapping methodologies have been used for decades as part of the researcher's toolbox to collect and analyze data from local communities around the world (Herlihy and Knapp 2003). Participatory mapping also has been used as a planning and social transformation tool, and is now widely recognized as a powerful methodology that allows communities to represent themselves and bring the issues affecting their territory and threatening their livelihoods to the attention of authorities and decision makers. Community mapping has been used as a strategy for analyzing issues in areas such as conservation, community planning, environmental conflict and territorial disputes (Sletto et al. 2013).

The type of participatory mapping described here is particular to the approach developed in Colombia known as social cartography. This social-mapping approach emerged as a result of the work of the FUNDAMINGA Foundation, a multidisciplinary group of practitioners, researchers and philosophers who, based on more than 30 years of experience working with indigenous peoples and Afro-Colombian communities, recognized the need and potential for developing a methodology to stimulate dialogue and social transformation based on the drawing of different types of maps (Andrade and Santamaría 1997; Restrepo and Velasco 1998; Restrepo, Velasco, and Preciado 1999).

The basis of the approach relies in the special relationship that local people have with their territory, which translates into an organic mapping process. During the mapping process, in addition to maps, other graphics and drawings such as calendars, diverse artistic expressions and oral traditions are also represented. That is why the term "social cartography," which emphasizes the use of cartographic maps, has been replaced, by FUNDAMINGA, with "social polygraphy" to include the use of multiple graphy that are any form of writing, describing, drawing and so forth, with which the participants feel familiar. Consequently, the process invites participants to use diverse tools and cultural elements to tell their story. The maps, which are now not only cartographic representations of the territory, that result from this process have the ability to reflect the complexities of indigenous peoples' cosmovisions as well as the life stories of local communities.

Theoretical, Conceptual and Methodological Basis of Social Polygraphy

From a theoretical perspective in the social polygraphy approach, the mapping process shifts from a positivist paradigm that typically dictates a well-controlled environment in the collection and analysis of information, to a postpositivist paradigm that rejects considering simply sticking to what we can observe and measure as knowledge generation. Thus, maps are not just built from cartographic data to represent a geographic depiction of the territory where the medium used in the social polygraphy activity must present a factual image of reality. The participatory mapping process is conceived in the postpositive constructivist paradigm in which each individual constructs their view of the world based on their perceptions of it. The drawing of maps in the social polygraphy process recognizes that people form their own understanding and knowledge of the world through having experiences and reflecting on those experiences. The role of the researcher under the postpositivist paradigm is to put aside their biases and beliefs and see the world as it really is, recognizing that we are all biased and that all of our observations are affected by our own views.

Social polygraphy, as any other participatory research tool, can be used in the entire spectrum of participation from extracting participants' information all the way to empowering individuals in search of their own solution to specific problems (Biggs 1989; Probst et al. 2000). This potential to empower people draws attention to this type of social-mapping process.

Conceptually and methodologically social polygraphy has been influenced by participatory action research (PAR), which developed as an answer to the failures of Western research to deliver appropriate results in response to the requests of local communities in the Global South (Martin and Sherington 1997). This type of research is characterized by its use of participatory methodology to meet local people's needs (Herlihy and Knapp 2003). PAR distinguishes itself from other types of participatory research in calling for (a) collaboration based on a participatory process, (b) acquisition of knowledge, (c) empowerment of individuals and (d) social change (Probst et al. 2000). One of the principles behind the utilization of this methodology is its bottom-up approach, which was influenced by the understanding that, in order to answer more effectively to the complexity, diversity and dynamism of any territory, knowledge has to come from within. Chambers (1997) calls this approach a reversal of realities.

Social polygraphy closely follows the PAR model proposed by the Colombian researcher and sociologist Orlando Fals Borda, who defines PAR as "action research that is participatory and participatory research that unites with action for transforming reality" (Fals-Borda and Rahman 1991). It is the process of involving local communities in generating knowledge about their own condition and how it can be transformed (Fals-Borda and Rahman 1991). It is important here to mention Fals Borda's critique of the positivist researcher. The critique calls for Western researchers to question themselves, and it demands a shift in research thinking and action:

We felt that colleagues who claim to work with "neutrality" or "objectivity" supported willingly or unwillingly the status quo, impairing full understanding of the social transformations in which we were immersed or which we wanted to simulate. We rejected the academic tradition of using—and often exploiting—research and fieldwork mainly for career advancement. (Fals Borda 2006, 29)

He argues that researchers should go through two stages. First, they must decolonize themselves by recognizing the traits and ideas planted in their minds and behaviors by the scientific learning processes. Second, they must search for a more satisfactory value structure based on praxis to give meaning to their research without overlooking scientific rules (Fals Borda 2006).

The role of the researcher in social polygraphy as compared to other social-mapping process changes into that of generating social capital, including empowering actors to join side by side in a research cycle of planning, acting and observing, and reflecting, which by repeating itself adapts and progresses in a continuum of change.

Through the PAR approach, local communities come to understand that their practices are a product of particular circumstances that happen under specific contexts, and that it is possible to transform or reproduce those practices through their current ways of acting or behaving. This approach can ignite changes in "a) what people do, b) how people interact with the world and with others, c) what people mean and what they value, and d) the discourses in which people understand and interpret their world" (Kemmis and McTaggart 2000, 279).

The purpose of social polygraphy is to engage actors in a process of reflection so they can reveal the knowledge acquired through their traditions, valuing their memory and daily activities. This mapping process provides a space where creativity and imagination can be the means for recognizing and recreating traditional knowledge and producing new knowledge based on collective action (Velasco 2012).

Social polygraphy is defined as

a conceptual and methodological proposal generated to explore, feel, and understand the complex and dynamic web of relations, and knowledge that exists in territories, these being recognize as depositories of information and memory [...] Social Polygraphy allows the parties involved to generate processes for reflection and production of knowledge with the people, as result of an exercise of virtual reconstruction of reality, which is understood as a web of multiple relations. (FUNDAMINGA 2012)

In this sense, social polygraphy is more than a research tool. It is an approach that is always tied to specific social processes in which community members interact to untangle the life story of communities, starting with the recreation of the past, followed by contemplation of the present and visualization of the future.

The "How-to" of Social Polygraphy

There are no set steps that can be applied regardless of context when it comes to social polygraphy; however, there are common procedures that are used to lead the participatory process. They include three phases: (1) diagnosis; (2) construction of maps; and (3) interpretation of the data collected (Andrade and Santamaría 1997; FUNDAMINGA 2002; Bastidas and Gonzalez 2008).

During the diagnosis phase, the facilitator or facilitation team of the mapping process meets with representatives of the groups participating in the social polygraphy exercise to review the goals of the mapping activities. Information is gathered through participatory techniques including observations, interviews, focus group discussions, rapid rural appraisal (RRA), transect walks and cartographic maps. The commonalities among these techniques are that they are a part of qualitative assessments and the cooperative participation of stakeholders, encouraging shared understanding of the social-mapping process.

The facilitator develops guides for the mapping, drawing and other contemplated activities. These guides are elaborated based on a set of questions relevant to the goals of the mapping activities. At this time, the logistics of the workshops are prepared to ensure that all stakeholders are represented in the process. This phase can take a couple of days to a couple of months depending on the context of the project. Objectives have to be clear to everyone in order to develop a cohesive process; therefore, it is critical to take the time to ensure that the different actors participating in the process feel ready to engage in the social polygraphy exercise. If this phase is not appropriately completed, the diverse interests of stakeholders and unbalanced power relations can drive the process to a halt or dissolution.

The role of the facilitator is critical throughout the social polygraphy process, but is especially so at this stage. As facilitator of the dialogue, their role is similar to that of an intercultural mediator. Given that local communities are heterogeneous, the process calls for a facilitator who can promote social integration of the different stakeholders, be they men, women, older or younger generations, local authorities, civil society groups, researchers and other outsiders who have a stake in the process. The facilitator becomes the third party, the mediator of the dialogue, who in addition to minimizing communication problems, helps decipher the jargon each stakeholder uses, but most importantly helps in preventing conflicts (Ury 2000). We have to be mindful that thinking about facilitation as a neutral activity rejects the social responsibility of the facilitator in supporting social change. The role of the facilitator in the social polygraphy process can be vested in a researcher, a community leader or a teacher if that the person possesses enough experience, practical skills and most importantly, is open to criticism and suggestions from actors participating in the process that might improve the execution of the facilitator role (Kemmis and McTaggart 2000).

The second phase consists of the construction of maps and other drawings. In this phase we see the bridging of the different views of the actors participating in the process. An essential part in this process is to have a unified understanding of the meaning of territory in the context of social polygraphy. Some of the common Western definitions for territory include the geographic definition: "any one of the large parts that some countries are divided into" (*Merriam-Webster Dictionary*); the sociopolitical definition: "an area of land that belongs to or is controlled by a government" (*Merriam-Webster Dictionary*; and the ecological definition: "an area often including a nesting or denning site and a variable foraging range that is occupied and defended by an animal or group of animals" (*Merriam-Webster Dictionary*). All of these definitions are rather narrow as compared with the local view of territory.

Indigenous peoples, for example, think of their territory not only as a piece of land but also as a cultural space where humans and nature coexist with their traditions and practices, engaging in a constant exchange. Their territory is not only a space that encompasses social groups, landscape, mountains, rivers, valleys and animals but also a space occupied by history, memory, dreams and the experience and knowledge of the people who inhabit that territory (Restrepo et al. 1999; Restrepo 2005; Andrade and Santamaría 1997).

Principles of systems theory and complexity theory help us understand territory as a multiple and complex relational space (Restrepo 1999). Territory is space and time that flows and remains, that is, it changes and sustains relationships between nature and humans, between past and present. Because territory is configured by relationships, when these relationships change there is also a transformation in the territory and its possible representations (Restrepo 1999).

Going back to the mapping exercise, this starts with the drawings of reality, beginning with the simplest concepts and moving toward a more complex field of networks and relations that allows for the translation of different versions of reality. The mapping activity uses diverse materials, ranging from simple markers, graphing paper and flip charts to, in more technological settings, computers and geographic information system (GIS) mapping equipment. The key to selecting the materials is that the participants find them easy to work with (Bastidas and Gonzalez 2008).

As social polygraphy activities start to unfold, uncertainty may be present in the minds of everyone participating in the process. Since there is no precise set of steps to follow or specific outcomes that can be predicted from the beginning of the exercises, there may be a feeling of unrest that the facilitator has to be sensitive to and deal with. We are all trained to expect to be told what to do and how to think, what is right and what is wrong. We expect to have a recipe delivered to us from someone who knows more than we do. Social polygraphy activities, however, provide the necessary conditions for discarding those expectations and becoming immersed in a process of the social production of knowledge. At the beginning it is difficult to change participants' frame of mind, but as activities progress and actors get familiar with the materials and are guided by questions that motivate their interest in sharing and learning from one another, the uncertainty transforms into a pleasant surprise when each of them discovers that there are many things that they know and can contribute to the process. This process of mutual learning empowers the participants; they no longer feel uneducated and powerless as compared to other stakeholders who are perceived as experts. This is how critical consciousness, as proposed by Freire (1970) is formed.

The activity should take place where participants feel most comfortable and where they can surround the drawing material in a way that always allows for horizontal dialogue. That is, if the majority of the group decides to work on the floor or on tables, all participants should be working at the same level. This prevents participants from feeling that different levels of power are established in the process. The groups are usually formed with a maximum of eight to ten participants, to encourage the participation of everyone but still have a good representation of diversity in the group. In each group, it is critical to select one person to document the logistics and dialogue that emanates from the process. This is very important since it is crucial to record the instances when production of knowledge and mutual learning occurs as the process develops (Figure 4.1).

The role of the facilitator in this phase is that of one who probes without giving norms of communication. The facilitator provides the spark for the creative process using the guides previously developed in the first phase of the process. The complexities of the systems analyzed require the use of several maps to decipher traditional knowledge. Depending on the purpose of the activity, different maps can be constructed. The first set of maps typically includes (a) people and nature, (b) infrastructure and (c) cultural and social relations.

The people and nature map displays the livelihood systems, including production activities. The farming system, which is composed of the production of crops and animals, gardening spaces and hunting and forest areas that

Figure 4.1 People from the community of Robles drawing maps. Photo by Elena Bastidas.

supply other natural resources important for the survival of the household, are all mapped out. This map shows the traditional farms in the context of the landscape of their territory. A systems perspective starts to evolve as different participants express how they see the relationships among each part of the system. These relationships can be drawn among production activities, natural resources and people resulting, in an economic-ecological map.

A second map shows the infrastructure, including services, that is, roads, health services, bridges, schools, churches, parks and so on. The contribution of different members of the group to the discussion around this map usually uncovers services that certain members of the community were not aware of. This motivates the participants to question each other and value their input.

The cultural and social relations map shows the networks as well as areas of cultural and spiritual importance, such as local markets, sites for cultural practices and sites that have a spiritual meaning for the community, among others. Again, the importance of having diversity within the group is highlighted here since it is usually the elders who can identify, unfold and tell stories about the sites represented in this map. There is a rich exchange between older and younger generations, who through the activity learn interesting aspects about their culture.

Figure 4.2 A young Afro-Colombian woman presenting the map constructed by her group. Photo by Elena Bastidas.

Each of these maps can be used to show different levels of analysis depending on the objectives of the exercise, from household to local, national and international scales, that is, going from the micro- to the macrolevel. Once the maps have been constructed, they can be superimposed to gain a holistic view and understanding of the multiple sets of relationships and processes present in the territory. Each map can be as detailed as needed according to the objective of the process. A first collective reading and interpretation of the maps can be done in a plenary workshop at this point in order to gather the different sentiments of the participants. The facilitator can assess the mapping process while the participants start building consensus about what they have identified in their territory and how it is now represented on the maps (Figure 4.2).

The time and space dimension is incorporated in social polygraphy when the maps are analyzed from a time perspective. Each map is constructed illustrating the past, present and future of each collection of maps. Incorporating the time dimension enables the analysis of the dynamic basis of transformation. The maps of the past, also called historical maps, focus on rescuing the collective memory of the community. They highlight the transformation of systems and processes, emphasizing the changes that have occurred in the territory while also detecting cyclical phenomena. The construction of historical maps allows community members to identify their territory and share its memory.

The present dimension helps participants focus on the current situations facing their community. The first set of maps (people and nature, cultural and social relations) is typically drawn in the present because they communicate the immediate reality in which the community members function. By comparing the present maps with the historical map, we can detect the evolution of the community. The maps of the future, also called "maps of dreams," depict how the community would like to be seen in the future. During this activity, participants dream, reflect on ideals and work toward a collective vision. At the end of the mapping process, the result is a chronological view of the past situation, the present reality and the promising future that incorporates the expectations and desires of all the actors participating in the social polygraphy process (Andrade and Santamaría 1997; Bastidas and Gonzalez 2008).

The mapping process reiterates the sense of belonging to a territory and identifies the fundamental interests in finding solutions to its problems. Depending on the situation and objectives of the mapping activity, different maps can be drawn by different groups, and they can be shared with all the participants during plenary sessions.

Maps representing conflicts, risks, vulnerabilities and capabilities can also be constructed during the process. Community conflicts related to natural resources (water, land, mining and so forth) can be highlighted on the maps to create a visual representation of the problem and start dialogue among the participants to, first, clarify the issues surrounding them. Participants have the opportunity to say what they know about the conflict and how they feel about it. This provides the opportunity for understanding the context of the conflict in a collective manner. The stakeholders can be represented in the maps along with their perceived "power." Not all stakeholders will be represented in the groups participating in the drawing activity. The important thing is to make sure they are represented on the map in order to be included in the analysis of the situation. Relationships among stakeholders can be drawn while analyzing each actor's positions and interests, allowing for a discussion that can provide opportunities for reframing conflicts and offering possibilities for conflict transformation. By mapping the conflict within its time dimension, the analysis can uncover its causes and also motivate the participants to look for ways to transform the conflict in order for it not to appear in the maps of the future.

More elaborated maps can be used to depict issues between communities or the conflicts between the community and enterprises with interests in the community area's resources. They can focus on environmental conflicts

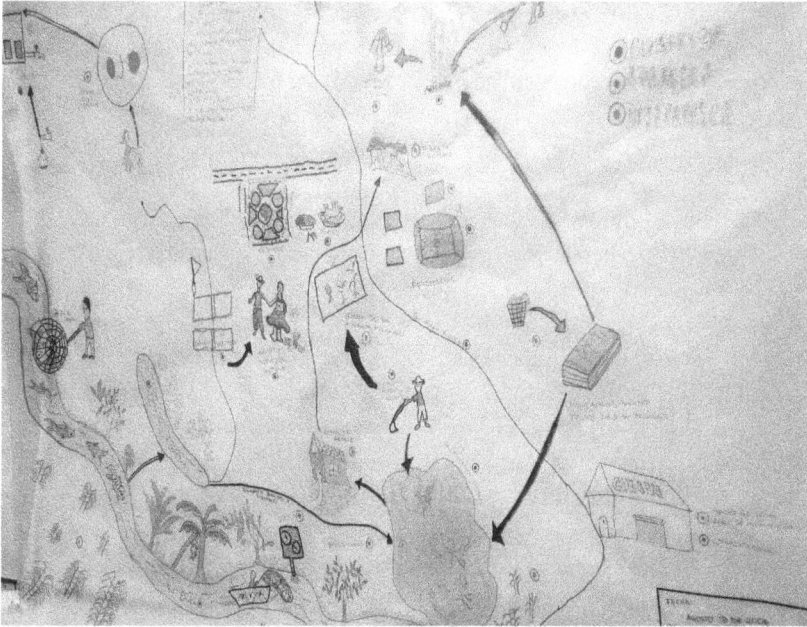

Figure 4.3 Map showing what things, relations and processes the community would like to make disappear, conserve and make appear in their future. Photo by Elena Bastidas.

associated with the risk of deforestation, erosion, flooding or climate change, or they can focus on internal socioeconomic and political issues (Figure 4.3).

During the third phase the participants share the process that took place in each group and highlight the most important moments of the drawing activity, including the logistics of the process, the conceptualization of relationships and disagreements on points of view. This phase includes debates and social creativity workshops (Habegger and Mancila 2006). During this phase, participants discover the abundant knowledge they have about their territory and their natural and social systems. Through the mapping exercises they reveal their own reality.

According to Velasco (2012), what is being represented on the maps weaves a fabric that mentally and emotionally threads together elements of context, social practices, artistic expressions, ritual celebrations and key moments in the life of the community. While the process of representation continues, the capacity to narrate, dialogue and comprehend improves gradually among the participants. The participants—who are now freed from fears and insecurities, and have the acquired ability to represent, relate and interpret—start to feel the need for actions destined to affirm their dignity and equality. As a result, they feel the need to communicate, learn, transform and relate to the world. The following are two reflections made by participants during a social polygraphy exercise led by FUNDAMINGA with the Afro-Colombian communities located at the riverbeds of the Rivers Mejicano, Chagüi and Rosario, located south of the Colombian Pacific Anden, in the Nariño Department, on the border with Ecuador. These are narratives that Velasco calls moments of lucidness.

> The elders would tell us, he said, that once there was a man who spent much of his life begging. When the beggar came to the final days of his life, a few friends accompanied him as he was dying, until he drew his last breath. One of his friends then took up the tray that the deceased had always used when he begged, and noticing it was very heavy began to clean it. The friend was truly surprised to discover that the beggar's tray was made of gold. He called to the others, who when they saw the tray could not believe that the man who had died had spent his entire life begging with a tray that was itself indeed a treasure. Even worse, he continued, is what is happening to us, because our own gold tray is the treasure we have seen and described today in making this map. We must not allow it to be viewed as nothing more than a paltry tray with which to go begging. If we take that path we will end up losing completely our liberty, our lands, our dignity and our culture, just as his own treasure was lost to the dead beggar. (FUNDAMINGA 2008 in Velasco 2012, 10)

Another participant on a lucid moment:

> Look at the map: our rights were born here in the land of our liberty, caring for nature, and learning to respect life. Our rights are sung and danced about here to the sounds of tambores and marimba. Our rights teach us what we do not learn from the law. I submit to the law, but my rights set me free. The law moves me forward, my very rights give me roots. (FUNDAMINGA 2008 in Velasco 2012, 10)

There is no telling where the social polygraphy exercise can take the community in terms of using the maps to change or transform the community's life stories. An example of that is presented in Box 4.1, where the community shows its assertiveness by giving me the opportunity to participate with one of my projects in their long- term community's life plan. On another occasion I got a lesson on project sustainability, see Box 4.2.

Boxes 4.1 and 4.2 describe just a couple of the examples that over the years have made me think about how the social polygraphy approach has empowered the people of Robles. I can see that the community has the ability to transform projects that start as short-term arrangements into long-term processes because they believe the whole community can benefit from them.

Box 4.1
Social Polygraphy in Robles

In 2004 I was introduced to the Afro-Colombian community of Robles. I was coordinating a community-based conservation and capacity-building project in which members of this community were active participants. During my first visits to the community, in the meetings held to discuss the project objectives and logistics, the community leaders would always come prepared with maps they had constructed about five years earlier in a social polygraphy workshop. The community members used the maps to present the community's overall goals and plans. I could see they were very proud and enthusiastic about using the maps to voice their life story. They also used the maps to make sure we—"our project team"—understood the expectations the community had about the conservation project and to discuss issues about activities they were concerned about. I could see that they had a very clear idea of the community's goals for the near and long-term future, and that they were making sure our project goals would fit into their overall plans in order to fully support the project. I felt the roles had been reversed. I felt I was being invited to participate in a small part of their community life story, although at the beginning, I thought I had chosen the community to participate in my project.

Box 4.2
The Teacher Training

I was ready to deliver a gender training targeted to the teachers at the local schools. As I was preparing to start the workshop, there were about 20 schoolteachers and about five children, ranging in age from 11 to 14, who were still in the room. I approached the community member who was going to introduce me and said, "I am waiting for the kids to leave the room so I can start the training." The community member, preoccupied, looked at me and said, "Why would you want the kids to leave? After all, they are the ones who will be delivering this workshop in the future." At that moment it became clear to me that the community was already thinking about the sustainability of the project and that training the younger generation was an important strategy for them. The community leaders are always including the youth in capacity building or planning activities to ensure that future generations feel part of and take responsibility for their common future. I have witnessed how the children who, ten years ago I tried to exclude from my workshops, are now leading projects and training younger generations.

That is the case for a youth peace project that started under the auspice of an international sponsor, as do many of the youth peace projects in Colombia, which usually only last a couple of years. In Robles, the youth peace project CULPAZCON has been in operation for more than 11 years and it is thriving, impacting the lives of the children and youth in Robles and the neighboring communities.

Limitations of the Social Polygraphy Approach

As with any other approach, social polygraphy has its limitations. One limitation of this process resides in the difficulty of its interpretation by people who were not part of the exercise. The information generated can be so complex that, without an appropriate systematization of the process, it is difficult to convey the richness of the knowledge gained during the social polygraphy process. In addition, we have to remember that the maps are a construct of cultural and symbolic materials; consequently, they have to be understood by taking into account the sociocultural setting in which they have been developed (Di Gessa 2008).

Another problem is that the amount of information generated during the process can be overwhelming if there are no clear objectives and purpose for each of the products delivered through the mapping activities. A parallel and simultaneous systematization process is critical. That is one of the reasons why there should be someone in each working group assigned the task of recording the process as well as the dialogue that emerges as part of the process. If the activities last longer than a day, the facilitator should make an effort each evening to evaluate the diaries of each group to guarantee the appropriate recording of activities.

Long-term commitment poses a challenge to the typical development project. For this approach to deliver the anticipated wealth of its results, community members and other actors must feel comfortable around each other and, most importantly, a certain level of trust must reign among the participants. It takes time to build trust and flexibility on the part of projects to work at the pace of the community. As mentioned earlier, it can take anywhere from a few days to a couple of months to be ready just to start the processes of social polygraphy. If we conceptualize this process to take place at the beginning of a development project, its effectiveness and specific project time lines might be compromised.

Integrating indigenous knowledge and Western science requires acquiring the capacity to recognize, connect and act in the specific spaces and contexts of each local community and thereby understanding its most profound reality. Social polygraphy provides a methodology for achieving the right set of conditions that will ensure leveling the field, providing equal status to both scientists as well as local people (Mazzocchi 2008). According to Agrawal (1995), in order to initiate a productive dialogue, it is necessary to retreat from the sterile dichotomy between Western knowledge and local people, recognize the heterogeneity of the groups and look for commonalities between multiple paradigms and views. Therefore, the process of mutual learning between different views must be based on respect for and acceptance of the individuals involved in the learning experience. This mutual learning approach emphasizes the importance of being open to others, of appreciating and respecting each other's knowledge and wisdom (Schmink et al. 2002).

Mutual learning calls for cooperation among its participants. It recognizes the value of exchanges of knowledge, experiences and information among different actors who come to realize that there is much to learn from and much to teach each other. Further, because there is so much we know and we don't know, at the same time it becomes vital to learn how to learn together. Social polygraphy provides a space for experiencing ourselves with the invisible, the relational, the complex and the diverse. When these are represented in the maps, we move from a perception to being able to touch and verbalize it.

Mutual learning can only develop when there is enough time to interact with others in a systematic way. Therefore, the need exists for a long-term perspective acknowledging that the social polygraphy exercise can be a point of departure for a process, but it should be repeated during different stages of a community's planning process. The ultimate goal would be for communities to internalize the methodology and use it as a way to check their progress and reflect on it, employing the maps of dreams they created during the process.

Alternative Forms of Communication and Mutual Learning

Meaningful dialogue between Western researchers and indigenous people must start with the realization that difficulties in communication are due to the inherently different ways of thinking and learning between them. Fruitful dialogue can only surface if we withdraw from the dichotomy between Western knowledge and local people. It is important to recognize that neither side can possible know it all, that it is critical to distinguish the differences between the groups, embrace them and look for ways to bridge multiple paradigms and views. One way of moving forward is to learn to put aside our own views and see reality through the "lenses of the others.".

How can we do that? First, we must acknowledge our fundamental differences within our ways of learning and thinking. Although we can argue that each individual has their own preferred learning style, the marked differences between how indigenous people and Western researchers think indicates that as humans, we exercise different parts of our brain hemispheres more than others. Since the 1960s, there has been a growing interest in neuroscience related to differences in how people learn and think. Studies pioneered by Dr. Roger Sperry focused on the specialized manifestations of the brain hemispheres. He discovered that each hemisphere processes information in different ways, each perceiving the world in a different manner (Sperry 1961). Since then, research studies have shown that functions of the left brain are characterized by sequence and order, thinking in words and its importance for language processing, while the right hemisphere shows dominance for visual-spatial processing, which is especially important in creating the rich sensory experience that goes together with the comprehension of language (Ocklenburg and Gunturkun 2012). Current research shows that some of these differences may be attributed to which hemisphere tends to be used in particular circumstances or due to individual differences in how the brain hemispheres are organized. People who share a common cultural background will also share certain strategies of acquiring knowledge, skills and understanding.

This scientific explanation of how people think and learn differently clarifies why researchers trained in the Western scientific method, and indigenous peoples who make meaning out of knowledge gathered through experience, have a hard time understanding each other. Recognizing this can also help us escape the trap of romanticizing indigenous peoples' views. As mentioned throughout the present book, indigenous peoples learn by discovering and using symbols and rich storytelling to record their history, and some even use dreams as a method to guide their lives. All of these are characteristics of right-hemisphere brain function. For researchers trained in Western ways of learning, it is easier to verbalize abstract ideas, use language to communicate in a linear way, think in a more systematic way and order things to later put them together in an organized whole. There is no mystery, then, in the fact that indigenous peoples like to draw and map things, and why it is easy for them to communicate through the process of social polygraphy.

Multidisciplinary teams

On the flip side, I believe that the same principles of social polygraphy can also be used as an exercise among multidisciplinary groups of researchers working on sustainable projects. People trained in different disciplines tend to focus on what they are taught to see. An agronomist will pay attention to the crops and start evaluating the cropping system. The zoologist will be more interested in the animals present in the landscape. In the same way, the gender expert will try to figure out how men and women relate to each other, and the rest of the socioeconomic and natural environment surrounding them. They could be witnessing and even experiencing the same phenomena, but interpreting them in a different way because of the different scientific training and theoretical frameworks they use to interpret phenomena.

The importance of working in multidisciplinary teams in the development arena is a concept that started in the late 1970s and that has gained popularity in most fields that deal with complex systems. These complex systems need to be studied through more than one lens or discipline to uncover the diversity and dynamism of these systems. However, the truth is that multidisciplinary teams can work together extremely well or they can be a total disaster. This is especially important to recognize when working with local communities.

Taking the time to go through a parallel exercise of social polygraphy among the team of researchers and practitioners working together provides an important opportunity for them to get to know each other on a deeper level, thus building trust within the team. In any type of collaborative process, being able to recognize each other's strengths and weaknesses allows the team to build on each other's expertise and contribute to the success of the project. Once researchers have gone through that process, they will be better prepared to come together with community members. At this point, social polygraphy offers a medium for deciphering knowledge in a similar way to putting together a jigsaw puzzle. Instead of using speech or language to communicate in a one-dimensional way, it uses a multidimensional medium to help people understand each other.

Enhancing partnerships

The success of a sustainable development project has to do more with the partnership and trust between community members and researchers than with the actual project activities themselves. Forming partnerships is a difficult process, but they can grow strong when the community realizes that the researchers have a true interest in the well-being of the whole community and that they are not looking out only for the benefits of their own project.

The social polygraphy process enhances the community-researcher partnership by fostering respect and mutual understanding among stakeholders. However, not all researchers get involved in the dynamics of the social polygraphy exercise. Some may be intimidated by the process because the type of participation it requires is usually out of their comfort zone. In some cases, the researcher typically watches the social-mapping process from a near distance and uses the opportunity to acquire information specific to the objectives of their project. This is clearly a missed opportunity to engage with other stakeholders and be active participants in the learning process. The role of researcher in the mutual learning process can guarantee the scientific validity of the knowledge produced through the social polygraphy approach without threatening the gained authority of the other stakeholders participating in the process. Fals-Borda (1987) explains, "the sum of knowledge from both types of agents [researchers and local people] permits the acquisition of a much more accurate and correct picture of the reality which we want to transform. Therefore academic knowledge plus popular knowledge and wisdom may give as a result a total scientific knowledge of a revolutionary nature" (332).

It is the role of the researcher to try to cross not only disciplinary boundaries but also cultural boundaries and learn to learn in a different way. The question arises: will researchers take the time to invest in incorporating this type of approach into their projects' planning stage?

Balancing the investment in social polygraphy

One of the advantages of social polygraphy is that at the end of the activities, the tangible products like the maps, calendars and other drawings stay with the community to be interpreted with different stakeholders, and reinterpreted at different points in time when new community goals arise. On the one hand, it might seem a considerable investment in terms of time and resources for short-term projects to engage in a participatory planning process such as social polygraphy before getting into implementation. On the other hand, this process might be the pathway to engaging in true partnership and understanding the meaning of sustainability across the actors involved that results in the success of the project.

Several characteristics of the social polygraphy approach make it a practical option for applying the VIEW framework and for reaching mutual learning. It uses a visual and graphic method of representation—an alternative form of communication suitable for working with indigenous peoples and encouraging mutual learning. It acknowledges that whoever inhabits the territory is the one who knows it, and there is the belief that it is possible to initiate a dialogue based on such knowledge. It encourages communities to question their long-term goals and position their present reality within their past and future. It allows researchers to see how their sustainable projects fit within the community's life story and context. And finally, it deals with power relations and distrust among groups participating in a process.

Chapter 5

EXPLORING THE
UNDERLYING VALUES

In the second part of this book I present a case study of the Trio indigenous people as they are facing climate change and participating in the national REDD+ development efforts in Suriname, South America. With this case study based on 12 years of fieldwork, I demonstrate how to unravel, group and present information by means of the VIEW framework to better understand the lens through which the community sees their future. The case study is presented in three chapters—5, 6 and 7—in which I describe the Trio values, meaning-making and sustainable decision-making process, respectively. The present chapter describes the values held by the Trios, which are the point of departure for the construction of their view.

The Trio Indigenous People

Indigenous people live in the Amazon forest, the largest remaining tropical forest today, which houses about one-fifth of the world's mammal, fish, bird and tree species. Trees of up to 50 meters in height reach out over the rivers. These rivers, along with the replenishment of water by the forest, make up roughly one-quarter of the freshwater resources available globally today (Hall 2012). More than 380 groups of indigenous peoples, who speak various languages and have greatly varying appearances, live along these Amazonian rivers. Their lands cover approximately 7.8 million hectares, of which 45 percent falls under some form of protection, primarily officially declared indigenous territories and protected areas (RAISG 2012).

The Amazonian groups domesticate food crops and hunt animals and fish to feed their families. Each group has developed a certain pattern of forest use, and their adaptation is largely dependent on locally available resources. Resource strategies are developed out of past experiences. Failure dictates which strategies indigenous peoples will use going forward. The longer an indigenous group lives in a specific location, the more the traditional knowledge

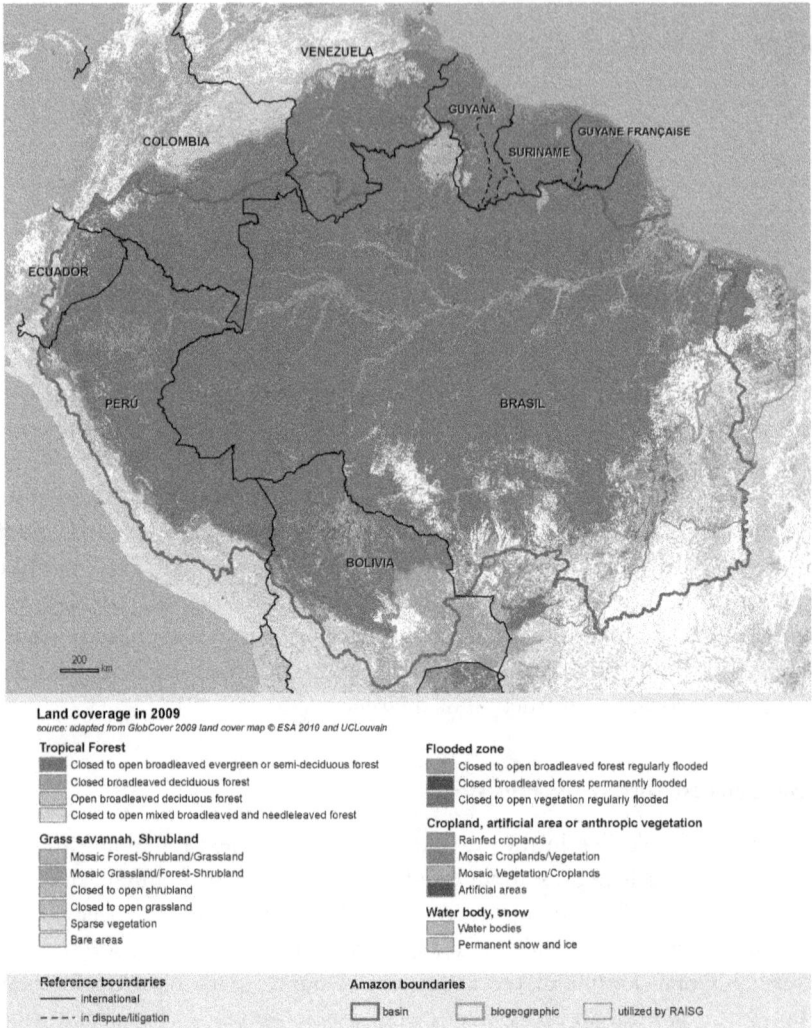

Land coverage in 2009
source: adapted from GlobCover 2009 land cover map © ESA 2010 and UCLouvain

Tropical Forest
- Closed to open broadleaved evergreen or semi-deciduous forest
- Closed broadleaved deciduous forest
- Open broadleaved deciduous forest
- Closed to open mixed broadleaved and needleleaved forest

Grass savannah, Shrubland
- Mosaic Forest-Shrubland/Grassland
- Mosaic Grassland/Forest-Shrubland
- Closed to open shrubland
- Closed to open grassland
- Sparse vegetation
- Bare areas

Flooded zone
- Closed to open broadleaved forest regularly flooded
- Closed broadleaved forest permanently flooded
- Closed to open vegetation regularly flooded

Cropland, artificial area or anthropic vegetation
- Rainfed croplands
- Mosaic Croplands/Vegetation
- Mosaic Vegetation/Croplands
- Artificial areas

Water body, snow
- Water bodies
- Permanent snow and ice

Reference boundaries
- ——— international
- – – –· in dispute/litigation

Amazon boundaries
- basin
- biogeographic
- utilized by RAISG

Figure 5.1 The Amazon rain forest and its boundaries. *Source*: Red Amazónica de Información Socioambiental Georreferenciada (RAISG 2012).

base is developed and the better prepared the group is for challenges arising from the surrounding environment (Moran 1993).

The Trio indigenous people live in the rain forest in the country of Suriname, situated along the north coast of South America (Figure 5.1) Their living spaces stretch into the southern region of the country in the vast and pristine lowland tropical rain forest. The Trios are a conglomerate of 1,500, with more than 26 subgroups who to a large extent share a history, culture and language. Many of these groups are named after their physical features. For example, the Pireujanas, the arrow people, are slim and have thin legs that metaphorically may be seen as arrows. Each group also has a specific specialty, for example, the Tunajanas are known as the water people and are fishing experts.

The recorded history of the Trio indigenous people goes back to before the seventeenth century, when they lived in small groups of four or five families consisting of men, women and children. Each group of families traveled from river to river to temporarily settle in a single place. The nomadic culture of the Trios was typical for South America. It is believed that the Trios first lived in the region of the Orinoco River, which is now situated in Venezuela. Subsequently, they moved to an area that extends to present-day northern Brazil and southern Suriname. The Trios usually were attracted to places with sufficient food resources, but also settled as far as possible from the contemporaneous intertribal wars (Koelewijn 2003).

Upon colonization, the Trios sheltered under a dense mass of trees that stretches out over plateaus, mountains and hills at elevations of less than 500 meters. Trio families prefer to settle in the vicinity of the most fertile soils, which are the imperfectly drained soils alongside the rivers (Teunissen et al. 2003). Here, they can plant a variety of food crops that provide for their nutritional needs. The Trio people are capable of taking care of themselves, in part because they have many skilled workers; they can make tools, crafts, medicines, boats and houses.

The Trios also highly value freedom, and thus situating themselves far from colonizing populations was a preferred and conscious choice, like that made by various other indigenous tribes in South America (Boven 2001). The historical record shows that many of South America's indigenous peoples have been slaughtered by colonizing forces, some to the extent that entire populations have become extinct (Salomon and Schwartz 1999). Today the Trios move around in an area as large as 40,000 km,² comparable in size to Switzerland. This so-called Trio territory is identified by locations with unique Trio names, each referring to the abundance of resources present in that specific area. For instance, as seen in Figure 5.2, in the vicinity of the village of Kwamalasamutu, there are creeks named after palm fruits (*maripa eeku*), caimans (*ariwe eeku*) and a crappie-like fish (*mokoko eeku*). In and around the creeks, the Trios capture these favored fruits and animals.

The integrity of the Trio culture has been buffered by the large expanse of tropical rain forest that separates the Trio from the modern cultures in the coastal strip of Suriname. Closely tied to their land, the Trios practice a traditional existence based on hunting, fishing and subsistence agriculture. Through careful observation and continuous experimentation, the

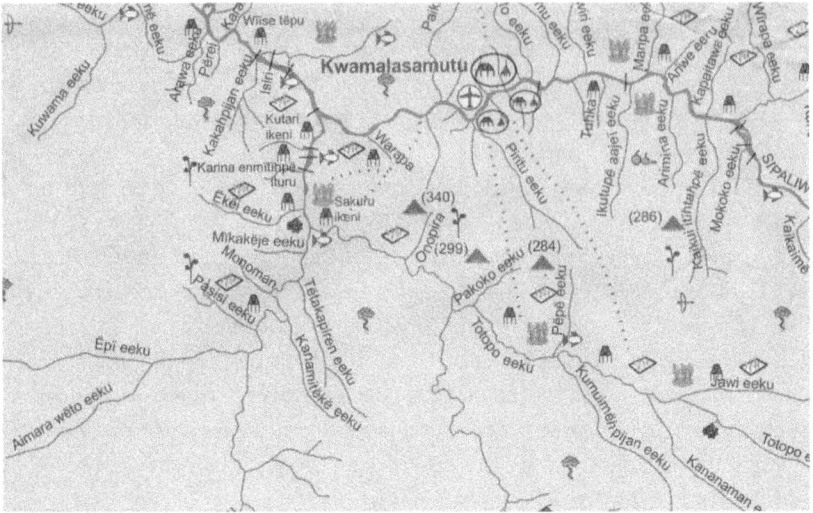

Figure 5.2 Local place names in the Trio territory near the village of Kwamalasamutu. *Source*: Adapted from the Land Use Map of the Trio Indigenous Peoples in Southwest Suriname (2000).

Trios have developed tools to adapt to uncertainty and disaster occasioned by climate change. The Trios are counting on traditional knowledge for planting food and hunting, knowledge that is still intact due to their rather slow acculturation process, which began in the 1960s (Heemskerk and Delvoye 2007).

Values Related to the Collective

The Trios function in their surrounding environment by constantly assessing risks and subsequently deciding whether to take action. Risks are assessed based on personal values and norms, a set of beliefs and awareness of the consequences of the risk (Slimak and Dietz 2006). Most of these factors are strongly linked to the past experience of the Trios; they have learned to cope with changing circumstances in the region since their recorded entry in the seventeenth century. These past experiences are important elements in shaping the Trio view. In the language of risk-assessment experts Slimak and Dietz (2006), this is a "system two" analysis—a process that reflects back on previous experiences over long stretches of time, which ends in a negotiated choice between the tribal members. In this process, less dependence on individual judgment exists than in "system one" decisions, which typically lead to action more immediately.

Togetherness

The first historical factor that shapes the Trio view is the ancestral primacy of togetherness, seen as one of the highest tribal values. A Trio leader describes togetherness to me as follows: "We, Trios, always need to walk like a herd. If one leaves the herd, he/she needs to be brought back." Togetherness also is reflected in the way that Trio families are structured in tight bonds around a central female figure. The family units usually live together in one village, but intangible borders often exist between them. For example, in the village of Kwamalasamutu, I have observed that different tribal groups coexist. These groups each have their own leader and sometimes a hut for performing cultural ceremonies. The hut provides a practical space for the group to discuss cultural issues in privacy, after which they may bring their outcomes to the larger setting in the village. This horizontal system seems to work well for the Trios, who have created a leadership structure with representatives from each of the larger kinship groups. In this way, the elders remain highly influential in decision making in their specific group without having to assume a central role in the tribe.

However, Trio history shows that the ties and relationships between kinship groups in Trio villages have not always been good. A famous Trio story describes how two groups, the Pireujana and the Mawajana, came together and created a bond by drinking each other's blood. In time, it became evident that the groups did not get along. The Trios believe that these groups are too different in origin, which prevents them from collaborating (Koelewijn 2003). This central story shows that tensions may exist between groups despite no direct evidence of conflict in the village.

In my experience, togetherness also is expressed in two other Trio activities: sharing of goods and traveling outside the village. The Trios share goods as a necessary survival activity in their village. This is typical for South America, where kinship is defined by giving rather than by biological relations between peoples (Miller 1999). Sharing is a fundamental part of life. In the Trio oral history, a moment is described when all the indigenous groups came together to settle permanently. One group, the Pianakoto, was unwilling to share its food crops and even today, the term "Pianakoto" refers to an individual who is unwilling to share and thus chooses to abandon the tribal togetherness principle.

The Trios also prefer to maintain social relationships through personal meetings and visit family members in other regions—such as Brazil, Guyana or French Guiana—at least once a year. This practice is viewed as mandatory in maintaining respectful and peaceful relationships. The visits are seen as necessary in order to share information about everyday life and family, to

Figure 5.3 The Trio indigenous peoples. Photo by Rachelle Bong A Jan.

provide help to others in need and to collectively develop strategies to adapt
to changing circumstances for surviving in the future. With respect to distant
travel, the Trios believe that togetherness is uninfluenced by distance because
they always return (Figure 5.3). The term "Tareno," the name that the Trio
people give themselves, is explained to me as "returning better than before
departure."

Religion

A second historical factor, I find, that influenced the Trio view was their
Baptist conversion as a group in 1960. Ever since that time, the United States-
based "door to life" gospel mission began gathering the small Trio groups
and persuaded them to live in one large settlement, called Alalapadu. The
ancestral spiritual rituals guided by Trio shamans were replaced with recita-
tions of the Christian gospel and Bible reading. As the missionaries translated
the Bible into the Trio language and continued their teachings, they made it
clear that the continued use of indigenous healing practices was unacceptable.
These traditional healing practices have been an integral part of the lives of
indigenous communities in Suriname since pre-Columbian times. Prior to the

modern era, indigenous healing was vital to their survival. The tribal healer, called a *piai* man (shaman), would use his knowledge to produce medicines to treat known illnesses and mediate encounters with the spiritual worlds. But the Trios were susceptible to the customs imposed by outsiders and gradually came to distrust their own traditional medicine and knowledge (Smith and Uiterloo 2007).

The role of the shaman as leader and healer of the Trios was replaced by an overarching chief and a religious leader in each village. Shamans symbolically and publicly swore off shamanism by handing over their *marakka* (rattles) to the missionaries. The indigenous healing system became dormant (Smith and Uiterloo 2007). The word of God became the new life script of the Trios, and they were promised a good life: they would learn to read, write and become "smart." The influential church also promised the Trios healthcare services that would prevent feared illnesses. This so-called good life goes on today, though it was briefly interrupted in 1978 when crops and bushmeat started to become scarce, causing the mission to relocate the Trios to a new village named after bamboo (*kwama*) and sand (*samu*): Kwamalasamutu.

The introduced discourse of the Christian gospel also affected the way that the Trios moved around in their territory. Before the arrival of the missionaries, Trio groups would relocate frequently because of the occurrence of disease, which sometimes eliminated entire families. The Trios believe that if more than one person dies at one location, it is due to spiritual powers, and they should move to a new location (Healy et al. 2003). Even today, when the Trios prefer living together in one place, they have clarified that disease is still a serious threat to the viability and survival of the tribe.

Frequently, the Trios have told me they believe that bad things are descending from the sky. For example, in recent years, Trio agricultural plots have been plagued by large red ants known as leafcutter ants. As the name implies, these ants consume the leaves of plants and can strip a cassava plot of 100 square meters overnight. The Trios think that the aggressive ants, which in oral tradition were sent to the sky in the past, are now returning because the Trios are not living the right way (Iejetuupe Malapï, pers. comm.). Similarly, an old Trio story describes how Jareware, the master of cassava planting, was abandoned to the sky because he wanted to kill his wife (Koelewijn 2003). Thus, the sky serves as a holding cell for beings that fail to behave well.

The Trios trust that punishment follows when one does not live according to the word of God. Although it would be expected that the Christian gospel influences the decision-making process, this is not always the case. Behavior that conflicts with church rules is widely accepted and described as the "Trio way." Almost every day, the majority of the Trios enjoy fermented cassava beer in the afternoon, a practice that has been strictly forbidden by the church.

Values Related to Social Behavior

The values that the Trios maintain for managing social relations influence their view. I think the Trios are a typical collective society in which they celebrate the "we" aspect (Augsburger 1992). This means that they generally behave in a way that promotes peace and harmony among members and ensures security for their long-term survival. Trio men and women must be obedient to their leadership and conform to the rules that are in effect (Triandis et al. 2001), even if this conflicts with their individual goals. It also means that Trios must maintain a constant association with each other that depends on their functional relationships, and assess whether members are "stepping out" of normative behavior. In the event that a Trio transgresses these tribal boundaries, as it appears, they are expected to apologize to make things right.

Face

In their social relations, it seems the Trios are very concerned about losing face as a society. Face is lost "if an individual acts in a manner that is inconsistent with his or her role and fails to fulfill reciprocal obligations" (Lewicky et al. 2007, 117). Trios seek to protect other Trios from losing face to outsiders or to Trios in another village or group. To protect face, I have seen conversations take place in a collective manner, and as Trio community members sit together in groups, they constantly assess the danger of weakening social relationships. In such power-balancing conversations, not surprisingly, the Trios believe it is socially acceptable to stray from the truth, because lying is a way for them to prevent "masks" from falling. Because of the many interdependent relationships in the tribe, the Trios can easily hold on to a variety of masks to keep or restore face (Box 5.1).

Another way that the Trios manage social relations and maintain power balances is through gossip. In my interaction with the Trios, one community member will launch a rumor in certain families or groups to save the face of another. The opinion of the one member then may quickly become the opinion of the entire village, and reputations so formed will have staying power. However, as I also experienced, the Trios are somewhat cautious with gossip and particularly bad-mouthing because they believe it is associated with punishment. This has a basis in an old Trio story: the Trios, who once had long legs, wanted to visit a man living in the sky. Because the Trios were bad-mouthing each other as they climbed a ladder to the sky, the ladder fell, breaking off their feet and leaving the Trio as short as they are now (Koelewijn 2003).

Box 5.1
The Missing Gasoline

The Trios explained to me that our organization's gasoline disappeared because the lock for the storage house was broken. The Trio men responsible for guarding the storage house knew the identity of the thief, but it was never revealed. Although the gasoline thief's mask of "good worker" had been destroyed, later in the same day, the same man came to eat in my group, where he was able to assume the mask of "friend." This is an example of how the Trios create room for wiggling between masks, indicating a broad approach to maintaining relationships with others (Lewicky et al. 2007). Thus, from a conflict resolution perspective, the Trios are negotiators who are primarily concerned about future relationships.

The importance of face-saving can occasionally lead to changes in semantics. In the previously described event, to compensate for the gasoline loss, I immediately announced sums would be subtracted from the monthly stipends of the Trios working on the related project. The Trios were furious, and one villager even attempted an attack with a machete and bow and arrow. The following day, a delegation of tribal leaders appeared at my hut to hold a meeting, which is an unusual practice. They thoughtfully contended that "stealing" is taking gasoline when nobody sees it. Although the majority of the villagers had seen Trios carrying tanks full of gasoline, the leaders concluded that the gasoline had not been stolen. The definition of stealing was thus transformed from the concept of "taking from others," as the Trios have learned from the Bible, to "taking from others secretly." Here, the Trios skillfully reframed the meaning of stealing to save face and protect togetherness.

Avoidance

When the prescribed cultural norms are not followed, the social relations of the Trios collapse. This means that the Trios usually avoid conflict and find subtle ways to begin rebuilding a relationship when it is under pressure. One of these tactics is the conveying of messages that build trust, for example, in my experience it involves reviewing history and demonstrating how important the other person has been across time. The Trios often prefer to warn a person when conflict is felt by indirectly noting discontent. For example, in a discussion with me regarding the proper amount of a raise in salaries of Trios working for the NGO, one Trio leader employed a metaphor: "You gave me the feathers, but not the meat." Moreover, I have also seen them smoothly hide behind language in uncomfortable moments of dispute, typically blaming the conflict on poor translation of key words.

A universal means of avoiding conflict is to focus on collaborative efforts that are going well and sidestepping those that are problematic. Avoidance is a conflict style associated with collectivity in which members of the collective have only one goal—to maintain relationships. The strategy of avoidance is largely reflected in Trio historical tales, and if conflict exists in human affairs, the Trios prefer to move away, especially if they are ashamed of their behavior. Remaining in the location of conflict would reinforce their shame toward the other and negatively influence the long-term relationship (Koelewijn 2003).

In Trio society, it seems, conflict will be addressed when a serious violation of behavior is presented that carries the risk of tribal disintegration. Conflict is always handled in a collective manner. The Trios meet in their round hut and discuss the different aspects of the conflict with each other, reaching decisions by consensus. I witnessed an excellent example of Trio conflict resolution in a diamond mining permission dispute (Box 5.2).

Box 5.2
A Diamond Mining Dispute

In 2008, the Trio leadership was approached by entrepreneurs who wanted to begin exploiting diamond reserves located beneath the forest in what is considered Trio territory. The smooth and tactical entrepreneurs gave the Trio leaders expensive gifts to persuade them to approve the plans so that the entrepreneurs could convince Suriname's government to grant them a diamond mining license. Two members of the Trio tribal leadership were instrumental in mediating between the entrepreneurs and the leaders, and ultimately pushed the leaders to approve the extraction plans. They convinced the most important tribal leader to sign the permission paper.

After this tribal leader signed the document, news spread quickly that the Trios had given permission to outsiders for diamond mining. The news reached me, and I immediately flew to the village for consultation. The bad news also had spread to all Trio community members, most of whom were upset and assessed the situation as very serious. A delegation of Trios went to one specific tribal leader to ask him about the decision. The community members' interest—keeping their land out of the hands of the extractive industry—was not aligned with that of tribal leaders. This type of conflict is constructed along the vertical dimension; it reflects the differences between the tribal members and a tribal leader. The vertical dimension is associated with a conflict style that is collective, in which group members are concerned about other individual members but are unwilling to sacrifice the group relationship (Komarraju et al. 2008). The Trios were more worried about instability within their group. The conflict over approval of the diamond mining plan was discussed in a series of meetings during the course of three weeks. In these meetings, some attended by up to 80 members, each participant had an opportunity to make a statement.

The Trios collectively decided that individual punishment was in order. A group of women denounced one of the tribal leaders who had pushed for acceptance of the plan, noting his earlier thefts. Following verbal condemnation, this leader was literally dragged from the hut. His behavior had violated the normative behavior expected by the community. Notably, the other tribal leader was permitted to save face, but now was expected to fix the problem. This tribal leader immediately overturned the decision and then traveled to the capital city, where he openly spoke to local media about his mistake. He was spared from "social execution," thereby both saving the face of the entire tribe and promoting group peace and harmony. The Trios typically ascribe equal value to the face concern of others and that of the self (Ting-Toomey 2001).

Values Related to the Environment

The Trio perspective on their territory is equivocal, depending on the values held by the community member providing the viewpoint. For example, a Trio shaman describes how the savannah, located in southernmost Suriname, was created by a spiritual bird, *busi skowtu*, that laid its feathers as a blanket over the trees. Then a person walked through the land and sketched the rivers with his hand. It is clear that the knowledgeable shaman is describing a spiritual connection between animals, humans and the land. A nonshamanic Trio man characterizes the creation of the same savannah in more naturalistic terms. He believes the Trios originally lived on the hills, and then the water came pouring down and the savannah was created because trees stopped growing (Smith 2013).

Notwithstanding the different perspectives, all Trios believe in an intrinsic connection between their peoples and their traditional lands, seeing themselves as a part of a world of animals, plants, water, soil and sky. Such a deep connection to land is seen in most of the world's forest-dwelling indigenous peoples (UNU 2012). The spiritual separation between animals and humans is no greater than that between individual humans. To illustrate, in my interaction with the community, a Trio man described an event when another Trio man was killed by a wild animal as follows: "the animal was hungry and needed food, and if the Trio is hungry, the animal simply will die." A lack of spiritual separation between humans and animals in the Trio viewpoint also is expressed in the names of tribal subgroups such as the Mawajanas, who are named after a type of frog (*mawa*) because they have short necks and are relatively plump.

Livelihood

The Trio livelihood is almost completely dependent on the forest and is broken out into customary gender roles. The women conduct planting and harvesting and carry heavy baskets with crops from the field to their homes. The women's responsibility appears greater than that of the men because the women also are in charge of cutting and carrying firewood, preparing food for their families and nurturing the children. Trio men, meanwhile, help the women cut open plots and are in charge of providing meat and fish for meals. The men also harvest trees for timber from which they build houses, boats and household tools (Heemskerk and Delvoye 2007). The men often must leave the village for long periods of time to carry out their responsibilities. Both men and women take several hours each day to provide for the simplest needs in life. The tasks assigned to men and women necessitate daily forest walks, thus reinforcing the cultural bond between the Trios and their environment.

When the Trios engage in livelihood activities, they take only what they need from the forest. Based on my observations, the Trios normally hunt for one day, eat the meat and return to hunt in the next few days. The storing of food is not generally practiced, in part because of the absence of electricity to run refrigerators and freezers. The Trios believe that everyone—animals and humans—needs to use the forest, and each must take a share. This sharing concept also is extended in time—they have designated areas for the provision of food for the next generation (Bong A Jan 2006). Such areas, located to the north and east of the village of Kwamalasamutu, are carefully chosen based on the availability of fertile soils and the presence of fruits and animals. Areas like this will be needed in the future because the Trio population is slightly growing and putting increasing pressure on the environment. This substantial increase in pressure was demonstrated through a comparative analysis of

Figure 5.4 The village of Kwamalasamutu. Photo by Gwendolyn Smith.

agricultural plots in an area of 121.5 km^2 in and around Kwamalasamutu (Figure 5.4). The average annual deforestation rate for the period 2004–2009 was almost triple that of the rate for 1987–2001: 1.6 percent versus 0.6 percent (Uiterloo 2011).

Threats to the land

Similar to other groups of indigenous peoples (United Nations 2009), the Trios feel responsible for the health and well-being of the land. Increasing evidence exists that local users, such as the Trios, protect the land. An analysis of forest cover in the Brazilian Amazon demonstrated that indigenous lands have the highest remaining percentage of forest in that region (Ricketts et al. 2010). However, prospects for conservation diminish when indigenous peoples live in poverty and cannot provide for their livelihood or when indigenous peoples become dependent on modern technologies and thereby on the market economy (Loomis 2000). In some of these cases, indigenous peoples significantly increase their take of forest products and meat to the point that these goods become scarce or even extinct (United Nations 2009; Wilshusen et al. 2002). Fortunately, as it appears to me, the Trios have not reached this point yet, although there are now fewer animals found than before. Taking into account each indigenous context is different and dependent on tribal interest, available natural resources, social organization and income generation alternatives. Assessments of an indigenous people's stewardship role should be made by researchers, taking all aspects of livelihood into account, including the provisional ability of the external environment.

Threats to the Trio land predominantly arise externally. Gold and bauxite mining activities in the region can pollute native environments and, more ominously for the Trio, increase exposure to new diseases. The Trios are very concerned about the effects of small-scale gold mining, debris from which turns their rivers brown and foggy, as seen in maroon and indigenous communities of eastern Suriname (Smith 2006). On several occasions, however, the Trios have been visited by gold miners with small-scale operations who are interested in exploring Trio territory. The Trios see this as a severe intrusion on their way of life, and they are scared about diseases such as malaria, poachers or any other destruction to their village system.

The first serious incursion of Brazilian gold miners in Trio territory took them by surprise at the end of 2006. The Trios quickly took protective action by working with an NGO in establishing a team of rangers in charge of nature protection. The rangers help monitor the environment through vigilance activities, measuring the impact of livelihood activities, water quality and indicators of forest change. I have seen rangers take part in nature awareness activities at schools, and also serve the valuable role of acting as the eyes and ears of the government, which is especially important because the Trios live in villages far removed from the sphere of government influence and presence (Smith et al. 2012).

The Trios also face threats from within their own society, such as an increasing illegal trade in exotic animals. In personal observations, some Trio men and women hide snakes, frogs and birds in small boxes together with food and other necessities destined for family members living in the capital city of Paramaribo. Designated family members sell these animals to traders in the capital Paramaribo or take them to the neighboring country of French Guiana, where they receive a relatively high payment. The monies received are used to buy modern goods such as clothes, condiments and electronics. Trio youth now wear fancy clothes, use hair products such as gel and coloring kits and carry portable music players (Figure 5.5). This was not the case even five years ago.

An increasing dependency on cash also puts pressure on the tribal leadership, because other figures gain power through income from illegal animal trafficking and stints in gold mines in the east. These new powerbrokers may become a threat to the existing leadership, adversely affecting maintenance of the "old ways." Because many Trio youth are not following the

Figure 5.5 A typical indigenous family from South Suriname. Photo by Rachelle Bong A Jan.

rules prescribed by the elders, the Trios believe that their society is on a downhill path.

Values Related to Development

The Trios explained to me the elements that are important to sustaining life in the forest are traditional knowledge, the health of the tribe, the health of the forest and a peaceful life with no interference from outsiders (Smith 2006). The Trio language lacks a specific word that describes the concept of development, and they told me that development is something that outsiders bring. They expect outsiders to help them with each small problem they encounter. The government of Suriname, which is perceived as "father," is especially expected to fulfill its paternalistic duty to provide for the same basic needs as the citizens receive in more urban areas. It is well known among the Trios, as well as the other nine Surinamese forest peoples, that for the last 150 years the government has favored the citizens living on the urbanized coast. Indigenous groups living in the forest belong not only to the groups with the lowest income in the country but are also the ones with the lowest levels of education and health-care status (ABS 2005).

Very little of the development is initiated by the Trios themselves and this "incapacity" brings in an extra dimension for the development organizations working with them. Each organization that supports Trio activities is perceived as a good friend and, in the Trio philosophy, friends always take care of each other. Caretaking is here defined as a holistic concept; it ranges from problems on the personal, family and village level as well as across different themes such as culture, religion, environment, health, education and others. Whenever the development organization violates this caretaking concept, for instance by withdrawing from assisting the Trios for one year, they will be unconditionally punished. One way is by putting the organization on probation, and as I have observed, the organization has to support lots of small activities before it returns to being in "good standing."

Development organizations like to partner with the Trios in establishing 1- to 2-year projects and, therefore, fund smaller activities such as training, workshops or the building of a structure. The Trios generally dislike short-term projects and favor development organizations that stay for longer periods of time. They expect these organizations to invest in buildings and offer jobs to local men and women (Figure 5.6, Box 5.3). With the money the Trio receive

Figure 5.6 Indigenous ranger post in the village of Kwamalasamutu. Photo by Gwendolyn Smith.

Box 5.3
The Real Development

In a leadership training for indigenous Trio leaders, my colleagues and I asked the leaders to identify what development projects existed in the village. For this exercise, we had drawn a traditional hut on a large piece of paper and asked the leaders to draw the projects that were active. To our surprise, only a few projects were drawn by the leaders. When we asked why only specific projects—a traditional health-care clinic, a ranger's post and a village office—were listed, they explained to us that these projects are real. It was then that I understood that development becomes a reality when there are permanent structures and associated staff on payroll. I have noticed that Trios like to visualize development activities. Another example is that rangers for nature protection are trained in six Trio villages, but only in the three villages where guard posts stand and the rangers are paid, is the program perceived as valid by the villagers.

from such projects, they can obtain expensive goods and radios, solar-powered lights and freezers.

With the increasing acculturation of the Trios, driven by more frequent contact with the capital city, individualistic desires—the acquisition of luxury products—are becoming more prominent. The Trios who enjoy higher status—such as tribal leaders, teachers, the community members working for Suriname's government and NGOs and the military—seem to set the trend for the entire village. When they begin using certain luxury goods, the rest follow. It has become increasingly evident to me that the Trios want to be like the people living in the capital city of Suriname called Paramaribo, an observation also made by another researcher (Healy et al. 2003). Thus, I observe the Trios follow a combined path in which they strive for collective development, including basic services such as water and electricity, while also pursuing individual goals specifically to obtain income and status.

Apart from the internal Trio perspective on development, I think it is also useful to look at the experiences of organizations that seek to assist the Trios through development projects. The relative success of projects that build on the everyday cultural activities of the Trios is exemplified in an NGO-sponsored program that has been underway since 2000: the "Shamans and Apprentices" program. This program prevents the disappearance of traditional knowledge by encouraging young apprentices to learn from elder shamans and to pre-serve the knowledge of plant-based medicines from the rain forest. Plant col-lection trips by the shamans with their apprentices result in the transmission of ancestral knowledge to younger generations as well as the renewal of the forest as a repository of healing. The program is implemented for the ben-efit of the community through traditional medicine clinics. These clinics are fully operated and directed by elder shamans and provide adequate room for several healers to practice medicine. In addition, the clinics provide facilities for apprentices—each paired with a shaman—to directly observe the elder healers practicing their medicine with opportunities for graduated clinical responsibility (Smith and Uiterloo 2007). The project organizes and supports a normal Trio activity: knowledge transfer. It is aligned with the tribal need for interest in traditional medicine. The work of the NGO and my personal experience provide evidence that the Trios cannot deviate too much from their traditional pattern, and that a need exists to skillfully build on the existing sys-tem when initiating development activities.

Education and income

Trio leaders initiate different activities to overcome the educational divide between the traditional and the modern world. In one such activity, Trio chil-dren are sent to the capital city to continue their education at the middle school level and higher. The Trios believe that with more children receiving a modern education, the community's participation in development is sup-ported. Education seems a priority, as I have seen the Trios self-initiate various education-related activities. One such activity desired by the leadership is the establishment of a vocational school for the operation and repair of machines such as outboard motors and chainsaws so that Trio community members can learn skills that they can apply in the village.

Until 2005, the Trios did not use money regularly, and would barter bush-meat for sugar and salt from the city. Money now is generated through scarcely available jobs such as the export of crafts and (exotic) animals, through tem-porary work in the gold-mining fields and by providing support to local activi-ties of Suriname's government and nature conservation organizations. Some Trios also export forest products, although this practice is hampered by the high costs of transporting goods from the villages to markets in Paramaribo. Such goods that have been exported on a regular basis—including Brazil nuts, bushmeat and ground pepper—have been supported by locally active NGOs and the government (Healy et al. 2003). The money that the Trios earn is used to obtain goods from the city, predominantly basics such as clothing and food items.

Negative identity

The Trios believe that outside development is superior to their way of life. This reflects the social identity theory of Tjafel and Turner (Pruitt and Kim 2004), which holds that, when groups with an inferior position compare themselves with other groups, they develop a negative social identity. This was demonstrated from a survey from Trio respondents in Kwamalasamutu, when they were asked whether the traditional or the modern type of knowledge was more useful. About half (53.3 percent) appraised both types of knowledge as useful; approximately one-fourth (26.7 percent) decided that modern knowledge is more useful because outsiders know more than the Trios; and the remainder (20 percent) called the knowledge of Trio elders more useful (Smith 2013). The survey outcome shows that approximately 80 percent of interviewed Trios consider modern knowledge to be equal or superior to their traditional knowledge. This clearly shows that the Trios respond to the influence of knowledge conveyed by outsiders.

Negative identity also is in view when the Trio tribal leadership holds meetings with outsiders. At such meetings, I observed that the tribal leaders dress completely in modern formal attire, including jacket and tie, shedding all traditional elements. Trio tribal leaders wear a traditional feather headdress only in official settings. And seldom have I seen that Trios living in the villages wear traditional clothing. To overcome their negative self-image, the Trios want to improve their social status position and become like those living according to the values of modern society.

The Trio also experience language problems when dealing with outsiders. It is evident that the majority of Trios speak a Carib-based language among themselves, and only a few Trios can speak Suriname's national language, Dutch, or the widely used lingua franca, Sranang Tongo. Concepts in the Northern frame are very difficult for Trios to understand, and it is generally believed that the Trios need a long time to process and comprehend such information, similar to many other indigenous communities (Cohen 2004). Their lack of fluency in mainstream languages puts the Trios in a weaker power position in negotiations, and I have observed this disparity sometimes misused by outsiders.

The Trios may initially accommodate ideas from outsiders when they seek to overcome their negative identity. Accommodation as a strategy is "unassertive and cooperative," because in it "the person gives in at any cost as a way to avoid conflict to maintain the relationship" (Folger et al. 2005, 66). When the Trios are accommodating, unfortunately, others can easily overrule and make decisions for them (Smith 2010a). The accommodative conflict resolution style can change into one of competition if the Trios deem their collectivity or livelihood to be in danger (Box 5.4).

Box 5.4
The Unexpected Tourism Resort

Around 2004, a private company was granted concession by the Suriname government to establish a tourism resort in the midst of the vast tropical rain forest. The place was beautiful, with large water rapids and seemingly untouched forest. So, the company decided to build lodges within the scenic landscape. The moment they started bringing in materials, the Trios immediately decided to settle near the future tourist site.

The Trios were furious about being kept in the dark about the tourism plan in "their" territory. With bows and arrows they went to the lodge holder to fight for the land and respect. Today, the Trios view the tourism operation not only as an intrusion on their collective privacy but also as a threat to the future food supply (Bong A Jan 2006). The resort holders, on the other hand, see the Trios as extreme opportunists, because they were absent at the start of the operation and settled only after the resort was constructed (Winston Gummels, pers. comm.).

Applying the VIEW Framework

In this chapter I have presented the values the Trios possess as a collective. The values were retrieved with a social polygraphy exercise, more specifically, by making a "map of the past." Generating a map of the past allowed the community to bring central themes to the forefront, such as religion, education and so on. It is then up to the researcher to discuss these themes with different men and women, representing the total of functional groups—women, youth, elders, hunters, fishers, agriculturists, processors, traders, rangers, teachers, traditional leaders—in the community. During such elaborate conversations, usually in the form of storytelling, it is almost certain that the values the community holds come to the fore: what is accepted and what not during the course of history. The questions available to the researcher to initiate a conversation about values are: why and how. An example of such a systematic discussion with the Trios is given in Box 5.5.

I have engaged with community members in several "map of the past" exercises to retrieve the historic values the Trios possess. Each of the maps was initiated and completed with different types of functional groups within Trio society. Environmental values were best described by the rangers, hunters, fishers, and crop caretakers. Social values were strongly held by tribal leaders

Box 5.5
Guiding Questions for Retrieving Historical Values

The community's elders drew a map of the village as it appeared in the 1960s. I noticed some strange lines in the right upper corner of the map, only was I clueless about what they meant. I was aware that in each object on the map lies a story filled with information about the values a community holds. So the first question I asked was framed as, why? I asked the elders, Why do I see lines in the corner?

An elderly shaman explained to me the following:

"In that region [pointing to the south in the village of Kwamalasamutu], there is a lot of lightning". Unsatisfied with the answer, I kept on asking why it was important to them. The shaman told me, "Lightning bring us problems, such as earthquakes. When we see lightning, we know that things are happening in another place [another part of the world]. It comes with lots of rain. If lightning moves [pointing to the north], it is bad. In the past, we all were praying that lightning would not move. It was *Warapa* [spirit]." (Smith 2013, 128)

The shaman automatically talked about the times when things had gone wrong, or in other words, when value boundaries were violated. The story shows that lightning was a phenomenon that the Trios valued as bad. When I continued with the inquiry to understand why *Warapa* is so important, the shaman told me the following:

He was bad and restless. He jumped a lot and caused dark clouds and rain. Then it was dark almost the whole day, the ground was shaking and we were praying with the shamans and their *marakkas* [rattles]. We did not know that it was God, now we know that it is God. Everyone was in the *paiman* [round hut] to pray so that bad things would not attack us. We were praying with two shamans, one was saying that we have problems and the other one was saying that there are no problems. Before there was a large frog, it was a God but not a serious one. He looked like a person [Trios believe that shamans can see animals as humans] and he killed people. We called him God. He was so big that he could look over the world and guide us. (Smith 2013, 128)

The information revealed by the shaman gave me a clue about the social space that the Trios think is acceptable. To better understand the strength of the "lightning" value, I ask a second question in the frame of, how? I posed the question to see how he coped with the lightning and associated bad spirit. The shaman answered,

> My mother and grandmother told me to be someone that can see the frog [shaman]. Then other people told me to do good things. Now I work with the stars and plants, not with the animals. I still see things in my dreams. (Smith 2013, 128)

This shaman's answer gave me an idea of how strongly "lightning" still influences the present day. Seemingly the shaman had woven the story into one of the gospels on his conversion by the missionaries, which happened in the 1960s.

and older persons with lots of knowledge about the tribe's history and journey. For economic values I relied on food processors, traders, youth and those with daily involvement in business. The data I gathered was carefully complemented by my own observations and valuable experiences with the Trios. But my own interpretations and findings were only useful after triangulating the data with my colleagues to get rid of my own distortion.

The gathered information was used to complete the value analysis of the VIEW framework, which consisted of three groups of values: environmental, social and economic. For environmental values, the Trios seem to fall back to a strong urge to protect their livelihood dependency through their surrounding environment. The concepts of "togetherness" and "religion" define the social values that Trios cherish, and these values are anticipated to become active in a situation of rapid change. These social values, important since early in their existence, were developed over centuries of dwelling in the area currently known as the south of Suriname and the north of Brazil. But presently, other types of values have come to the surface. It is evident from the analysis that modern, Western cultures are appreciated by the Trios, but they approach them with a (perceived) negative identity. This same modern world is highly valued because there is a potential opportunity of economic advancement. For example, Trio children should receive an education in order to be able to find income through modern jobs (Figure 5.7).

So, what can we do with this first outcome of the VIEW analysis? The value analysis can help researchers better explain certain motivations and behaviors of a community. For example, an economic value may be a main driver for a community that sells forest goods in the market economy, while a social value

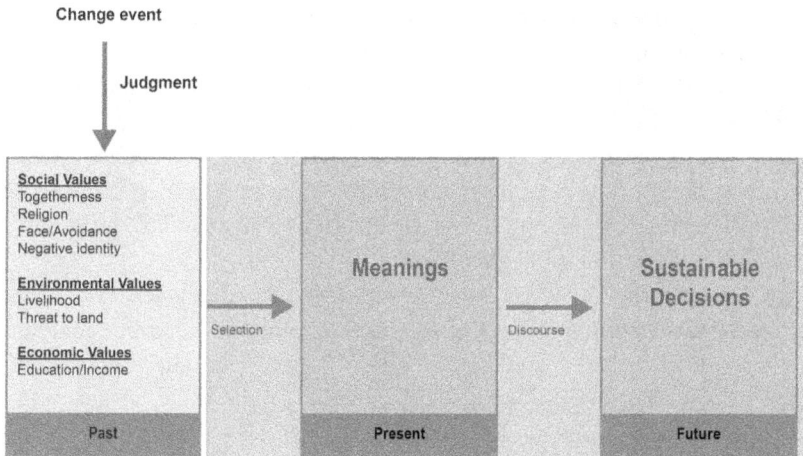

Figure 5.7 Values held by the Trio indigenous peoples across the dimensions of sustainable development.

clarifies a typical way a community behaves toward other outsider groups. Because values are typically developed over a long time, they serve as the stable foundation on which a community depends when it is undergoing some kind of social or environmental change. Exploring these deeply rooted morals improves our understanding of how the Trio community makes choices.

Values and sustainability

During my years of community work I have learned that a project's sustainability can be promoted when a community's values are, in fact, addressed by the researcher and respectfully engaged the project. Following this vague and potentially argumentative statement, every good researcher will ask the next question: how do we know the community values are sufficiently engaged in a project?

I normally check a project's design against the values that came out of the analysis. Although this practice sometimes occurs automatically, it makes me aware of potential discrepancies the project has with the values the community embraces and gives me a chance to correct the mistake I habitually make: designing a project based on my own Western frame of thinking. A project, for instance, that supports individual entrepreneurship would run into problems because the Trios hold on to a strong value of togetherness. Value proofing this project in the design phase would allow me to anchor the project activities onto the community's togetherness values, which in turn, may lead to improved project outcomes.

I have developed several practical indicators that helped me and that hope-fully can assist other researchers who follow the value-judging processes. Every indicator works along a continuum. On the left side of the continuum I present the lower end, which resembles a state in which there is limited vigor to make a project sustainable. On the right side I show the higher end, which is the most effective state for promoting the sustainability of the project. Particular actions that are intermediate in supporting the project's sustainability are found in between the lower and the higher end.

For example, the VIEW framework helps the researcher assess the commu-nity's internal capability of judging the climate event, knowing that judging is a tedious and concealed cognitive process. When a researcher notices that a community cannot make this so-called value judgment, these intrinsic values may remain hidden and undetected by the researcher. Under this peculiar circumstance, I have quite often seen a conflict arise between the community and other project partners. In the event that a value judgment is made, the community progresses in the view making and the project has a higher poten-tial for sustainability.

Chapter 6

MAKING SENSE OF THE WORLD

Like other indigenous peoples, the Trios constantly track changes in their surrounding environment by making comparisons between historic and present events (Byg and Salick 2009). This attests to the specific nature of indigenous peoples' observations in space and time, and to their evaluation of deviations from normal over time, even discerning between a few "odd" and more long-term trends. Groups like the Trios are the first to observe and experience changes occurring in the forest, which they seem to interpret as both local and global phenomena. Most Trios have never heard of the term "climate change," let alone what it entails. Climate change comes across as a mental construct created by the developed world.

The Trios understand climate change at the level that the forest presents risk to their livelihood. The risk system is based on an assessment—they constantly walk in the vicinity of their village to assess the forest, and use their senses of sight, taste, sound and touch to compare and contrast situations from the past with current phenomena. After thorough assessment, the Trios create an image of risk that is directly linked to the way that they see the world. Subsequently, they make a decision on how to act, based on the levels that they define as acceptable (Weber 2006).

Such images of reality are known to play a fundamental role in the assessment of risk and subsequent behavior, and define the organizing concept through which the tribe views local climate-related changes. For a researcher like me who seeks to understand the Trio view of climate change, information must be collected for describing the present-day reality in which the Trios live, the so-called map of the present. This information becomes relevant for the VIEW framework by answering five relevant questions: 1) What is real? 2) How is the "real" organized? 3) How do we know what is "real"? 4) What is valuable or important? and 5) How should we act? (Nudler 1993). When these exploratory questions are answered, I can draw a complete picture of how the Trios interpret and create meaning of climate change.

Table 6.1 Organization of information for understanding the process of meaning making using the VIEW framework: A case study of the Trio indigenous peoples

Questions for Reality Description (Nudler, 1993)	Questions Attuned to the Trio Case Study	Categories for Analyzing Conflicting Views
What is real?	What observations make up the Trio view on climate change?	Interest
How is the real organized?	How is Trio climate-change knowledge organized in the community?	Interest
How do we know what is real?	How is the Trio climate-change detection system organized?	Interest
What is important?	What role do values have in the Trio view on climate change?	Values
How do we act?	What attitude and strategies do the Trios have with respect to combating climate change?	Strategies Attitude

As seen in Table 6.1, the collected information is organized into conflict categories. Such distinct categories are necessary for analyzing a potential conflict between the Trio view and the view held by others, such as the development organization. Four conflict-related categories seem important for studying such opposing views (Carpenter and Kennedy 2001): interest, values, strategies and attitude (Table 6.1, third column). These categories are now further discussed in detail.

The Trios' Interests

The Trios are interested in harmoniously living with the forest to survive and facilitate the next kin to progress through time. On several occasions when the tribe was in danger, their shamans gathered the entire community to engage in rituals to divert the bad weather. Elder tribal members also can recall songs that shamans sang to redirect clouds and repel water monsters that could cause unwanted floods (Koelewijn 2003). Besides rituals, the Trios appear to possess and preserve knowledge they need to survive, which suggests that their knowledge resembles their interests (Habermas 1971). Following this thought, it can be said that Trio knowledge and interests are embedded in their traditional system, which is typically operated by two types of assessments: spatial and temporal. The spatial assessment apparently relies on seasonal indicators and the temporal assessment on observations over long periods of time.

Indicators for seasonality

> The forest is still good in the place where I live. [...] But when we plant crops, the crops deteriorate faster than before. In the past we could get any fruits from the forest, all that we needed, but now we have different seasons. *Nerie* (insect) is not making noise in time for the dry season and in November the rainy season does not start on time. Before you could exactly see when the rainy season started. Now we can't predict it anymore making it difficult to plant our crops. (Smith 2013, 173)

The Trios have the unique ability to detect seasonal shifts with their traditional knowledge, centered on a set of physical and biological indicators. Seasons have always played an important role in the life of the Trios, because they were used as a time measure before the Trios learned about the modern calendar. As I was told, a traditional Trio year would end when leaves began falling and when flowers started sprouting in unison (Smith 2013). Now that the Trios have converted to the Western calendar, two different seasons are distinguished in Kwamalasamutu: a dry season that runs from August through November, and a rainy season that runs from December through July. In both seasons, the temperature is fairly constant, on average between 26 and 28.2 degrees Celsius respectively; this constancy is a well-known feature of the tropical rain forest ecosystem (Heemskerk and Delvoye 2007).

Today, as in the past, seasons are instrumental in the planning of Trio livelihood activities. Seasonal forest change is detected by the Trios using 52 indicators (Table 6.2). The indicators are carefully selected along the small paths the Trios walk to and from their agricultural plot or any other forest location where they collect livelihood goods. Each indicator seems linked to the seasonal calendar. For example, one set of indicators predicts the outset of the dry season. Certain species are active during the first phase of the dry season, when the amount of rainfall decreases rapidly to almost zero. Other indicators thrive in the midst of the drought season when it is completely dry, and the third group of indicators is vigorously active only at the end of the season. A similar pattern is distinguished in the rainy season, only now the indicators are associated with rainfall instead of drought.

The seasonal indicators in Table 6.2. are chosen from the locale in which they live and represent the spatial component of the Trio traditional knowledge system. Indicators seem to be selected based on their availability and, more importantly, the ability to perform a specific function, of which the Trios assess five types: (1) predictors, (2) indicators to detect a nuance in the rainy season, (3) indicators for soil health, (4) indicators for forest health and (5) indicators to detect changes in the microclimate.

Table 6.2 Names of seasonal indicators used by the Trio indigenous peoples to detect local climate change. Plant and animal names identified by the National Zoological Collection of Suriname, National Herbarium of Suriname and ethnobotanist Mark J. Plotkin.

Function	Trio Name	Scientific Name	Type	Season	Action	Characteristics for Seasonal Change
Predictor	Nerie	*Felicina sp.*	Crawling insect	Dry season	Makes noise	
	Poko poko	*Gryllidea sp.*	Crawling/flying insect	Dry season	Makes noise	
	Nirïï	*Cicadeae sp.*	Crawling insect	Dry season	Walks	
	Ékui aki	*Pseudosphinx tetrio*	Caterpillar	Dry season	Walks	
	Weipereru	*Phoebis sennae marcelina*	Butterfly	Dry season	Flies	Low water level
	Taparara	*Loadamia \ loadamia*	Butterfly	Dry season	Flies	
	Oroi	*Anacardium occidentalis*	Plant flower	Rainy season	Flowers	
	Emepeke	*Cochronella oyampiensis*	Frog	Rainy season	Makes noise	
	Moman	*Taurus*	Star constellation	Rainy season	Disappears	In the west
	Mopé	*Spondias mombin*	Plant fruit	Rainy season	Ripens	
Nuance in rainy season	Arimai	*Taralea sp.*	Plant flower	Rainy season	Flowers	With little rain
	Akanopatoro	*Herrania kamukuensis*	Plant flower and fruit	Rainy season	Flowers and fruits	Flowers with little rain and fruits with lots of rain
	Kura	*Rhinella sp*	Frog	Rainy season	Makes noise	End of rainy season, high river water level
	Muru	*Bufo sp.*	Frog	Rainy season	Makes noise	Start and end of rainy season, high river water level
	Marakau	*Ceratophrys cornuta*	Frog	Rainy season	Walks	Start of rainy season, high river water level
	Minute	*Unknown*	Scorpion	Rainy season	Walks	With highest river water

	Local name	Scientific name	Type	Indicator	Season	Description
	Kijapoko	*Ramphastidae picoformes)*	Bird	Makes noise	Rainy season	With little rain that keeps on going
	Suri	*Cyanerpes caeruleus*	Bird	Flies	Rainy season	When it keeps raining
	Kito	*Eleutherodactylus fenestratus*	Frog	Makes noise	Rainy season	When it is dark
	Wapuri	*Sapatoceae sp.*	Plant fruit	Fruit ripens	Rainy season	With little rain; otherwise, fruit rots
	Jareware	*Gemini*	Star constellation	Disappears	Rainy season	In the west, highest river water level
	Otojaramëtephë	*Orion*	Star constellation	Disappears	Rainy season	In the west, lots of animals, high river water level
Soil health	Urukuja	*Passifloracea cf. serrulata*	Plant flower	Flowers	Rainy season	In fertile soil after planting cassava
	Karau Alawata	*Inga sp.*	Plant fruit	Fruits	Rainy season	In fertile soil
	Anakara	*Inga sp.*	Plant fruit	Fruits	Rainy season	After dying off in dry season
	Jalan	*Sapindaceae sp.*	Plant flower	Flowers	Rainy season	In fertile clay soil
	Marajaimë	*Geonoma sp.*	Plant flower	Flowers	Rainy season	In wet soil
	Ëmumoimë	*Passifloraceae sp.*	Plant flower	Flowers	Rainy season	In fertile decaying soil
	Kamaki	*Ambelania acida*	Plant flower	Flowers	Rainy season	In dry fertile soil
Forest health	Mikakë	*Atta sp.*	Crawling/flying insect	Walks / Flies	Dry season / Rainy season	In large groups
	Tëtëkë	*Isoptera sp.*	Crawling/flying insect	Flies	Rainy season	
	Tënmiren pereru	*Lystra sp.*	Butterfly	Flies	Dry season	
	Karosiwa aki	*Urania leilus*	Butterfly	Flies	Dry season	
	Tamu	*Morpho achillus achillus*	Butterfly	Flies	Dry season	In abundance

(continued)

Table 6.2 Continued

Function	Trio Name	Scientific Name	Type	Season	Action	Characteristics for Seasonal Change
	Aturaimë	*Cayaponia ophalmica*	Plant fruit	Rainy season	Fruits	
	Karaiwëimë	*Bignoniaceae sp.*	Plant flower	Dry season	Flowers	
	Eru eru këei	*Unknown*	Plant flower	Rainy season	Flowers	And breaks open when it becomes dry
	Jekara	*Combretum sp.*	Plant flower	Dry season	Grows and flowers	
	Adikanama	*Theobroma sp*	Plant fruits	Rainy season	Fruits	
	Tamo	*Coccoloba sp*	Plant fruit	Rainy season	Fruits	With the highest water level
	Piaiman	*Allophryne ruthveni*	Frog	Rainy season	Makes noise	With lots of rain
	Pepekane	*Ameerega trivittata*	Frog	Rainy season	Makes noise	In the morning and at night
	Tamatupë aroki	*Phallus sp.*	Macrofungi	Rainy season	Visible	In extreme drought
	Sadie	*Gudua sp.*	Plant	Dry season	Yellowing	
	Pirakirii	*Lachesis muta*	Snake	Rainy season	Visible, walks	
	Pemëime aki	*Unknown*	Caterpillar	Dry season	Walks	In large groups at the end of the dry season
	Tamo Piriku	*Unknown*	Plant fruit	Dry season	Fruit ripens	When the rain stops
	Marasi ena	*Passifloraceae sp.*	Plant flower	Rainy season	Flowers	
Sensitivity to microclimate	Kuweimë	*Unknown*	Snail	Dry season	Walks	In complete drought
	Koimëme	*Araceae cf. philodendron*	Plant flower	Rainy season	Flowers	In high mountains
	Sikiman wetu	*Fabaceae sp.*	Plant fruit	Rainy season	Fruits	In high mountains
	Kaikui norepiriki	*Clusiaceae sp.*	Plant fruit	Dry season	Fruit falls	In high mountains

Figure 6.1 The predictor Poko Poko (*Gryllidea sp.*). Photo by Jonathan Sapa, indigenous ranger of Kwamalasamutu.

Predictors

The first functional indicator type the Trios differentiate is the species that predict the start of seasons. Poko Poko, an insect of the family *Gryllidea*, is a popular indicator for the onset of the dry season. Poko Poko announces the new year, as I was told by the Trio elders (Smith 2013). Poko Poko prefers living in a yellow-blossom tree known as the Poko Poko Udu tree. The pupas, found in groups of 30–40 in dry clay soil on the hills and mountains, emerge from the ground in the drying weather of August. The insects set out to fly and sing vibrantly when it becomes completely dry in September. Intriguing is the sound made by Poko Poko, a feature also well known to other forest communities. But when the singing is over and the rainy season starts, Poko Poko disappears (Figure 6.1).

Another central predictor species is Ëkui aki (*Pseudospinx tetra*), a red-yellow-black-striped caterpillar of the *Sphingidae* family. The Ëkui aki actively crawls on a specific tree (Ëkui) just before the dry season begins. The light-loving caterpillar prefers to move in groups of approximately 20. The captivating sound Ëkui aki makes from eating leaves from the Ëkui tree at night is an indicator for the dry season. After becoming dormant in leaf-covered sandy soil,

Figure 6.2 The predictor Ëkui aki (*Pseudospinx tetrio*). Photo by Jonathan Sapa, indigenous ranger of Kwamalasamutu.

the caterpillar transforms into a bright yellow butterfly that disappears subtly when it starts raining.

The Trios revealed to me that Ëkui aki is not only a favorite predictor species but also a fish provider because its droppings are eaten by popular fish (Paku and Murëkeïmë). The link between caterpillar and fish can also be found in a Trio legend that describes how Ëkui aki deposits its litter at the base of the Ëkui tree, which ultimately transforms into a fish named Siwiri (Smith 2013). In such stories about transformations, knowledge and belief may cross paths. For example, after seeing Ëkui aki, the Trios begin cultivating their agricultural plots, after which, it seems, they can catch the fish Siwiri in the river flowing underneath the Ëkui tree. Indicators like Ëkui aki thus are tied to more than one event because of their association with the belief system (Figure 6.2). The belief system is thus crucial for backing up community knowledge and consolidating the actions that must be taken (Berkes 2008).

Nuances in the rainy season

The Trios opt for indicators to detect subtle changes for which they need to possess extensive knowledge of the species' life cycle. Both men and women

Figure 6.3 The nuance indicator Akanopatoro (*Herrania kanukuensis*). Photo by Jonathan Sapa, indigenous ranger of Kwamalasamutu.

can notice nuances in the rain with the indicator Akanopatoro. Scientifically known as *Herrania kanukuensis,* this 2- to 3-meter-high tree grows on leafy soil beneath the taller trees. The bark is used by various indigenous groups as a medicine to counter the sting of the Irake (a black insect used for a rite of passage test when males reach adulthood). An interesting characteristic is that the tree's buds simultaneously produce flowers and oval-shaped fruits. During a period of little rain in December, Akanopatoro shows more flowers. Alternatively, during a period of excessive rain in January, the tree begins producing fruit. Akanopatoro functions as an indicator to determine whether rainfall will continue or whether there will be a short dry period during the rainy season (Figure 6.3) (Smith 2013).

Subtle changes also are detected through other types of species. Frogs make sounds during the rainy season, and according to the Trios, they do so playing in the tiny pools that are formed by the rain. One Trio man describes the frog sounds as follows:

Rain comes when the frogs start singing [making the frog sound]. When the big rains come the frogs keep on singing. They don't stop! They

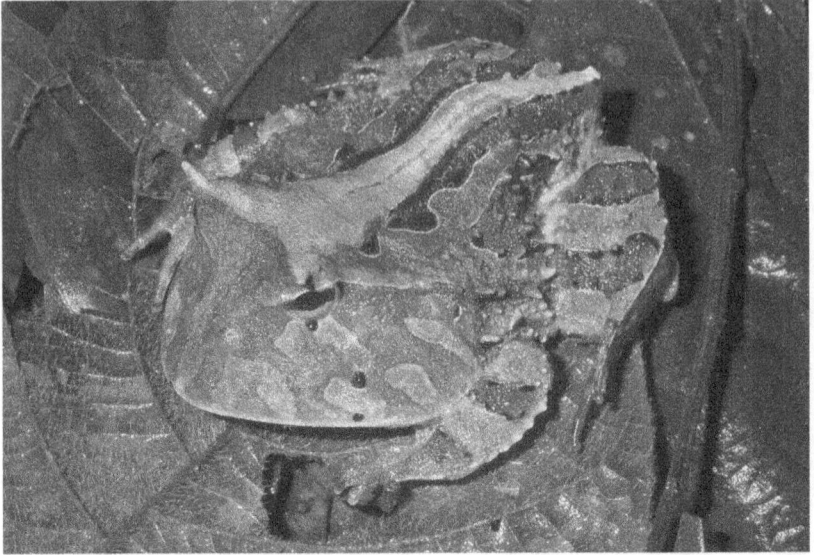

Figure 6.4 The nuance indicator Marakau (*Ceratophrys cornuta*). Photo by Raffael Ernst/Senckenberg.

indicate that you cannot go to the forest, because it is going to rain, so it is inaccessible. (Smith 2013, 161)

A particular frog sound that the Trios use to signal the highest river water level in the rainy season is from Marakau (*Ceratophrys cornuta*). This scary-looking frog prefers to stay in dark and moist places and only emerges from its hole when a high river water level is observed (Figure 6.4). Then the frog is forced to walk around in the forest because its holes are underwater (Smith 2013).

Also during this time of high water, I observed the Trios avoid walking in the forest for long periods. They are afraid of dangerous scorpions that actively move around seeking a mate. Scorpions are only seen when the star constellation that we know as Scorpio is observable in the sky, particularly in the west. The correlations between these phenomena—frog presence, highest river water level, scorpion presence and constellation visibility—exemplify the connectedness of different indicators (Figure 6.5). It appears that Trio indicators often are assessed in combination rather than singly, demonstrating a traditional knowledge system with numerous interconnections (Smith 2013).

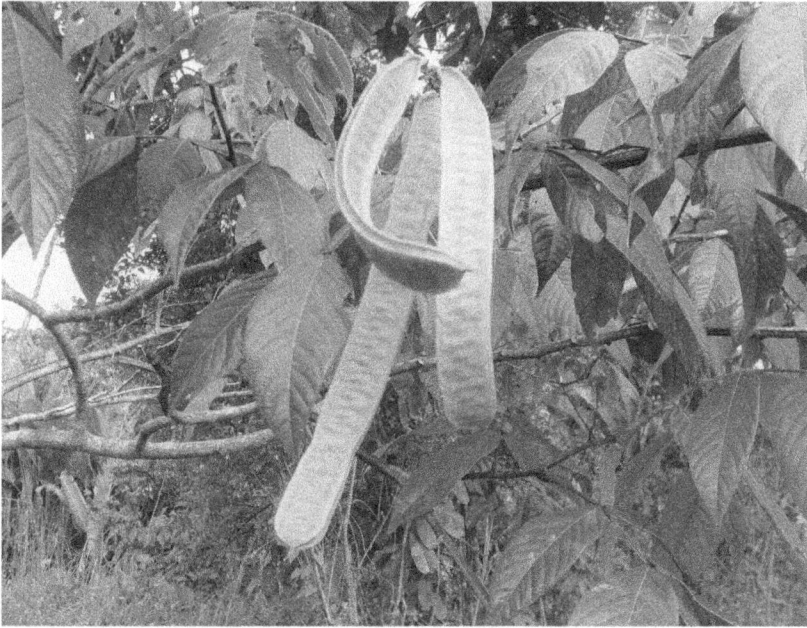

Figure 6.5 The soil health indicator Karau Alawata (*Inga sp.*). Photo by Jonathan Sapa, indigenous ranger of Kwamalasamutu.

Soil health

The Trios use certain plant species to determine whether the soil is suitable for planting food crops. Karau Alawata, a plant from the *Inga* family, grows well only when soils are fertile. This means that this pod-bearing species grows in yellow-brown sandy soils, which are considered excellent for planting the most desired Trio crops, such as cassava and other roots, plantains and corn. The Trios particularly look for Karau Alawata when picking their subsistence plots in the forest, and in some cases plant Karau Alawata to determine whether a new plot is fertile or when the fertility of a used plot has been restored. Besides its indicator function, Karau Alawata also is important to the Trios as fire-wood and as an attractor of different game species (Smith 2013).

Forest health

The Trios also perceive the forest as a whole. They distinguish several species that serve as indicators for a healthy forest, including insects, frogs, plant flowers and fruits, fungi and snakes. When these species appear, the Trios trust

Figure 6.6 The forest health indicator Tamo (*Coccoloba sp.*). Photo by Jonathan Sapa, indigenous ranger of Kwamalasamutu.

that the forest is vigorous and healthy and that no immediate danger to their livelihood exists.

By far the most popular Trio indicator for a healthy forest that I have learned about is the presence of fruit-bearing trees. Tamo (*Coccoloba sp.*) belongs to this group. The small and narrow tree of 1.5 meters in height is only found in dark places in the forest (Figure 6.6). Flowering starts when the first drops of rain fall and, a few months later, the purple-colored fruits appear in the peak of the rainy season. The amount of available fruit is a trivial input in their risk assessment process: when the forest is unable to produce sufficient amounts of fruit, the Trios perceive a poor and unhealthy forest that they assess as a high risk to their livelihood (Smith 2013). One Trio man describes this situation:

> If you don't see fruit than you know something is wrong. If one thing is wrong then everything will go wrong. (Smith 2013, 165)

Sensitivity to microclimate

A distinct set of Trio indicators is associated with very rare and special forest conditions. These are plants that fruit or flower, or animals that are active under specific climate conditions, hereafter referred to as sensitive species.

Figure 6.7 The sensitivity indicator Kuweimë (unknown scientific name). Photo by Jonathan Sapa, indigenous ranger of Kwamalasamutu.

One of these species is Kuweimë, a 10-centimeter-long snail that walks on trees when they are extremely dry (Figure 6.7). It is rarely seen in the forest because tree dryness is a rare event. Kuweimë seems to have transformative capacity: the large snail transforms into a poisonous snake in the dry season, according to a Trio legend (Smith 2013).

The five types of functional indicators discussed here show the extensiveness of the Trio knowledge system. The assessment reveals, as expected, that their seasonal indicators are closely associated with their most important livelihood activities. Indicators related to prediction of seasons seem to be extremely important as well as those on soil health (Smith 2013). Both these groups of indicators are needed for safeguarding the Trio food supply and security. Such strong links with agriculture are often seen when studying the views of indigenous peoples on climate change (Berrany-Ford et al. 2011; Roncoli 2006; Turner and Clifton 2009).

Observations in time

In the past, the water would become so low that we could pick the fish out of the water. Now the water is not lowering anymore. The water vanished in a large hole. Then we moved to another village. Not now.

Now there is water! The young boys can jump from the shore in the water. (Smith 2013, 173)

The Trios have gathered, compared and contrasted information from the forest over an estimated 4,900 years. Scanning elements that surrounds them—the forest with its animals and plants, the soil, water and sky—to detect changes in the cycles of life, rain and other natural events is normal Trio practice. As a rule, the Trios make associations between all these elements, which is the only way that the Trios understand local climate change (epistemology).

The assessment of temporal change refers to a continuous process of assessing differences between past and current knowledge and practice (Alessa et al. 2008; Pierotti 2011). It enables Trio men and women to link current events with events they experienced as youth and to connect them with ancient tales. This system of observation for recognizing anomalies complements the Trio spatial system, which is evidently more focused on monitoring the seasons in order to optimally execute livelihood activities. Observations run on a longer time frame than the seasonal indicators, typically on a scale of years rather than months.

The inimitable ability to observe also is dependent on the sensitivity of the observer. Specialization in observation is the logical result of the Trios' experience with the forest—hunters will have more knowledge about animals, women about crop plants and shamans about the behavior of living and spiritual beings. The majority of Trios I have engaged with told me that the forest has worsened, explicitly meaning that the forest as a whole is unable to provide as much fruit and game as before. Even though the Trios think that the forest is deteriorating, I find from my research that they foresee that it will continue to provide a sufficient amount of food for the future. This indicates that the forest hasn't reached its threshold for an immediate livelihood risk.

The Trios are particularly knowledgeable about the rainy season, more so because it presents an abundance of fruits and meat as compared to the dry season. Tribal men and women now sense more rainfall than before, and this conclusion is based on four separate events. The first event is the natural shedding of leaves from trees during the dry season. Quite a few trees naturally shed their leaves; however, in the last few years it has been too wet for this to occur. The Trio women, who are able to detect this change, view this episode as a means of forest replenishment. They find that the ongoing climatic changes prevent the forest from restoring itself, leaving it to deteriorate. A Trio woman describes these circumstances:

When the rain stops, all the leaves fall. Then the dry season begins, so we know that the dry season begins. This is also the time that the forest will replenish itself. Now there are not falling many leaves, I see it in the wind. (Smith 2013, 171)

A second event that the Trios use to assess change in rainfall is the exact time when agricultural plots can be planted. Agricultural plots are selected and burned in the dry season between September and November, just before the planting of crops in the second half of November. But recently, most Trios have felt that their plots are staying too wet for burning in the dry season. The reasons for this are the intensified rainfall and the reduced hours of sunshine, which by and large contribute to the soil turning insufficiently dry to facilitate the burning process.

Third, for many years, the Trios have watched the sky as a guide to the beginning and ending of rainy seasons. They cunningly distinguish several star constellations, of which Moman, Jareware, and Otoijaramëtephë are the most profoundly and widely used. When each of these assemblages reaches the western sky, the Trios believe that the flow of rainfall is supposed to change. Momam[1] is the first constellation seen when the rainy season launches in April. Traditionally in May/June, Jareware[2] disappears in the west, which the Trios connect with the highest river water level. This time mark is connected with deer, rabbits, turtles and other animals that become fat and appear in abundance. The Trios associate the vanishing of Otoijaramëtephë in the west with the profusion of a pig-like animal named Peïnjeke (*Dicotyles pecari*). Otoijaramëtephë represents the jaw of this Peïnjeke (Koelewijn, 2003), and perhaps is part of the star constellation Orion, which fades away in May. Although this tracking system has effectively worked for centuries, today, however, the Trios note different conditions: asynchrontity between rain and the appearance of these star constellations in the west. The Trios make the following observation:

Rain starts falling before certain stars reach the west.
When the stars reach the west there is more rain than before.
(Smith, 2013, 172)

Fourth, the Trios examine the water level of the village's river for a change in rainfall. A lot of different activities are carried out on the river such as fishing, bathing and the washing of clothes and cookware. Higher water levels are now perceived than in the past—the Trios can drink the river water because it is clear rather than muddy, and fishes survive instead of die

---

1 Presumably part of the star constellation Taurus.
2 Presumably part of the star constellation Gemini.

during the dry season. Trio members also witness that the water level now remains high, and changes dramatically overnight instead of there being a gradual increase during the rainy season. High water level resulted in disastrous flooding in 2006. Although serious flooding occurs every 25–100 years (Amatali 2012), a sudden water level rise of several meters took the Trios by surprise.

As my analysis demonstrates, the Trios examine the changes in the local forest and detect those changes through their traditional knowledge system, which integrates a variety of indicators, observations and stories. I now explore the Trio traditional knowledge system by trying to answer the logic-based question "How is this 'real' organized?" In indigenous communities like those of the Trios, traditional knowledge usually is transferred via practice and through the telling of stories by elders to youth (Pierotti 2011). The strength of the system is, therefore, mainly dependent on the distribution of knowledge between the community age groups and between genders.

The Trios seem to possess a strong and reliable knowledge system: the Trio younger and older generations hold the same amount of knowledge about seasonal indicators, demonstrating excellent knowledge transfer. Transfer occurs in multiple ways: elders and offspring work and examine the forest collaboratively, knowledge is conveyed through stories and knowledge is put into practice through livelihood activities (Smith 2013). The Trio youth may have discussed the forest changes with their elders to gain understanding, thereby classically linking old and new phenomena. Another possible explanation I put forward is that the Trios always stick together as a family, and by putting their concept of togetherness into practice, they effortlessly facilitate interaction between elders and youth. The family setting also contributes to women and men having similar amounts of knowledge about seasonal indicators, even with very distinct customary roles.

In summary, the knowledge system the Trio indigenous peoples possess is of high integrity and actively dispersed among the community members. I believe the Trios are generally interested in advancing their livelihood with the forest and, therefore, have developed a set of indicators by which they monitor their surroundings. Based on these observations, they ultimately decide how to adapt to changes and what strategies to employ.

The Rules for Survival

> If you take too much meat from the forest, it will deteriorate and you will not find food when you go hunting next time. You cannot hunt too much or you will be punished. (Smith 2013, 178)

My quest to understand the Trio view on climate change continues with the axiologically based question "What is valuable or important?" It seems that prioritizing food-security activities over any other activity is a viewpoint the Trios share with other indigenous peoples (Pierotti 2011). The rules necessary for preserving healthy populations of plants and animals appear to be of high value. The first lesson Trio men and women learn is that animals should be taken one at a time for consumption and that killing young or pregnant animals is therefore strictly forbidden.

By community rule, the Trios are allowed to kill two to three animals in and near the village, but when going further into the forest they may shoot only one animal at a time. This firm and persistent rule seems to reflect the Trio belief that animals running in close proximity to the village are excess and may be consumed. The survival of animals that live far from the village is necessary to maintain steady and healthy populations for the future Trio food supply. Such rules, I have learned, are specifically designed to ensure the continuation of the food supply for the community. The Trio rule that only certain types of animals may be slaughtered can be compared to the classic conservation concept of "endangered species" held by the scientists trained in the Western orientation.

Besides animals, the Trios place high value on selected forest constituents. Certain fruit-bearing palm trees—Maripa[3], Mauritie[4] and Koemboe[5]—may not be cut down for nonlivelihood reasons, as these are valuable food sources when the Trios undertake lengthy travel. I have also noticed that some areas of the forest may not be touched at all, constituting a "habitat taboo" (Colding and Folke 2001). A demarcated area in the vicinity of Kwamalasamutu is designated by the Trios as sacred. This holy place, called Werephai, consists of century-old rock tunnels with petroglyphs that contain an important part of Trio history. Hunting and plant extraction here are strictly prohibited by the Trios.

Quite a few Trio rules are based on their prior experience with resource scarcity (Parlee and Berkes 2006). On two past occasions, when living in the villages of Samuwaka[6] and Alalapadu,[7] the Trios were forced to collectively relocate because of a fruit and meat scarcity. Alongside such environmental factors, the Trios also center risk on their script of togetherness: they should maintain social contact to survive the dreadful cycles of the forest. In times of food shortage, Trios from Kwamalasamutu may receive cassava from

---

3 Scientific name: *Attalea maripa*.
4 Scientific name: *Mauritia flexuosa*.
5 Scientific name: *Oenocarpus bacaba*.
6 Located in what is now known as Northern Brazil.
7 Village of Alalapadu is located in South Suriname.

Trios who live a two-day walk and boat ride away. One can now imagine the lens through which the Trios define risk.

The Strategies for Adaptation

Grandma told me that one day there will be no food anymore, nothing will grow and we will fight. (Smith 2013, 184)

The impacts of climate change on the Trio way of life should be placed within the context of their historic experience with respect to overcoming environmental shocks. The Trios now must constantly adapt themselves in response to the pressure from climate change. It responds to the ethically based question "How should we act?" The Trios operate in a remote traditional setting, so they do not commonly experience significant interference from outside forces in their interaction with the forest. I think it is, therefore, likely that the current Trio adaptive activities result from local climate change. This hypothesis also is supported by records that suggest that the majority of Trios who have been interviewed, perceive local climate change as affecting their current livelihood (Bynoe and Liddell 2013).

When I asked about the general impact of climate change in their village, the Trios responded by saying that food production has become problematic. The Trios learned that climate change progressively degrades their soil, and they must now work much harder to cultivate it. In urgent pursuit of finding new fertile soils, some Trio families started planting crops along hillsides at higher elevations. Several other Trio families now open additional forest plots in order to grow more food per season in recognition that a portion of their crop may surely deteriorate (Figure 6.8).

Crops seem to be first attacked from climate change. The Trios observed that the cassava crop rots more easily due to the higher occurrence of disease in their crops (Smith 2013). The roots of the crop die off before it has grown to its full potential. As a response, the Trios adjusted the timing of planting seasons, and it has become evident to me that some Trios have begun planting and harvesting crops at an earlier date. An alternative strategy employed by indigenous peoples like the Trios in handling climate change is the diversification of the resource base (Byg and Salick 2009): the Trios are supplementing their main cassava crop by growing plantains, purple sweet potato and other smaller stable crops.

The Real Attitude

The year is different now, the sun comes in September instead of August. Now it is different, it is dark, and the old people think that problems are about to come. Our cassava does not grow just as kids do not grow well in women's belly anymore. People do not listen anymore, they are confused. Before, the old people were calm. (Smith 2013, 185)

In order to draw out a better understanding of potential mitigating actions the Trios might take against climate change in the future, I continue exploring the ethically based question "How should we act?" Not only do the Trios consider climate change as a major problem that is occurring now but also they predict that the weather will continue to change—it will become darker, and there will be a great deal of rain and high water (Smith 2013). The current weather changes are experienced as a parallel to the traditionally described apocalypse, and they believe that a trajectory to the end of existence has commenced (Box 6.1). Climate change is thus blueprinted in an ongoing tale about the end of their existence on earth, as one Trio men explains:

Before the life was good, but when we will reach the end we will have changes in the forest. We drink, commit suicide and that's why it is happening. (Smith 2013, 184)

Figure 6.8 Subsistence plots on hillsides as an adaptation strategy. Photo by Gwendolyn Smith.

Box 6.1
The Apocalypse

In the past, the Trios lied, bad-mouthed and killed. Trios also died for no reason, and they had sex during the daytime. The spirits who were living among the Trios warned them of the apocalypse. The Trios did not listen. The shamans, at that time tribal leaders, directed all the Trios to take sufficient food and immediately move to the hills. Soon clouds covered the sun, and it became pitch dark for days.

The rain started, the river water rose and all the villages and rivers flooded. The Trios were stuck on the hills and felt hopeless. They offered children to the water monster, whom they believed would help them. Then the light returned. The spirits instructed the shaman of the Trios to sing a riddle about shooting away the clouds and at the same time the Trios needed to shoot arrows in the water. At that time the water started to move away. The moral of the story is a warning for the Trios to behave well (Koelewijn 2003, 532).

Making a strong link between bad behavior and climate change is common to many indigenous peoples. In East Kimberley, Australia, the Miriwoong traditional community expectedly links climate change to biological indicators and the negative attitudes of community members, but sees development pressures also as a cause of climate change (Leonard et al. 2013). In another emic study regarding the view of indigenous peoples on climate change in Tibet, certain Tibetans were blamed for triggering climate change because of their religious misconduct and violation of taboos (Byg and Salick 2009).

The Trios draw a similar conclusion and think that their excessive drinking and incidental suicide is contributing to reaching the end of their existence. They assert that the influences of this catastrophe will be seen in the weather and felt in the production of food. The tribe firmly believes that their plants will rot because the soil is turning soggy. Although soft soils are generally associated with heavy rains, the Trios refer back to their story of the apocalypse, in which it becomes hard to grow food and all live in extreme poverty. Receiving such brutal punishment, the Trios now must plant many more crops to survive than before (Smith 2013).

The community perception of a current path of misbehavior is also seen as a big problem for the next generation of Trios. While some Trios think that their offspring will get sick and eventually die, others think that women will bear children who are handicapped, malformed or just unhealthy. Quite a few Trios worry that the children will continue to misbehave to the extent that they will fiercely fight with each other and their parents. This raises a critical question: if the Trios believe that the consequences of bad behavior are harming the next generation, how can they stop this trend? To answer this question, I examined the Trio attitude with respect to combating climate change.

In this journey of climate change, the Trios appear to stick tightly together as a collective. This interconnectedness is seen in the Trios helping each other rather than letting their individual interests prevail. The robust practice relates to Durkheim's concept of common consciousness: kin-based societies share a collective consciousness, which, in turn, leads to a strong solidarity among its members (Ritzer 2008). Finding solutions to current climate problems appears to reside within the kin, and during my five-year-long climate discussion with the Trios, no one ever mentioned or asked about ways to combat climate change. The Trio portfolio seems to purposely leave out immediate strategies to escape climate change, for example, relocation to another site somewhere in the forest. Relocation is probably an ineffective solution because, as the Trios jointly clarified to me, climate change is happening everywhere.

It seems that the discourse regarding the apocalypse is the starting point for the Trios in identifying a solution vis-à-vis local climate change. Climate change appears to be part of a catastrophic process that is impossible to delay or terminate. One might think that this discourse originated from the Baptist church, but my research clearly shows that most Trios heard the apocalyptic tale from their elders, such as grandfathers and grandmothers (Smith 2013). It is unlikely that the Trios have been influenced by outsiders in their description of the apocalypse.

Applying the VIEW Framework

The VIEW framework was put in practice by responding to the five reality questions developed by Nudler (1993). The reality questions were answered using cognitive maps of concepts generated by the Trios. A cognitive map is a qualitative model that represents "a mental image made by human individuals and groups of their environment and their relation to it, involving not only the rational aspects of attitude and behavior but also the values and belief components that shape human perception" (Laszlo and Krippner 1998, 26). These maps are made based on qualitative information analysis rather than parameter estimation: questionnaires, written texts, drawings and interviews (Figure 6.9). Cognitive mapping was applicable in this research because it captured the complexity of the Trio indigenous system (Berkes and Berkes 2009; Özesmi and Özesmi 2004).

Figure 6.9 A Trio man and woman working on cognitive maps. Photo by Rachelle Bong A Jan.

The data collection started with mapping the climate indicators in small focus groups and conducting a community-wide survey.[8] The maps were complemented with semistructured interviews, which is the preferred methodology for obtaining information in indigenous communities (Alessa et al. 2008; Byg and Salick 2009; Ford et al. 2006; Huntington 2000; Tucker et al. 2010). Knowledgeable Trios,[9] including elders, hunters and fishers, adolescents, women and shamans, were approached and interviewed on livelihood and climate change. The selected Trios responded with lengthy answers to the predetermined guiding questions (Box 6.2). These interviews turned out to be useful instruments for me to better understand the cultural context (van Aalst et al. 2008), which was vital in creating an accurate map of the present.

The main outcome of my analysis is that the Trios have decided to adapt and survive for now while knowing that they are on their inevitable way to the end of existence. When looking closer at this outcome, I can distinguish a short- and long-term division. For the short term, the Trios create meaning by assessing the forest, and to do this, they maintain a traditional knowledge system with a set of indicators and rules. It seems that they rely largely on

---

8 A total of 238 persons were surveyed, a representative sample of the targeted community in Kwamalasamutu from a sample of the population of 600 subjects above 12 years.

9 A total of 62 persons were interviewed from the community in Kwamalasamutu.

Box 6.2
Guiding Questions for Meaning Making in
Climate Change

Livelihood systems

1. What activities do you engage in when going to the forest?
2. Are there tribal rules concerning how to do your activities in the forest?
3. Do you get any advice from your family when there are problems with the forest?
4. Does the tribal leadership give advice on how to manage the forest?
5. Do you receive advice from other people, besides your family and the tribal leadership?
6. Whose advice is valid/invalid?
7. Do you think there are enough resources for everyone in the forest to live?
8. Is the forest now better than, worse than or equal to before?
9. In the past, what did you do when there were insufficient resources available from the forest?
10. If the forest cannot provide you with resources, what are you going to do in the future?

Climate change

1. In the dry season, is the water level in the river higher or lower than in the past?
2. In the rainy season, is the water level in the river higher or lower than in the past?
3. Is there more, less or an equal amount of lightning seen as compared to the past?
4. Is the strength of the wind greater than, less than or equal to that in the past?
5. Is there more, less or an equal amount of time available to burn your plot as compared to the past?
6. Is there a greater, a lesser or an equal amount of fruit available from the forest as compared to the past?
7. Do you think the rainy season is the same, longer or shorter than before?
8. Do you think that more water falls from the sky during the rainy season as compared to the past?
9. Do you think the dry season is the same, longer or shorter than before?

10. Do you think that there are more floods as compared to the past?
11. Do you think more or fewer leaves are shedding in the dry season as compared to the past?
12. Are there an equal number of, more or fewer leaf cutter ants on your plot as compared to before?
13. Do you think that the star constellations are still coinciding with the seasons of rain?
14. Have you experience all the above-mentioned problems before?
15. Did you hear about these problems from your ancestors/elders?
16. Since when have you had these problems?
17. Are these problems affecting your children's life?
18. Do you think these problems are only in your village or also elsewhere?
19. Is this a large or a small problem?
20. Who is the cause of these problems in the forest?
21. Do you think there will be more problems in the future?
22. How do you think we can stop these problems with the forest?
23. Have you ever heard of climate change?

their environmental values of livelihood protection and threat management. Taking care of the land and their food supply are their most significant tasks during this temporary journey. For the long term, the Trios will depend on their social values of togetherness and religion, and have to suffer, all because of their own bad behavior. Therefore, they have decided to stick together and help each other in this ending journey. So, as I demonstrated with the case study, the social values of togetherness and religion are strong drivers in the Trio meaning-making process.

After organizing this meaning-making information in the VIEW framework (Figure 6.10), it became apparent to me that the Trios have created meaning from climate change only based on their social and environmental values. The Trio economic values—education and income—were excluded from the meaning-making process. It seems to me that Trio meaning making in climate change centers on their internal knowledge rather than on foreign concepts.

The VIEW analysis helped me systematically lay out the Trio sustainability context. The outcome would be less clear, I think, if the community were approached differently. If looking from a typical environmental perspective, in which the focus is on the human-nature interaction, I would unquestionably have missed the strong link to the apocalypse. When analyzing the view from a development context, I would primarily focus on the livelihood assets of the Trios' system needed to cope with climate change and potentially overlook the

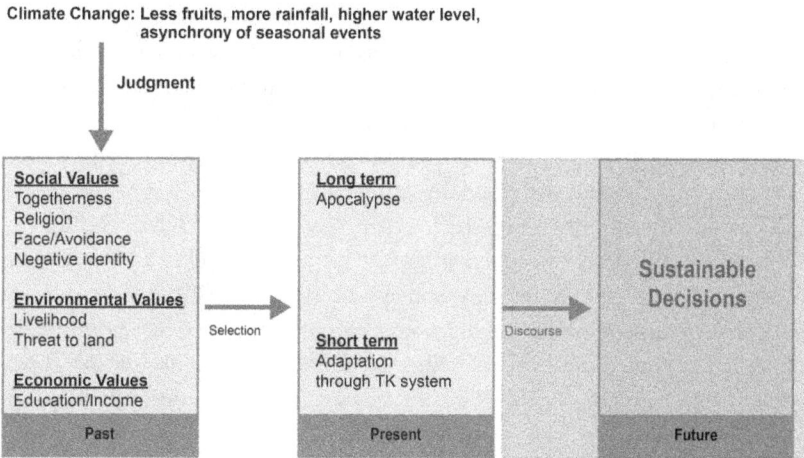

Figure 6.10 Meaning of climate change generated by the Trio indigenous peoples.

importance of past values such as togetherness and religion. It seems like the VIEW framework allowed me to get deep inside the community's system and illuminate the Trios' sustainability focus without fitting the community into a conventional research paradigm.

I could look through the eyes of the Trios in their effort of making meaning of climate change because of my step-by-step organization of information. Such analysis would be very difficult when only looking at the end of the chain of events, when communities are already in the conclusive process of making decisions. Countless times I have tried to go backward—from decision making to meaning making (top-down approach in Figure 3.2A), but I kept struggling in finding explanations for the decisions a community takes. Then I would simply guess what a community thinks and make false assumptions. My experience has taught me that it is this kind of practice that contributes to project extension and failure.

Meaning Making and Sustainability

I have learned that projects in which the community cannot entirely complete the meaning making often have significant problems in the execution, such as delay or sometimes even ceasing. Communities that are still occupied with meaning making are usually very cautious about partaking in projects, and if they do, it seems to be out of pure opportunism and not a real desire. Such communities, when engaged, often keep changing their opinion on the course they want to take during project life. This change of mind comes after identifying risks and hazards that the community wasn't able to identify before. The "wobbling" of a community can be very frustrating for a researcher, and it is therefore beneficial to a researcher to have a notion of how far a community has progressed in the meaning making.

Now a researcher can track how the meaning-making process evolves after a community is overrun with climate change. I have shown that for developing a full position on the climate episode, a community like the Trios identifies and selects useful information. But if a community cannot successfully complete this key process, a researcher may notice that its members start postponing or even putting up barriers to talking about climate change. It is also quite possible that the community might withdraw from making sense of the climate experience. Although a worst-case scenario, this specific community might just ignore climate change happening in its village and go on with everyday life.

Chapter 7

SUSTAINABLE DECISIONS

At some point a community will want to convey its constructed view to people outside the living place where its members normally socialize. Socialization typically includes a community's attempt to identify (potential) areas of compatibility and conflict with the so-called outsiders. It is a similar route to what I take when I choose to make a new friend and started seeking, maybe unconsciously, for one or more things I have in common with the person, such as experiences, values, goals and aspirations. Just like me, every indigenous community will go through this natural testing phase, in which it defines a specific position and develops a series of tactics on how to negotiate its view to the outer public. Comparing and contrasting is a vital task in order for an indigenous group to craft decisions that are satisfactory with both the outside world and its own life plan. It is a process of ensuring sustainability.

In this chapter, once again I hone in on the case study to research how the Trios compare and contrast information to the realm of REDD+ projects in Suriname. I applied the last step of the VIEW framework—sustainable decisions—to unravel the messages buried in the Trio public conversation. I directed particular attention to appreciating the position the Trios take in the REDD+ debate and how they skillfully maneuver and take decisions for reaching long-term sustainability.

Conflicting Views

In this section I try to put together all the information gathered so far. At the outset I place the climate-change view of the Trio peoples juxtapose with that of the development organization, more specifically comparing each party's interests, values, strategies and attitudes (Carpenter and Kennedy 2001). This information helps me understand the context of the differences in the two views before going deep into the last phase of the VIEW analysis.

Conflicting interests

Researchers from development organizations typically express interest in activities that inform them about the causes of climate change and ways of fighting it. The global-level analysis seeks to determine an average for the warming activity on earth. Since the 1800s, the average global temperature has risen due to the increased release of greenhouse gases, to the extent that nine of the last ten years have been the hottest years on record. The impact of the rising temperature is noticeable in the melting of ice in the polar region, and subsequently, this melting water contributes to the rise of the sea water levels (Parry et al. 2007).

Researchers also look at the regional level and study the Amazon rain forest, in which the habitat and life forms of animals and plants are potentially affected (Clark 2007; Root et al. 2003). Even more significant, researchers find changes in the regional rainfall pattern (Borchert 1998). Specifically, the length of the dry season is identified as the key indicator for tropical forests (Hutyra et al. 2005). Researchers estimate that between 30 and 50 percent of Suriname's tropical forest is projected to gradually convert into savanna due to changes in annual rainfall and seasonality that disable plants' ability to survive the dry season (Cook and Vizy 2008; Hulme and Viner 1998; Oyama and Nobre 2003; Nurmohamed 2008). Most of these climate calculations are made for periods between 20 and 100 years.

The indigenous Trios, in contrast, have no clue about this highly scientific analysis. They have an obligatory interest in traditional knowledge because it is part of their everyday guidance in long-term survival. Using a comprehensive and embedded system of indicators, the Trios are able to align and adjust their crop planting and other livelihood activities with the changing seasons. Observing events in their surroundings—such as rainfall, the fruit bearing of trees and the position of star constellations—gives helpful hints to the Trios about the health of the forest and consequentially the tribe.

The closest that scientific evaluation and indigenous knowledge align is through the assessment of the natural system based on the identification of indicators (Berkes and Berkes 2009). Both the Trios and scientists use indicators to identify changes in the natural ecosystem, but in such efforts, indigenous peoples focus on indicators that are important for survival, such as food security and reproduction, while scientists are more interested in the behavior of animal and plant species.

Although scientists agree that traditional knowledge on climate variability is handy for efforts to improve adaptation to new circumstances (Berrang-Ford et al. 2011), the tribal knowledge has rarely any value in the REDD+ discussion and apparently fades away in these projects that just concentrate on carbon trade (Table 7.1).

Table 7.1 Overview of the conflicting goals and issues between the Trio indigenous peoples and development organization in REDD+ projects. The + sign shows the elements supported by REDD+ projects.

Conflict dynamics	Trio Indigenous Peoples (Traditional View)		Development Organization (Northern View)	
	Goals and issues	**Cultural characteristics**	**Goals and issues**	**Cultural characteristics**
Interest	Food security Forest health (animals, plants) + Tribal health	Long-term orientation	Emissions trading + Climate change modeling + Drivers of deforestation +	Short-term orientation +
Values	Forest rules (animals, plants) + Togetherness Religion	Traditional society Survival	Positivist view + Academic information + Peer review +	Rational society + Self-expression +
Strategies	Adaptation: Planting at higher elevation Diversifying of crops Timing of crop planting Larger plots (area)	Culture of "being"	Mitigation +	Culture of "doing" +
Attitude	Climate change is linked to the apocalypse High investment	Femininity Accommodative	Top-down institutional process + Technocratic solutions + Medium investment	Masculinity + Competitive+

The strong Trio interest in the forest can be better classified as a need. Needs are aspects that are critical to a person's life. In the words of Abraham Maslow, humans "are motivated by the desire to achieve or maintain the various conditions upon which our basic satisfactions rest" (Maslow 1943, 394).

Maslow describes human motivation in a hierarchical manner, listing four levels of needs that must be met before self-actualization may be achieved. The lowest level consists of physiological needs, such as housing, clothing and, in the Trio case, the safeguarding of food, which is a fundamental need for survival in the remotely located forest. The Trios also are motivated to fulfill their security needs, especially human and forest health, which is part of the second level of the Maslow hierarchy. Both physiological and security needs are strong motivators for action and the initiation of conflict, because needs are rooted in a species' psychological drive for survival (Katz et al. 2012). The other two levels in Maslow's system, social needs and esteem needs, can be attained only when the lower levels have been satisfied, which is not the case for the Trios.

Developing organizations working in the area of climate-change mitigation typically have an interest in the forest, but this is not an immediate need. In addition to REDD+, they have the option of exploring other avenues for advancing the reduction of emissions, such as planting trees or promoting the use of renewable energy sources. Consequently, a fundamental power difference exists between the interests of development organizations and the needs of the Trios: the interests of the organization are negotiable and optional, while the Trios' needs are nonnegotiable and mandatory.

I have seen that, when all the interests/needs of the community clash with those of the organization, the parties are far apart. Such projects have a seemingly lower potential for sustainability than projects where only one or a few interest(s)/needs of both parties remain unaligned. This situation resembles the case study: both the Trios and the development organization have a stake in protecting the forest. Development projects lean toward high sustainability if all the interests/needs of both parties match.

Conflicting values

As shown in chapter 5, the Trios value a set of tribal rules to effectively manage the forest and keep it in balance with their own livelihood necessities. Development organizations see such tribal rules as a subsidiary tool for keeping the forest intact and thus averting or halting its deforestation and degradation. Tribal rules appear to have an indirect value in the REDD+ schemes. Thus, it seems to me that the Trios possess a value reference point that largely falls outside the context of a REDD+ project (Table 7.1).

Development organizations, in the abstract, perfectly match with REDD+ projects due to a strong focus on the expression of self-interest. They typically value the economic development paradigm that supports carbon trade between countries. Factual information on the drivers of deforestation, more specifically, the exact measures on the amount of standing forest and the annual rate of losing trees, is important to them. The fact that the values held by development organizations are applied to the structure of the REDD+ project is problematic and brings about unevenness in power.

Power disparity between indigenous groups and development organizations feeds into a situation of inequality. Whenever the lower-power party starts feeling threatened, especially when the values are challenged, they can become highly protective of their boundaries. For example, in 2012, I noticed that the Trios purposely postponed participation in REDD+. On several public occasions, one Trio leader had stressed that the tribe was curious about how participating in REDD+ would affect their livelihood and caretaking of the forest. This information was crucial for the tribe to approve the REDD+ project (Smith and Lachmising 2012). Thus, the Trios obviously had defined a boundary while in a value conflict about the forest.

When values are challenged, it is likely that communities will enter into conflict. There is a way to track the level of conflict between the values of a community and a development organization in project implementation. Projects become incredibly tricky in cases when two parties possess divergent values and one party, usually the one with the least power, starts defending its own values to the other. A better circumstance is when the values of both parties are compatible, for example, when the Trio community and the development organization are both enthusiastic about trading carbon credits. Projects like this have better operational success and outcomes.

Conflicting strategies

In the Northern view, approaches for combating climate change are divided into two separately held streams: mitigation and adaptation strategies. Mitigation can be considered a more globally oriented strategy, focusing on a combined effort of nations to trim greenhouse gas emissions (Locatelli et al. 2011). Development organizations are here trying to induce indigenous groups like the Trios to prolong their effort of protecting the forests, and minimize deforestation-promoting activities to stabilize or lower the net release of emissions globally. From the view of this highly conceptual framework, communities like the Trios that live traditionally should strive to gain access to the so-called emissions trading market, so they can benefit from a new stream of money that promises economic growth. This money will bring development to the Trios, according to the "mitigationists," since they are one of the lowest-income groups nationwide with an unemployment rate of almost seven times higher than the average of that of the total population (ABS 2005).

An adaptation strategy, in contrast, includes those activities the Trios employ to cope with climate change at the local level (Locatelli et al. 2011). The men and women typically acclimatize by choosing different kinds of crops, changing the time and place of planting and amplifying the size of their agricultural plots. It is clear that the adept strategies falling under the umbrella of adaptation, however, are useless in the current, strictly demarcated, REDD+ framework, which operates only from a mitigation viewpoint. But when a community like the Trios actually becomes engaged in mitigation activities, the focus likely shifts to emissions trading, and local efforts of forest conservation and adaptation may be overlooked. Yet, then mitigation is seen as a "foreign" strategy that may have the potential to hinder their ongoing adaptation efforts (Locatelli et al. 2011).

The dichotomy between mitigation and adaptation, I think, is unfortunate. Progressively researchers advise against implementing the strategies separately because conflict can emerge easily between them (Laukkonen et al. 2009; Locatelli et al. 2011; UNU 2012). They argue for the simultaneous pursuit of adaptation and mitigation to endorse the synergy between them. Of course, this is easier said than done. I have learned about a simple technique to sort out the strategies held by actors: identify the source of the problem from the perspective of each actor. When applying this to the case study, the principle problem for the Trios is that in their belief system, the long-term journey to the apocalypse has begun. At the same time, they are identifying improved ways to adapt to the forest changes until their existence ends. Meanwhile, the development organizations seek to retain the Northern high-energy-use lifestyle by taking steps to compensate for its emissions by reducing global emissions elsewhere. Such a source analysis enables me to align the reasons for action that groups like the Trios and the development organizations may have.

To assess the gap between the strategies of two parties, a researcher can also look at the size of the problem as the parties experience it. A problem that is vaguely defined often hampers a community estimating the size of the problem. Such a situation was observed in the Trio case: as the tribal members were clueless about REDD+, it was impossible to identify and delineate strategies that temporarily held them back from participating in REDD+. Another scenario plays out when problems are very big in the eyes of a community, and then the members may delay or even halt developing novel strategies. This ultimately works against the sustainability of a project, as I have experienced.

Conflicting attitudes

From the case study findings, it is evident that the Trios' belief system, which links current events to their traditional story of the apocalypse, sees no pre-determined solution to climate change. My interaction with the Trios taught me that the Trio culture is centered around upholding the status quo. Such a "feminine" attitude is much softer than that of entities like development organizations, which celebrate effectiveness and are less emotional and more asser-tive, expressing a "masculine" culture. Keep in mind that the ruling attitude of the majority of development organizations is to find a technocratic solu-tion, which typically includes getting help from experts possessing scientific knowledge and expertise. The technocratic advice appears favored that comes from institutions that hold the Northern view and that encourage its use in a REDD+ project.

The Trios seem to adhere to a culture of "being" (Kluckhohn and Strodtbeck 1961). They emphasize the culture itself and associate spontane-ous actions with the situations they face, such as climate change. Development organizations have a "doing" ethic. One researcher explains that "in a doing culture, people tend to view work activities as the core of their existence, and attach much importance to achievement and hard work" (Yeganeh 2011, 230). Such a difference in culture reflects on the attitude each actor proposes for combating climate change.

One way of analyzing the attitude of the Trios is through their previous investment in the forest (Carpenter and Kennedy 2001). Once there is a sub-stantial investment in the forest, REDD+ may be experienced as bigger than it really is or appears to the Trios. Contrastingly, if little investment in the forest exists, Trio community members may move away from the problem more eas-ily. Following this thought, the Trios have invested a great deal by living deep in the forest for centuries. They cannot imagine their own existence without the strong forest connection. A Trio tribal leader describes his relationship with the forest in a discussion about the construction of a hydropower dam:

> I do not want to have a dam. I'm afraid that the water will become high and the villages get flooded, just like in *Afobaka* [a large hydropower dam providing for the majority of Suriname's electricity]. I'm worried because the Government has no idea how we live in the interior. I rather die than to lose the forest to a dam. (Smith 2006, 3)

The high stakes in the forest may even contribute early on to a negative attitude on the part of the Trios toward REDD+ projects. No comparable high investment in the forest is made by the development organizations. They have only paid attention to the forest in the last few decades and mainly for the purpose of serving the industrialized world.

Attitudes are also reinforced by differences in conflict styles. While the development organizations use their expert power to shape REDD+ projects according to their aims, the Trios consciously choose to be disengaged or to avoid confrontation (Pruitt and Kim 2004). They have a tendency to deflect attention deliberately from the main issue in a conflict and manifest this by avoiding certain kinds of expressions in language, such as naming things and persons and preferring to provide vague descriptions of events. Besides the Trios evading immediate confrontation, I have also seen them shun judging others on their behavior, or on the opposite end of the spectrum, instruct others how to behave according to the Trio rules (Carlin 2004). Both these aspects lead to withdrawal rather than the expression of real interests, resulting in a situation where limited means of cooperation exist with respect to process, goals or issues.

Decision Making under Uncertainty

The intrinsic inequality in the design of REDD+ is difficult to ignore. When looked at through the eyes of the Trios, the REDD+ project may be too dominant because it operates in a purely scientific paradigm, which is incompatible with their traditional view. In the eyes of the development organizations, it seems, the project has certain rules and obligations with which the Trios have limited scientific and technical capacity to comply. In the event that the Trios wish to assert their opinion about the project, a development organization can contest this by using a nondirect mode of power through the project design. Such hidden power tends to avoid matters of interest to the Trio peoples by emphasizing the project design and rules for planning, execution and evaluation. So the next question I like to answer is, how do the Trios make sustainable decisions in a situation of inequality?

Understanding the discourse

The Trios make strategic choices under climate change in the wider context of national REDD+ efforts. The last step of the VIEW framework—sustainable decisions—is useful to fully understand the decisions the Trios take and, most importantly, how these decisions are crafted. Specific thoughts on sustainability are projected to come alive in the words and expressions the Trios put forward during the REDD+ talks and negotiations. The discourse gives a researcher a gamut of information on what push and pull factors they experience from both inside and outside the tribal setting. It shows how the Trios take in all the influences from the environment, conduct a risk assessment and ultimately line up goals in their own journey of sustainable development. Therefore, I analyze three Trio discourses relevant to our discussion since the national REDD+ discussion with communities seriously started in 2012.

First discourse, October 2012

In this first discourse, the Trios were observant and listened to the project's ideas and intentions. Quite a number of meetings later, after they were asked about their opinion, the Trio leader frankly expressed their inability to understand the mechanics of REDD+. The Trio peoples appeared unsure REDD+ could mean anything in their future, and this was explained with a striking analogy: "When you have to weave a basket for your family, you have to know how to do it." The leader's metaphorical explanation of having a lack of information suggests that the Trios are stuck in the selection process. The Trios potentially need more information on what the possibilities are when preparing and implementing REDD+ so they can select what may be relevant to reaching their goals and aspirations. So, as I would have done myself, the Trio leader bought time. He cleverly directed the discourse toward other, less important things, such as his duty of information sharing among the tribal members (Smith and Lachmising 2012). The decision to buy time suggests that the Trios are willing to engage in REDD+ because they neither purposely avoided the topic nor fell back on their perceived negative identity to position themselves as less powerful.

Second discourse, January 2013

In the second discourse, the Trios were ready to convey a message to the government of Suriname, which works together with the World Bank and the United Nations Development Program in leading the national REDD+ effort. The Trios made clear to the government that they have for centuries protected the forest and been utilizing it in a sustainable manner. But in this effort, in reality, they fear outside intimidation and intrusion into the territory, which directly links to their social value of togetherness. The Trio leader continued the lengthy monologue by elucidating their efforts of drawing a land use map and how crucial this map is for obtaining land tenure rights before engaging in REDD+ (Smith and Lachmising 2013). To me, the Trio discourse seemed clearer than before because they conveyed a position: what they want. The words spoken are given proof that they had progressed in the meaning-making process and were adept at selecting useful topics for their future journey. The information they selected was twofold: they like to use

Figure 7.1 Trio leaders participating in the national negotiations. Photo by Forward Motion, Suriname.

the forest in a sustainable way, of course, and they need to have land rights to prevent invasion from others.

Third discourse, December 2014

The third discourse emphasized the future. The Trios clarified that they now grasp REDD+ and that it can potentially deliver positive results, but only if their collective land rights are acknowledged. Again, similar to the second discourse, the Trios' fear of plundering and land grabbing by outsiders was put forward. But this time, suddenly the Trios started talking about their offspring: Trio children should become Western educated so they can earn a decent living with new income-generation activities that should be introduced by REDD+. The Trio leaders rationalized that the children are the next generation, so elders are obliged to take action now, because they will not live forever. With these words, the Trios finally expressed their real interest, namely the catastrophic finale (Bong A Jan and Smith 2014).

Two years after the first discourse, the Trios apparently had made a decision. The discourse demonstrates that the decision is made up of three levels. For the long term, the Trios explained they will not live forever, thereby referring to the coming apocalypse. For the medium term, they want to have education and income-generation opportunities for the next progeny. For the short term, they will depend on their rich culture to sustain their livelihood and synchronously adapt to climate change. All three decisions refer back to historical Trio values, such as religion, education/income and livelihood, respectively.

Any researcher should be alert that during discoursing, a community is tactfully maneuvering in a negotiation arena, which is full of others who are also defending their own interests. Through careful assessment of the words spoken by the group members, a researcher obtains clues about the community's decision making. The genuine way a community begins its discourse is by expression of values and sometimes also value boundaries. Once the community can verbalize and argue its own position about climate change, the discourse has slightly matured. The best case scenario, in my experience, is when the community conveys explicitly its future interests and goals.

Applying the VIEW Framework

As shown, the discourse offers worthy information on how the Trios interpret climate change, how they linked it with their values and how they connect it with the decisions they need to make for the future. I obtained data for this analysis from sitting in various national meetings and carefully analyzing the words, intonation and body language of the participants. Looking back at the film recorded at meetings was another suitable way of gathering the ideas put forward by the Trios. I also engaged in "back-room" talk and sat with the Trios to hear what they thought outside of the meetings. In all of these settings, I used a set of guiding questions to filter out the parts necessary for the VIEW analysis (Box 7.1).

The discourse analysis complements the "map of the future" generated by social polygraphy. The map is a very suitable instrument to initiate and elaborate a rich discussion among different types of community members such as women, men, youth, elders and so on. The expected outcome of the discussion is that the community's mutual interests, which are then thoroughly discussed, are symbolized by the drawings on the map. Most central to this mapmaking is the community's discussion on what strategic choices to make for the future. It is then that the common vision especially comes alive. However, in the case study, the Trios stalled on making a map for the future, and only vaguely mentioned some future goals during the mapping process. It became clear to me that they were generally unenthusiastic about openly sharing their future plans (maybe because of the apocalypse). Without having the physical map, I relied on the discourse analysis as the only means of gathering information.

Box 7.1
Guiding Questions for Retrieving Information for the
Discourse Analysis

Themes

1. What theme is dominant in the discourse?
2. What themes came up and have been discarded?
3. What themes came up and stayed?
4. What themes are wanted for the future? (position)
5. What themes are being avoided for discussion?
6. What themes make participants uncomfortable?
7. What themes are being tested?
8. What are the reasons mentioned for choosing a specific theme? (interest)
9. What are the experiences/values mentioned for choosing a specific theme?
10. What are the themes dominating in the back-room talk?

Decisions

1. What are the reasons mentioned for (not) making a decision?
2. What are the experiences/values mentioned for (not) making a decision?
3. What decisions are being avoided for discussion?
4. What decisions are being tested?
5. What are the prerequisites mentioned before taking any decision?
6. What decisions are dependent on input from other actors? (coalitions)
7. What decisions are accommodated? And to whom?
8. How are the decisions being made—with or without internal deliberation?
9. What decisions are being made under pressure?
10. What decisions made by others make participants uncomfortable?
11. What decisions are being stalled or postponed?

With the VIEW framework, I was able to carefully unravel the process of how the Trios build on their existing values for creating sensible meaning and making future-oriented decisions. During the breakdown, as seen in Figure 7.2, I observed that the Trios included a new (medium-term) strategy in the

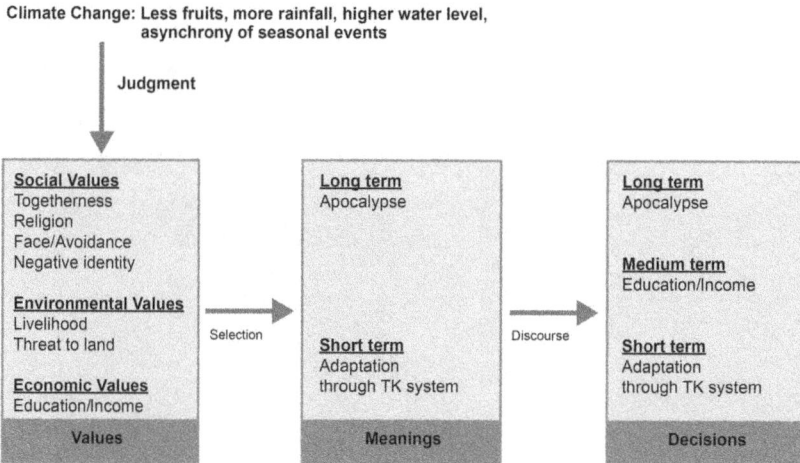

Figure 7.2 View of the Trio indigenous peoples on climate change analyzed with the VIEW framework.

decision making, consisting of aspects of education and income. So for me, the Trios fell back on these values and added those, maybe opportunistically, in the REDD+ project at the last stage of view making. Including the economically oriented values seems an important part of the Trio journey toward sustainable growth. This example shows how crucial it is for a researcher to first assess values to really understand how the community's view is assembled.

A researcher should be very patient when employing the last phase of the VIEW analysis. For an indigenous community to take actual decisions usually requires a considerable amount of time. Especially when an indigenous community, like the Trios, is highly accommodative, it tends to sway between the different options presented to them, making decision making a lengthy process. In this "swaying" act, the Trios also consider their lower-power position and try to find ways to secure their goals and aspirations in the REDD+ project. For them, time is never of the essence. And time also should not be determinative for a researcher who really wants to sense the community's decision-making process.

Chapter 8

WORKING WITH COMMUNITY VIEWS

In this book I have taken the reader on a journey of "sustainable develop-ment" through the eyes of the Trio indigenous community. I have also tried to explain how researchers like myself unconsciously make assumptions on sustainability when studying such an indigenous community in development projects. And this mismatch develops organically. Researchers and practitio-ners traditionally lean on the definition of sustainable development put for-ward by the modern world: "sustainable development is development that meets the needs of the present without compromising the ability of future generations to meet their own needs" (Brundtland 1987, 41).

Local communities like the Trios see "sustainable development" quite differently. In a journey through time, they thread together events from the past and present, and from there strategically craft their own life goals for the future. Although this approach seems to have the same past-future orientation as the Brundtland definition, there is a fundamental difference. The under-lying motivations make the Trio concept of development contrast that of a researcher: the Trios operate from caretaking while researchers follow a para-digm of economic growth/exploitation. It is therefore imperative for research-ers to be conscious of this divide rather than making a wrong assumption that the community wants to develop according to the (foreign) goals stipulated within the economic paradigm. Acquiring sufficient insight into the views of a community will further prevent failures in making the project a reality. It can help researchers and practitioners be aware of the assumptions they automati-cally make based on their Western perspective.

Promoting Sustainability under Uncertainty

This book concludes that in situations of environmental uncertainty, the com-munity's first action is to find new solutions that fit its own life goals. It is apparent that the origin of a sustainable decision lies in matching the values a community possesses with the development project: values related to keep-ing to its traditions (history), its social relations and its relationship with the physical environment, and pursuing its development. Understanding these values, as well as the community's related interests, strategies and attitude, are part of the view construct, and exploring this view is crucial for initiating and promoting sustainability.

I have illustrated how values have a durable influence on Trio decisions. The Trio belief in an eventual catastrophe seems a strong cognitive factor that has been passed down through generations and influences both their present and future activities. It is a solid value that can be easily labeled as the "past rule." Such rules are gradually developed from the human assets (knowledge and education), and social assets (internal group organization) needed for continued existence in the living environment of indigenous communities from the time they come into existence.

A case in point is that a good researcher should search for values that can provide some clues about the current and future reality of a tribe. Especially in nature-dependent communities, such as the Trios, historic events play a larger and more lasting role than future events (Humphreys 2005). Although these historical values are normally hidden, there is a need to reveal and study them to justly appreciate a community's view. Approaches from the fields of environment and development had insufficient research depth to uncover the tribal values. The selective focus from these fields tends to neglect the stories that have played an important role in the past. The VIEW method, in contrast, permits a researcher like me to thoroughly assess these historical events, as was illustrated with the illuminating importance of the apocalypse.

When I started my research on the Trio climate-change view, I had already partnered with the tribe for five consecutive years. My mission included, among others, designing, executing and managing a wide range of grassroots projects in the areas of protecting biodiversity in the forest, and preserving the Trio culture and traditional health system. Interacting and exchanging ideas with the Trios, then, was my daily routine. But only when I started posing targeted questions about the tribe's history to the Trio members was I able to discover the true significance of the Trio apocalypse. The moral of this confession is that the link between climate change and the expected catastrophe did not surface until I had completed a value analysis with the VIEW framework.

Thus, by studying values, a researcher like me could make a better prediction about the strength of the Trio view. Without such analysis, the reasons for the community's current behavior would have remained unknown and the strength of its view perhaps would be revealed only when the parties were openly in conflict (Docherty, 2001). Conducting a value analysis is thus a sine qua non for a complete recognition of the view of collective groups like the Trios, with deeply rooted and sometimes hidden values.

The VIEW framework

The VIEW framework presented here provides a single alternative to the conventional method of researching how a community makes decisions through choice or livelihood models. Researchers now have a bottom-up tool to unravel a community's view and subsequently have a systematic understanding about the decisions a community prepares. The framework assists a researcher in tracking multiple actors in the system rather than emphasizing only the viewpoint of the community or development organization. Views of different actors can be simply compared to widen a researcher's understanding of how the views can conflict. Particular situations of discrepancy have a higher probability of being detected and resolved with the VIEW framework than without knowing the rooted characteristics of various players in the system.

The VIEW method allows research to extend beyond the popular modernity paradigm. For a researcher trained in this contemporary world, the intention—probably unconscious—of the researcher is then to direct the project toward some form of capacity building, in turn, making the community integrate into the modern society. The VIEW framework is a point of departure for a researcher to professionally transform beyond such familiar approaches. It helped me look at sustainability from the inside out and desist from framing it into an economic growth concept. And opened my eyes to the Trio craftsmanship of sustainability: a path toward reaching their own long-term goals of providing for upcoming generations.

The VIEW framework can apply to communities with more economically driven orientations as well. By being individualistic oriented, these communities might carry faded life scripts and possess cultural values that together have only a small effect on their view. In groups like this that possess little collectivity, the bond between history and the present will surely exist but may be too weak to permit full assembly of a strong view, even when such groups possess a set of values, which in this case are of economic origin. The framework can then apply to assess the community's economic values and potentially link them to more contemporary decision-making mechanisms.

One limitation of the VIEW method is that it centers on a community after it is affected by some sort of environmental change event. The assumption I made is that the entire community's livelihood is impacted by such an unfortunate incident. But this may not be the case. For example, if only a few members' houses collapse with a strong wind on one side of the village, only those members will try to acclimatize to the new situation. Then it is unlikely that the whole community will build a new view, and the VIEW framework may not be appropriate to get an understanding of the entire community's outlook.

Bridging Differences in Views

In this section, I present a way to align the views of the Trio community and the development organization in a REDD+ project. For the Trios, the REDD+ project can fit within their development path when their interests in education, income generation and adaptation to climate change are fully considered. For the powerful organizations, the ideas of the Trios are far from compliance with the (inter)national REDD+ rulebook. Herein, as dictated by the global rules, a community's REDD+ performance is calculated based on amounts of carbon dioxide captured in the forest. Providing education, creating income-generation opportunities and engaging in adaptation fall outside this scientifically driven scope of managing the drivers of deforestation.

Conflict resolution theory and practice suggest that a difference in view can sometimes be overcome when the parties are "reshaped." This means that the parties must reorient themselves and have enough empathy, build trust and find ways to cooperate (Robards et al. 2011). Reshaping can occur when the cultural background of the parties is not too different and has some kind of common ground. In the case of REDD+, the assumption underlying the view of groups like the Trios is very different from that of development organizations. The Trios assume that the survival of the forest depends on a nondominant relationship based on caring and sharing. Development organizations, in contrast, assume a position of control when they approach the forest from a standpoint of rational decisions and instrumental relationships. Overlap of the two views is unlikely to occur.

In conflicts that might potentially arise between the Trio indigenous people and development organizations promoting REDD+, an inability exists on the part of both parties to look past their own view and understand the other's view. It is evident that the Trio view is formed from the inside out (Bayart 2005; Lewicky et al. 2007): it relates to their own particular interests, values and beliefs, which are obviously incongruent with the human needs of individualistic societies. Such sturdy and powerful views cannot be easily influenced—for example, the Trio belief in a coming apocalypse prevents them from taking any mitigation action against climate change. And the development organizations seem incapable of entering the perception of the Trios. The views seem to be too far apart, as demonstrated in Table 7.1, and none of the parties has the ability to "cross over" to the view of the other party.

In the field of conflict resolution, the divide caused by view difference is understudied. The topic is usually shunned because it is seen as an intractable conflict based in deeply rooted values and beliefs (Carpenter and Kennedy 2001; Moore 2003). One way to address view conflict is to holistically bridge the view of the Trio community and the development organization. Four specific things I have distinguished as crucial for bridging views at the project level are (1) creating holism, (2) creating shared goals, (3) establishing trust and cooperation between both parties, and (4) enabling meaningful participation of each party in the project.

Creating holism

Indigenous peoples like the Trios often view REDD+ as a conservation effort, in part because the conservation paradigm has dominated forest protection in the past two decades (Angelsen et al. 2012). The communities are thus maneuvered into a position of having to make difficult choices with REDD+ projects. Once the Trios choose to participate in, for example, a species conservation project instead of REDD+, a consequence may be destruction of the forest to build a research station and trails, which in turn limits the community's options for obtaining REDD+ sources of income. By trading off forest conservation for the larger climate goal, the community is long-term bound to the principles defined by the REDD+ project (Ring et al. 2010). The competition between climate-change mitigation and biodiversity conservation goals can be addressed when researchers approach REDD+ from a sustainable development perspective.

The Trio study indicated that if the REDD+ project had a more sustainable development focus, it could have amply included the Trios' economy-related interests in education and income. But REDD+ projects typically deal with drivers of deforestation, making it hard, or even impossible, to attend to the Trio interests. Thus, once the project's architecture can include the interests of both the community and the development organization, it is likely to have much greater prospects for sustainability than when only the interests of one party are embraced. Higher levels of sustainability manifest in projects that can include both the present and the future goals of the two parties.

Creating shared goals

As a researcher in conflict resolution, I am tempted to apply the conventional conflict resolution practice of finding some kind of commonality between the Trios and the development organizations. This seems rather difficult given the directly opposing views with no obvious commonalities that would facilitate a crossover, and therefore other means of cooperation should be sought (Pickerill, 2009). For creating a cooperative link between the two views, I refer to the work of conflict scholar Louis Kriesberg (2003), who proposes to search creatively for shared goals between the Trio community and a development organization.

An agreement on shared goals can be viewed as a small but vital step for the Trios and the development organizations in the management of their view differences. For example, a shared goal might be adapting to climate change, in which the parties can seek options that lead to the rapid recovery of opened subsistence plots. The Trios then have more land to adapt to climate change, and the development organization serves their interest in a lower level of deforestation. Keep in mind that shared goals are only fruitful in bridging views when there is enough negotiation room for all parties and when the development organization, as the key initiator of development, provides assistance to promote those ideas into the project implementation.

A researcher can evaluate how each party articulates its self-defined interests and the goals it shares with the other party. The most ideal and favorable situation is when each party is thinking in terms of project outcomes and thus prioritizes the overall goals of the project (Smith at al. 2014). This situation is rarely found in real practice. A more common situation is when parties automatically start by expressing their own interests in such a way that they are thinking about themselves first while they are unwilling to surrender or make any concessions. This obviously leads to lower project sustainability.

Establishing trust and cooperation

The Trios and a development organization can engage in an effective system of cooperation to negotiate a shared goal, even in a context of uneven power. Effective cooperation often is dependent on the level of trust between the parties. I build on previous research to discuss the three necessary elements in the trust-creating process: (1) communication, (2) awareness and (3) social learning (Smith et al. 2014).

The first key element is communication. Communication should be respectful so that the community and the development organization can debate topics and move into developing shared goals. Respectable communication happens when both parties feel secure and have respect for each other's opinions, and communicate their positions (what they want) and their interests (why they want it) (Smith et al. 2014). In many development projects, nevertheless, communication between the parties is often far from ideal. Development organizations usually employ a dominating communication style toward the community. I have seen such situations result in silence, nonexpression by the community or the use of several communication blockers—changing the topic and evaluating—to defend its lower-power position (Smith at al. 2014).

The second key element in a cooperative system is awareness. Awareness refers to a continuous interpretation of the observations that one makes to appraise what cultural constructs are at work, and which will create a better understanding and acceptance of the other party (Avruch and Black 2001). If one party wants to start cooperating with another, it first needs to be fully aware of the other party's culture and ideas regarding the project. A party can be so empathetic it starts thinking in the reality of the other party while making suggestions for improving the other party's circumstances (Smith at al. 2014).

Awareness can be structurally promoted, for example, when the scientific concepts of climate change used in REDD+ projects are simplified and made comprehensible for groups like the Trios. Contrastingly, the development organizations can also heighten their understanding of the indigenous traditional knowledge base and how that can feed into the REDD+ negotiations. But if a party is insensitive, it may stick to describing its own reality and simply acknowledge some ideas and opinions expressed by the other party. Living in its own perfect world, this party finds it tremendously challenging to position itself in the reality of the other.

The third key element of a cooperative system is social learning. A development organization naturally will have greater knowledge of a REDD+ project's content and will find the Trios' lack of understanding of the broader project goals to be a serious constraint (Angelsen et al. 2012; UNU 2012). To prevent an organization from forcing its viewpoint upon the Trios, I suggest a social learning process, which "occurs when new information and knowledge is processed, making it one's own and focused into the project" (Smith et al. 2014, 12). Development organizations and groups like the Trios thus must try to learn together in each step of the project, especially because REDD+ is still a worldwide experiment.

Social learning truly occurs when a party is willing to learn about itself, about the other party and take these new discoveries, discuss them with the other party and mutually decide to insert them into the project (Smith at al. 2014). A researcher can track whether this process initially occurs, and if so, can evaluate whether it is successful. Ineffective social learning happens especially when one party only wants to learn about itself, or learn about itself and the other, without including those lessons into the project. Then, social learning becomes an "empty" experience with no value added to the process.

Enabling participation

It is clear that there are various definitions of indigenous peoples' participation in climate change in circulation today. One definition includes new forms of social cooperation with indigenous peoples for securing the goals set in a climate-change project (Hulme 2010). A more community-based definition describes participation as collaboration that captures the rights and well-being of an indigenous community (Erni 2011). Although no common definition exists for such community participation in climate-change projects, I think two general assumptions are (silently) made by development organizations.

The first assumption is that the participation of indigenous peoples automatically promotes the sustainability of a REDD+ project. Often an indigenous community is viewed by researchers as an entity necessary to transfer global carbon-trading goals into the locale rather than a primary decision maker. Numerous carbon projects end in failure or are unable to attain the projected outcomes because of the community's lack of local voice in decision making (Nelson and De Jong 2003; Sikor et al. 2010).

Second, quite a few organizations think that indigenous participation is fully driven by the benefits coming from the REDD+ project. Indigenous communities are thus likely to engage based on their expectation of receiving some money from trading carbon credits. However, the case study showed that the Trios ultimately decided to engage in REDD+ (silently) knowing they cannot do anything to mitigate climate change. Thus, it seems to me that the underlying reason for participation is to fulfill their own goals for protection of the forest for their progeny in the years to come, and for the protection of the living place against the unwelcome invasion of outsiders.

Community participation is discussed here along a continuum in time with "short-term, project-related participation" on the low end. Typically, local communities only participate during the project life and then withdraw from any type of follow-up activities. This is very different from "long-term, beyond-project participation," which stands on the high end of the continuum. This form of participation envisages a long-term relationship with the community that extends after the project ends. The community and development organization then continue to partner in nonproject-related activities, such as knowledge sharing and giving feedback on the final outcomes of the project. Participation for the long term will likely promote sustainability in projects, as I have observed.

Community participation in a project is expected to have improved sustainability when it builds on the view of the community itself (Smith et al. 2014). When a researcher initiates an earnest conversation with a community on the subject of interests, it can permit much more equitable participation than if this does not happen. Less participatory action of a community is expected when only certain interests are included in the project. I have noticed that those are usually pushed for by the higher-power party. The least participation that I have seen, is when a community's view is only acknowledged but not associated with any of a project's activities.

Participation is also dependent on the flexibility in the design of the project. In case of an environmental change event, the community's view has to change rapidly. A researcher has to make adjustment to the project to include the new view (and interests) of the community (Smith et al. 2014). Only then does the project have a chance of becoming a sustainable effort. When a project is rigid and fixed in design, it commonly cannot adjust to potential changes in the community view.

Designing a model

There is an opportunity to bridge the opposing views of the Trios and the development organization by creating a model for collaboration. The starting point for designing such a model in the Trio case study is the shared goal of protecting the forest. I found six thematic opportunities to include in the project that will quite equally address the view of both parties: (1) the Trios desire to have their basic human needs met, such as clean water, food and security in the form of land rights and safety from intruders; (2) the Trios are also adapting to climate change, which is their primary way of surviving the current weather-related changes; (3) the Trios would like better education and income opportunities, and like to become empowered in these prioritized areas; (4) the development organization is in fact interested in mitigating climate change by collaborating in a REDD+ project with the Trios; (5) the development organization wants to provide assistance to reach progress in development; (6) the development organization wants to give continued feedback, follow-up and guidance in case the Trios join the REDD+ project.

The points brought forward so far I have fitted into a model for collaboration (Figure 8.1). This bottom-up model is founded on experience and concepts that were developed by my colleagues and me for analyzing conflict in development projects (Smith et al. 2014). The idea is that by building on the interests of the lower-power party, the Trios' view, conflict situations have a higher probability of being resolved than when a development organization implements activities from the top down.

The model also provides a useful point of departure for developing a negotiation process between the two parties. A community and a development organization should keep an open discussion about their goals as they may shift with changing conditions. It is not hard to imagine that without negotiation about the shared goals or if these fail after the project starts, there is a great possibility for conflict in case of a difference in opinion. The parties should engage in multiple tracks of negotiation to successfully manage the risk of conflict (Edmunds and Wollenberg 2001). One reason for having multiple avenues is the Trios possess power because they have a suitable alternative for participation in REDD+: the Trios can adapt locally to the effects of change, just like they have been doing for centuries. It is, therefore,

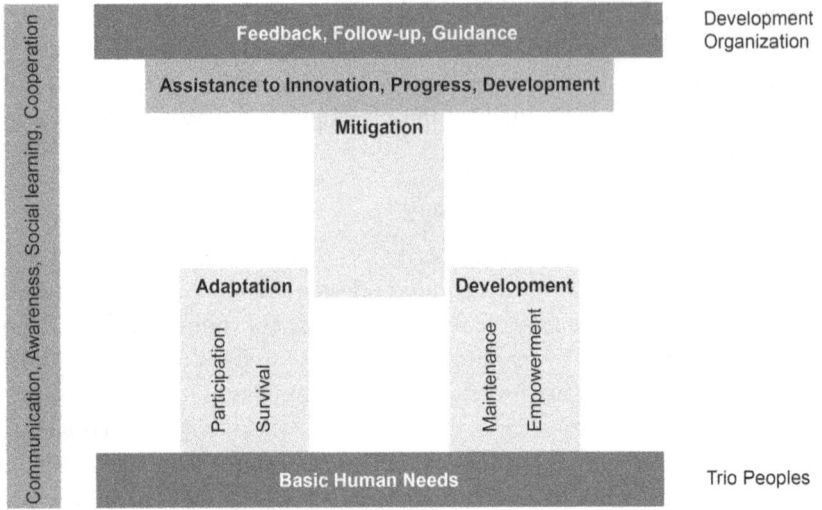

Figure 8.1 Model for collaboration of Trio indigenous peoples in REDD+ projects based on view differences (Smith 2013).

important to include the needs and interests of the Trios in the multiple-track negotiation—tracks of both development and adaptation will address the Trio needs and interests and create enough social space for decision making. The Trios can then continue working with development organizations even when some form of disagreement exists.

Focusing on the nature and character of communication, the Trios and the development organization can negotiate a narrative around the shared goal of protecting the forest. Creating narratives moves away from the prescriptive methodology approach, often used in models and tools for resolving conflict. John Winslade and Gerald Monk, the pioneers in narrative interaction, see a shared narrative as a way of opening space for parties to put an emphasis on reality rather than facts. According to them, narrative interaction is "a useful tool for depersonalizing conflict. It helps see how systems of meaning, or fields of knowledge and belief, shape not only people's perspectives, agendas, and desires but also the very nature of the conflict" (Winslade and Monk 2001, 42). Negotiating such narratives fits well with the Trio view, which is distinct from mainstream society and founded on orally transferred knowledge, values and beliefs.

Third-party intervention may also be useful in creating a narrative. The role of the conflict resolution practitioner is to engage the less powerful party, promote dialogue, build trust and ensure transparency and equity in the conversation. Thus, the conflict practitioner should try weaving together a narrative that includes the interests and needs of the parties in the different topics presented in the model in Figure 8.1.

Thus, the model explained here provides one solution to bridging views and balancing power at the local level. With an increased level of collaboration and equality, I expect the development organization and the Trio peoples to better frame their issues and express their actual interest about REDD+. Positions may soften, as both parties are more interested and become more cooperative in recognizing each other's interests. Researchers should be well aware that indigenous peoples also have other nonviolent strategies for acquiring more power in the REDD+ framework through negotiations, for example, by building strategic alliances with other partners. I have observed the Trios making such alliances with other indigenous peoples and NGOs in Suriname and abroad. In this way they create relational power as one important strategy to fight for equality. Researchers can address these influences by including them into the narrative, for instance, by asking the parties to review and revise the narrative.

The model contributes to a new way of transforming environmental conflict, a subdiscipline focusing on resolving complex conflicts over natural resources. For each conflict, a researcher can perform a VIEW analysis and design a holistic model for collaboration. Once a model is developed from the bottom up, it allows the aligning of view differences between the interacting parties. The approach assumes that managing these aspects in a relationship between the parties will lead to conflict management and ultimately transformation.

Principles for Researchers and Practitioners

Researchers working in the "pro poor development" track like to improve the deprived situation of local communities, who are currently also pressured by environmental change. As I have tried to illustrate in this book, a researcher is the key link between a community and the organization initiating the development, and is the only one who can initiate the change needed for having better bottom-up and sustainable projects. For me, real community change can only happen when a researcher first self-transforms and is capable of seeing things through the eyes of a community rather than as an outsider.

Not on every occasion, I realize, is a researcher (also read practitioner) adept at making such an ideological change. It is common practice that projects have fixed goals, and only very few projects have wiggle room to fully address community interests. Researchers from development organizations, on their part, are also bound to rules that are heavily influenced by global politics and the availability of funds. Nonetheless, I believe researchers and practitioners can start with adhering to a set of principles that guide them toward a more equitable and reflective research process with local communities.

Ethics

Ethical practice requires a researcher to ask permission from a community for conducting a development project. The researcher seeks verbal or written consent after thoroughly laying out the details of the project to the community. In this permission-seeking process a researcher normally designs a consent form in which the goals, objectives, research questions, methodology and expected outcomes are explained. Many times researchers and organizations violate this delicate practice. Even in my own experience, I have partnered with researchers who regrettably concealed relevant project information when seeking consent. Those researchers stressed the benefits to the community but purposely left out the potential risks and problems that were expected to arise during the course of the project.

To avoid such mistakes I have learned to become much more reflective in the consent seeking. In each engagement, I trained myself to assess my own view with the VIEW framework and subsequently ask three fundamental questions: (1) Is the project relevant for the community? (2) What will the community directly and indirectly gain from the project? and (3) Is there a balance between what the community gains and what the researcher gains from the project? With this bottom-up mind-set, I visit the community, discuss the project idea and creatively seek ways to enter the community's stake in the original project design. By the time I have answered all three questions, usually after six months, I have automatically looked at the project through the eyes of the community.

After my project is community proofed, I typically seek supervisor approval and then return to the community to initiate the approval process. Seeking consent is a very tedious practice and, as a general rule, I request community permission for every activity I anticipate doing in a project. For example, in a particular community project, I received consent for interviewing several women in the village. It was after talking with one powerful and wise woman that I realized her picture would contribute significantly to the quality of her testimonial. I had to ask the community for permission to take this picture rather than assuming a go-ahead was included in the first approval.

Research with indigenous peoples even goes beyond this type of consent-seeking process. Indigenous peoples expect researchers to show the ultimate respect for their lifestyles. They insist on researchers valuing nature the way they do, thereby stressing a harmonious and balanced relationship between humans and nature. Indigenous peoples also count on researchers to have respect for their rights, such as the right to self-determination, right to self-expression, right to free use of land and right to direct their own development. Indigenous peoples' rights are laid out in the United Nations Declaration of the Rights of Indigenous Peoples (UNDRIP), which is an important tool for preventing discrimination and marginalization of the planet's 370 million indigenous peoples (UNESCO 2008).

At times, a researcher can refuse to deal with pressing issues in an indigenous community that have, according to the researcher, no relevance to the project. I have seen a researcher talking with a community about conservation efforts while the tribal members did not have enough food to eat. The researcher simply ignored this community need because it was not written in the project. Another time I witnessed a period of two years during which several researchers from conservation NGOs would avoid getting involved with an indigenous tribe's fight for obtaining land rights. Although land rights is a requisite for good forest conservation, they argued that the tribe's fight for land rights fell outside their agenda. It is this type of avoidance that is often tactfully intermingled with a researcher's enthusiasm to engage with the community on the project.

Equality

Researchers like me want, as much as possible, to engage a community as an equal partner in the development process. This looks easy but is not. Many local communities and indigenous peoples have a strong suspicion against researchers and other outsiders, often validated by previous unpleasant and sometimes even damaging experiences. A typical community researcher has to do plenty of extra work to overcome this historic barrier and keep motivating the community when realizing a project.

Researchers may want to become close to the community by learning the local language and connecting with community members in everyday livelihood activities. But as I have noticed, a higher level of researcher engagement does not automatically mean that the community's interest will be adequately addressed. Sometimes researchers work closely together with the community, only to open the gateway for employing their own agenda. Such a process is different from that of researchers who are trying to find true ways to help the community, and then collaboratively design a project in which both community members and the researcher learn and move forward in obtaining their goals (Smith 1999).

The way I connect with a community is to consider them my extended family, which allows me to get rid of my Northern distortion and genuinely open up for collaboration. This practice permits the building of the necessary trust needed for true partnership. I do this by interacting with the community on a

Box 8.1
Photographs by a Trio Ranger

In my research with the Trios, I collaborated with the community in identifying the physical indicators for climate change. My initial plan was to ask the Trio peoples to point out which plants are useful indicators when we walked the forest together. Then I could take pictures and highlight each plant's flowers, seeds and leaves, a practice that I had learned during my previous botany training. But when I gave my camera to a Trio ranger, the story of collaboration became fairly different. The ranger photographed the same plants in quite a distinct way, showing only the whole plants from the soil up to the crown. For this indigenous man, it was important to see the physical place of entire plants in the forest.

project from the beginning. In practice, it comes back to applying the VIEW framework, asking questions and listening well to ensure that my Northern view is constantly being challenged with the view held by the community. Working together like this in every aspect of the project, I have learned, initiates a process of mutual learning (Box 8.1). Ultimately, the project gives more fulfilling outcomes for both the community and the researcher.

This example Box 8.1 shows how I could come closer to the community when sharing my expert power: I engaged the indigenous ranger as an equal researcher, which is a strategic way to gather the right type of data, to process data in a cultural sensitive way and to validate research outcomes (Smith 1999). Adhering to such a true collaborative process, however, took years of challenging myself. First, I had to lower the shield of my own Western thinking system, which felt like undressing in front of a large crowd. Then I had to gain trust in the indigenous peoples as researchers, and this happened only after opening myself up to their traditional knowledge system. Returning to the example in Box 8.1, "pretend" collaborative researchers might want to let the indigenous man take pictures of the forest plants, but they will ultimately interpret these pictures themselves. Such phony actions are unlikely to promote equality in research.

Accountability

Every community should have some kind of accountability for the success or failure of the project it is engaged in. This is tricky to realize when almost all projects are initiated and driven by development organizations. But the power of a researcher for boosting accountability shouldn't be underestimated. Researchers are in a fortunate position to intervene and make suggestions, so the community can take more responsibility for the project's execution and outcomes. My absolute preference for promoting accountability is to involve different types of community members in the project, such as women, men, youth, elders, teachers, shamans and leaders of an indigenous community, for example. Engaging these functional groups naturally promotes a two-way interaction: a horizontal interaction among community members of one functional group and a vertical interaction between the community members of different functional groups.

Communities can become more accountable when they believe the project can resolve a problem they are struggling with on a daily basis. So when I asked about the perception on climate change, Trio women and men would stop me to tell me enthusiastically about their experience. They would even go beyond the climate question and explain about other changes they have encountered in the village, such as suicide and violence among youngsters. The simple interrogation technique seems to work quite well when the problem is of high importance; however, the discussion would be less intense if I had chosen a trivial topic, such as how to plant cassava rootstocks.

Apart from topical discussions, I also like to engage community members in the processing and interpreting of data. This is one practice in which researchers are particularly more comfortable working alone. Researchers typically visit the field to gather piles of data and then return to their offices to process this data into scientific or other reports. Repeatedly, I asked myself if this routine is effective enough to elevate the community's accountability for the project until I had a life-changing experience. I was searching for answers to a research question on what techniques an indigenous community prefers to use for growing its food crops. After gathering a heap of qualitative and quantitative data during a few weeks of research, I returned to my desk to sort out the data. With my reports under my arm, I went back to the village to discuss my outcomes with the community members.

I can still remember that day as if it were yesterday. While standing in front of the community and presenting "my" results, I could see the indigenous men and women becoming restless and irritated because my conclusions were far off from reality. Since that embarrassing moment, collaborative data processing has become a standard activity when working together with local communities. The meek practice endorses that community and researcher both become true partners in the project. When a result is then presented, the community members feel more accountable, and this is seen when they may even defend the research results. They become vigorous supporters instead of distant observers.

Another important moment to partner up with a community is during the project evaluation. Project evaluations are typically designed from a Northern perspective, in fact, with indicators sketched along the theme of human development. Such indicators emphasize well-being, as in the level of education, health status and level of income, among others. But I have learned that projects also have major positive impacts on other aspects of the community, for example, bringing different community members closer together or building bridges with other groups. Because such indicators are seldom contemplated in a regular evaluation, I like the community to bring forward their own indicators, so they feel more responsible for the change a project makes within their social setting.

Adaptation

In their career, researchers are encouraged to develop and run projects. To do this, they are expected to know the on-the-ground situation in the community. However, in many communities, there are hidden values that only surface when there are problems (Box 8.2). Researchers frequently seem unprepared for problem situations, but they have to handle them to ensure proper continuation or closure of a project. The project should be adapted, which means that either the focus or activities are changed, the time line adjusted or the budget amended. Such alteration requires a balancing act in which the researcher has to rematch the interests of both the development organization and the community.

The example in Box 8.2 shows that the project should become adaptive to the internal dynamics of a community. And being adaptive includes a responsibility on the part of the researcher to explain the changed plans to the development organization. But what would the donor in Box 8.1 say if the researchers told them that the project halted because of a power imbalance between men and women? They would typically be sensitive to reasons of force majeure, for example, a natural disaster, but power balance may be too farfetched. Or the donor would say that this community feature should have been known to the organization. The researcher from that organization had a real dilemma.

Researchers seldom learn about dealing with such dilemmas in their academic career, and thus have no clue how to deal with them in practice. I have discovered by trial and error that when the local reality was clearly explained, donors would be sensitive to the community's circumstances and would agree with the proposed change. However, in the case that donors were extremely scientifically oriented, it might take a more thorough reality reconstruction. Then, I would let the community speak for itself and explain the situation to the donor, which until now, has always softened its position.

Box 8.2
The Women Pepper Producers

The women in an indigenous village have been making a powered pepper product as part of their traditional diet. An organization, which worked in the village for seven years, was interested in commercializing the pepper product so the women could earn some income. The organization talked with the women several times, and took approximately one year to carefully draft the project, focused on building capacity in propagation, production, processing and administrative and financial management. When the project started, about 30 women were participating enthusiastically, which led to the opening of a small selling point at a store in the capital city. The pepper jars would be produced in the village, flown to the capital city and sold, after which the women would receive their income. The organization also decided to build a processing center where the women could weigh and package pepper and store their tools. The project ran well, and every month pepper jars would be sent to the city. After approximately one and a half years, the pepper production ceased abruptly. The organization met with the pepper women several times, but was unable to understand why the women stopped working. Later it became evident that the women were receiving too much money, which was a threat to the men in the village. The organization tackled this problem by slightly changing the project so that the men were given some sort of power. Men were given responsibility for the storage of tools and supplies. Then the power balance was restored.

Communication

The views of a community and a development organization in projects may differ, or sometimes even conflict. It then becomes difficult for the two parties to hear and understand each other. Researchers are then in a position to mediate between the parties, something they haven't learned during their degree-seeking education. This is the right moment to apply social polygraphy, in order to better communicate with indigenous communities that are not directly expressive in language. The community can go through a self-reflection process and candidly sketch its thoughts and ideas on paper. Collecting information with community members' self-made maps can help a researcher conceptualize the reality in which that typical community lives.

I experience the clarity of communication with a social polygraphy methodology during data collection for the Trio case study. The Trios took pictures
of climate-change indicators while walking in the forest. All indicators were
further explored with a focus group that lasted approximately 45 minutes,
during which Trio men and women explicitly described the indicator, such
as its preferred location, life cycle and function. The resultant cognitive maps
were a pure representation of what the Trios thought was important about
each indicator. Every map was unique: a few maps highlighted information
about spiritual use, some about location, while others illuminated specifics
about the indicator's life cycle or function. If I had approached this project without communicating and giving the freedom to the Trio peoples to
express their own views, the outcome would have been very different. I would
have never learned about the distinctive characteristics of each indicator.
The indicators would be comfortably framed within my own systematic view
rather than a holistic description covering the spiritual, biological and human
dimensions.

Social learning

Groups can learn from working with each other during the course of a project. Social learning only occurs when a researcher and a community exchange
individual views and knowledge in such a way that the path of future action is
positively changed (Johnson et al. 2012). This intuitive practice can only happen when a researcher is skilled enough to understand the reality of the community, and the community is able to understand the reality of the researcher.
This means that a researcher should be open to a community's interests and
values. Apparently, this is not always easy (Box 8.3).

The example in Box 8.3 refers to a true social learning process in which
both parties not only exchanged ideas but also altered the direction of the collaborative learning process itself. The VIEW framework can come in handy to
initiate such social learning—to assess the values, meaning-making and decision-making processes in the community—which may trigger the researcher
to open up to the community's sensitivities.

Time sensitivity

A development project is usually designed by a development organization in a
wider framework of global policies. Development organizations are typically
insensitive to changing a project's format and adhere to strict time regimes
in the planning and execution of projects. Exceeding such a time frame is an

Box 8.3
A Frog Tale

I recall several years back when a few Trio men were telling me a frog tale. For four long and boring hours, the Trios were making frog sounds in their attempt to explain the difference between several types of forest frogs. It was then impossible for me to even slightly understand the relevance of this lengthy Trio narrative. However, little by little, the frog story started making sense to me. The frog tale was an example of the Trios to explain how an indigenous system works. Since then, I have become much more sensitive to the Trio way of sharing their knowledge and ideas and this happened as soon as I understood the frog metaphor. And the Trios spontaneously responded to my enthusiasm by bringing more information to the forefront. During this genuine interaction, the Trios and I started comparing different knowledge systems with each other: Trios from their traditional knowledge and I from scientific knowledge. The social learning process really took off when the Trios and I made significant changes to the research method as a result of this knowledge exchange. Including old frog stories in the research was suggested to me by the Trios. It was then that I discovered, in addition to speaking with several Trio men and women, frogs were previously spiritual leaders who led the tribe in making vital decisions in times of war and environmental uncertainty.

indicator for poor project management by the researcher. Yet, working alongside a community in a bottom-up way will regularly extend a project's time span. It takes me on average twice as long as the "normal time" I would have worked with a community in a project. So how can a researcher please both the community and the development organization?

Researchers like me would think of community development in terms of a change process. I like to get an idea of the community's goals (with the VIEW framework) and then develop a long-term process in which we line up different smaller projects, each trying to fulfill a specific subgoal of the larger community goal (Box 8.4). Time can thus be used more effectively because the community has a clear understanding of how each project fits within the larger process, so in each smaller project the community and the researcher need less time to deliberate. Motivating the community to participate, which is a tedious and time-consuming activity, will also take less time.

Box 8.4
The Indigenous Ranger Program

I applied this methodology during a process for establishing an indigenous ranger team between 2006 and 2012. Community members were going to be trained to protect the territory against intruders and polluters. Men and women needed to observe the territory, and gather, process and transfer the environmental data necessary for monitoring and guarding the area. For achieving this overall goal, several smaller projects were carried out over the course of seven years. The first project aimed at studying self-protection models in the region, so a curriculum for training of rangers could be developed. In the second project, indigenous rangers were recruited and trained in several villages, using both a classroom and a field format. The third project was targeted at building housing and equipment—boat and outboard motor, computer, solar panels, two-way radio—to carry out territorial surveillance.

Once the rangers were operational, my colleagues and I started writing projects that could help the rangers develop some more research capacity. One project was envisaged to teach rangers how to test water and soil pollution. Another project aimed at building ranger capacity in using basic computer programs so they could use the Internet to transfer pictures and send letters and other data. Rangers were also trained to use global positioning devices to map important locations. With this scientific knowledge, they could perform basic monitoring tasks that ultimately would support territorial protection. Together the Trios and my team have implemented projects in a wider process of the community change. With this example, I demonstrate a route for a researcher to line up projects to reach a broader community goal.

A Message for Policy Makers

Through this book, I hope to contribute to an understanding of community views and provide insight into how to make the sustainability of development activities more effective. The book is a tool to stimulate the thought process for policy makers to address sustainability from the bottom up and from the inside out. The VIEW framework presented here has shown the importance of assessing community interests, values, strategies and attitudes in an analysis of views. Such a deep analysis brings up issues of inequality and power differences.

Often the policy makers possess the power to claim the truth, while the lower-power party, such as communities, has no such ability. The surmounting of power differences usually is promoted through processes of collaboration in planning, management and policy making (Li et al. 2012). All of these processes envisage giving voice to less powerful communities and promoting the relational aspect in order to bring greater equity to solutions (Foley 2007). The VIEW framework provided insight into a local view, which in turn can provide greater understanding regarding the reasons for their behavior in conflict situations. Then, the policy maker can better address the community/development organization power relationship.

It is well known that policy development in the social sector is more an "arts and crafts" situation than is any other type of policy. The VIEW framework can be useful in providing evidence to policy makers on the social welfare and equality of communities when they are undergoing environmental change processes. For example, in making climate-change policies, the best practice REDD+ project design is still being developed, and thus the design is evolving worldwide. The VIEW framework can thus potentially help identify conflict at the local level before it expands and subsequently transfers to the national or the global level. A policy maker can assess the views of the community, development organizations and other groups in REDD+ to identify what policies will be supported or resisted. A similar case can be made for using the VIEW framework for view conflict identification for policy development in disaster relief. The approach assumes that when a policy maker better understands the views in a relationship between a development organization and a community, it will lead to better policy making.

Specific for climate change, I have noticed there is growing interest in validating indigenous peoples' viewpoints globally (Alessa et al. 2008; Frank et al. 2011; Sutton and Tobin 2011; Tucker et al. 2010). Following this movement, I like to encourage policy makers to also acquire information from the local level, even if it does not always fit in the highly academic policy frameworks in REDD+. A policy maker can, for example, propose the participation of groups like the Trios from the outset of a REDD+ project so that the power differential between the managing development organization and the indigenous group can be balanced throughout the project and the views can be bridged. Working this way also provides a new means of examining power differences between different actors in the playing field.

REFERENCES

ABS (Algemeen Bureau voor de Statistiek). 2005. *Zevende Algemene Volks: En Woningtelling in Suriname. Landelijke Resultaten: Volume I. Demografische en Sociale Karakteristieken.* Paramaribo, Suriname: Algemeen Bureau voor de Statistiek/Censuskantoor.

Adger, Neil W., Nigel W. Arnell and Emma L. Tompkins. 2005. "Successful Adaptation to Climate Change across Scales." *Global Environmental Change* 15 (2): 77–86. http://dx.doi.org/10.1016/j.gloenvcha.2004.12.005.

Agrawal, Arun. 1995. "Dismantling the Divide between Indigenous and Scientific Knowledge." *Development and Change* 26 (3): 413–39. doi:10.1111/j.1467-7660.1995.tb00560.x.

Agrawal, Arun, and Clark C. Gibson, eds. 2001. *Communities and the Environment: Ethnicity, Gender and the State in Community-Based Conservation.* New Brunswick, NJ: Rutgers University Press.

Aitken, Mhairi. 2012. "Changing Climate, Changing Democracy: A Cautionary Tale." *Environmental Politics* 21 (2): 211–29. doi:10.1080/09644016.2012.651899.

Alessa, Lilian (Na'ia), Andrew (Anaru) Kliskey, Paula Williams and Michael Barton. 2008. "Perception of Change in Fresh Water in Remote Resource-Dependent Arctic Communities." *Global Environmental Change* 18 (1): 153–64. http://dx.doi.org/10.1016/j.gloenvcha.2007.05.007.

Amatali, M. Armand. 2012. *Second National Communication to the UNFCCC: Technical Paper Present Profile; Water Resources.* Paramaribo, Suriname: Ministry of Labor, Technological Development and Environment.

Anderson, Mary B. 1999. *Do No Harm: How Aid Can Support Peace or War.* Boulder, CO: Lynne Rienner Publishers.

Andrade, Helena M., and Guillermo Santamaría. 1997. "Cartografia Social para la Planeación Participativa." In *Memorias del Curso: Participación Comunitaria y Medio Ambiente*, edited by Proyecto de Capacitación para Profesiones del Sector Ambiental, 185–212. Colombia: Ministerio del Medio Ambiente & ICFES.

Angelsen, Arild, Maria Brockhaus, William D. Sunderlin and Louis V. Verchot, eds. 2012. *Analyzing REDD+: Challenges and Choices.* Bogor, Indonesia: Centre for International Forestry Research (CIFOR).

Armitage, Derek R., Fikret Berkes and Nancy Doubleday, eds. (2007). *Adaptive Co-Management: Collaboration, Learning, and Multi-Level Governance.* Vancouver, Canada: UBC Press.

Augsburger, David W. 1992. *Conflict Mediation Across Cultures: Pathways and Patterns.* Louisville, KY: Winstminster/John Knox Press.

Avruch, Kevin. 1998. *Culture and Conflict Resolution.* Washington, DC: United States Institute of Peace.

Avruch, Kevin, and Peter W. Black. 2001. "Conflict Resolution in Intercultural Settings." In *The Conflict and Culture Reader*, edited by Pat K. Chew, 7–14. New York: New York University Press.

Bäckstrand, Karin, and Eva Lövbrand. 2006. "Planting Trees to Mitigate Climate Change: Contested Discourses of Ecological Modernization, Green Governmentality and Civic Environmentalism." *Global Environmental Politics* 6 (1): 50–75. doi:10.1162/glep.2006.6.1.50.

Barr, Stewart, Andrew Gilg and Gareth Shaw. 2011. "Citizens, Consumers and Sustainability: Re(framing) Environmental Practice in an Age of Climate Change." *Global Environmental Change* 21 (4): 1224–33. http://dx.doi.org/10.1016/j.gloenvcha.2011.07.009.

Barron, Patrick, Rachael Diprose and Michael Woolcock. 2007. *Local Conflict and Development Projects in Indonesia: Part of the Problem or Part of the Solution?* http://econ.worldbank.org/WBSITE/EXTERNAL/EXTDEC/EXTRESEARCH/EXTPROGRAMS/EXTPOVRES.html.

Barry, John. 2007. *Environment and Social Theory.* 2nd ed. New York: Routledge.

Bastidas, Elena P., and Carlos A. Gonzales. 2008. "Social Cartography as a Tool for Conflict Analysis and Resolution: The Experience of the Afro-Colombian Communities of Robles." *Peace and Conflict Studies* 15 (2): 1–14. http://shss.nova.edu/pcs/journalsPDF/Winter_2009.pdf.

Bavinck, Maarten, Lorenzo Pellegrini and Eric Mostert, eds. 2014. *Conflicts over Natural Resources in the Global South: Conceptual Approaches.* London: CRC Press.

Bayart, Jean-François. 2005. *The Illusion of Cultural Identity.* Chicago, IL: University of Chicago Press.

Bercovitch, Jacob. 1996. *Resolving International Conflicts: The Theory and Practice of Mediation.* Boulder, CO: Lynne Rienner Publishers.

Berkes. Fikret. 2004. "Rethinking Community-Based Conservation." *Conservation Biology* 18(3): 621–30. doi:10.1111/j.1523-1739.2004.00077.x.

———. 2008. *Sacred Ecology.* 2nd ed. New York: Routledge.

———. 2009. "Evolution of Co-Management: Role of Knowledge Generation, Bridging Organization and Social Learning." *Journal of Environmental Management* 90 (5): 1692–702. http://dx.doi.org/10.1016/j.jenvman.2008.12.001.

Berkes, Fikret, and Mina Kislalioglu Berkes. 2009. "Ecological Complexity, Fuzzy Logic and Holism in Indigenous Knowlegde." *Futures* 41 (1): 6–12. http://dx.doi.org/10.1016/j.futures.2008.07.003.

Berrang-Ford, Lea, James D. Ford and Jaclyn Paterson. 2011. "Are We Adapting to Climate Change?" *Global Enviormental Change* 21 (1): 25–33. http://dx.doi.org/10.1016/j.gloenvcha.2010.09.012.

Biggeri, Mario., Renato Lobanora, Stefano Mariani and Leonardo Menchin. 2006. "Children Conceptualizing Their Capabilities: Results of a Survey during the First Children's World Congress on Child Labour." *Journal of Human Development and Capabilities* 7 (1): 59–83. doi:10.1080/14649880500501179.

Biggs, Stephen D. 1989. "Resource-Poor Farmer Participation in Research: A Synthesis of Experiences from Nine National Agricultural Research Systems." OFCOR Comparative Study Paper, *ISNAR*, The Hague, 3–37.

Bolton, Robert. 1979. *People Skills: How to Assert Yourself, Listen to Others and Resolve Conflicts.* New York: Simon and Schuster.

Bonan, Gordan B. 2008. "Forests and Climate Change: Forcings, Feedbacks, and the Climate Benefits of Forests." *Science* 320 (5882): 1444–49. doi:10.1126/science.1155121.

Bong A Jan, Rachelle. 2006. *Land Management in the Trio Indigenous Community of Suriname.* Paramaribo, Suriname: Amazon Conservation Team Suriname.

Bong A Jan, Rachelle, and Gwendolyn Smith. 2014. *"Substantial Report Inception Workshop Redd+ Prodoc."* Paramaribo, Suriname: Attune.

Borchert, Rolf. 1998. "Responses of Tropical Trees to Rainfall Seasonality and Its Long Term Changes." *Climatic Change* 39 (2–3): 381–93. doi:10.1023/A:1005383020063.

Boven, Karin. 2001. *Samuwaka Herdacht: Een Geschiedenis van het Trio Volk.* Paramaribo, Suriname: Amazon Conservation Team and Center for Support of Native Lands.

Brennan, Mark A., and Glenn D. Israel. 2008. "The Power of Community." *Community Development* 39 (1): 82–98. doi:10.1080/15575330809489743.

Brundtland, Gro Harlem. 1987. "Our Common Future." Report of the World Commission on Environment and Development. http://www.un-documents.net/our-common-future.pdf.

Budjeryn, Mariana. 2012. "Survivors of the Tsunami." http://www.culturalsurvival.org/publications/voices/mariana-budjeryn/survivors-tsunami.

Burton, John W. 1990. *Conflict: Human Needs Theory.* Baltimore: Macmillan.

Bush, Robert A. Baruch, and Joseph P. Folger. 2005. *The Promise of Mediation: The Transformative Approach to Conflict.* rev. ed. San Francisco: Jossey Bass.

Byg, Anja, and Jan Salick. 2009. "Local Perspectives on a Global Phenomenon—Climate Change in Eastern Tibetan Villages." *Global Environmental Change* 19 (2): 156–66. http://dx.doi.org/10.1016/j.gloenvcha.2009.01.010.

Bynoe, Paulette, and Jewel Liddell. 2013. "Indigenous People, Livelihoods and Climate Change: The Guyana Perspective." Final Technical Report CIFOR/Iwokrama.

Byrne, Seàn, and Neal Carter. 1996. "Social Cubism: Six Social Forces of Ethnoterritorial Politics in Northern Ireland and Québec." *Peace and Conflict Studies* 3 (2): 52–72.

Cameron, Emilie. 2012. "Securing Indigenous Politics: A Critique of the Vulnerability and Adaptation Approach to the Human Dimensions in the Canadian Arctic." *Global Environmental Change* 22 (1): 103–14. http://dx.doi.org/10.1016/j.gloenvcha.2011.11.004.

Carlin, Eithne B. 2004. *A Grammar of Trio, a Cariban Language of Suriname.* Frankfurt am Main: P. Lang. http://www.eithnecarlin.nl/publications/grammar-trio-cariban-language-suriname

Carpenter, Susan L., and W. J. D. Kennedy. 2001. *Managing Public Disputes: A Practical Guide for Government, Business, and Citizens' Groups.* 2nd ed. San Francisco: Jossey Bass.

Carrero, Gabriel C., Vasco M. Van Roosmalen and Claudia S. Vitel. 2012. "Traditional Community-Readiness for Carbon Projects: Lessons Learned from the Surui Forest Carbon Project." Paper presented at the Climate Change Mitigation with Local Communities and Indigenous Peoples: Practices, Lessons Learned and Prospects, Cairns, Australia.

Chambers, Robert. 1983. *Rural Development: Putting the Last First.* Oxford, UK: Pearson Education Limited.

———. 1997. *Whose Reality Counts? Putting the First Last.* Warwickshire, UK: Practical Action Publishing.

Chan, Kai M. A., Robert M. Pringle, Jai Ranganathan, Carol L. Boggs, Yvonne L. Chan, Paul R. Ehrlich, Peter K. Haff, Nicole E. Heller, Karim AlGhafaji and Dena P. Macmynowski. 2007. "When Agendas Collide: Human Welfare and Biological Conservation." *Conservation Biology* 21 (1): 59–68. doi:10.1111/j.1523-1739.2006.00570.x.

Clark, Deborah. A. 2007. "Detecting Tropical Forests' Responses to Global Climatic and Atmospheric Change: Current Challenges and a Way Forward." *Biotropica* 39 (1): 4–19. doi:10.1111/j.1744-7429.2006.00227.x.

Cohen, Raymond. 1997. *Negotiating across Cultures.* rev. ed. Washington, DC: United States Institute of Peace.

———. 2004. *Negotiating across Cultures: International Communication in an Interdependent World.* rev. ed. Washington, DC: United States Institute of Peace.

Colding, Johan, and Carl Folke. 2001. "Social Taboos: 'Invisible' Systems of Local Resource Management and Biological Conservation." *Ecological Applications* 11 (2): 584–600. http://www.jstor.org/stable/3060911.

Colfer, Carol J. Pierce. 2011. "Marginalized Forest Peoples' Perceptions of the Legitimacy of Governance: An Exploration." *World Development* 39 (12): 2147–64. doi:10.1016/j.worlddev.2011.04.012.

Cook, Kerry H., and Edward K. Vizy. 2008. "Effect of Twenty-First-Century Climate Change on the Amazonian Rainforest." *Journal of Climate* 21 (3): 542–60. http://dx.doi.org/10.1175/2007JCLI1838.1.

Corbera, Esteve, Nicolas Kosoy and Miguel Martinez Tuna. 2007. "Equity Implications of Marketing Ecosystem Services in Protected Areas and Rural Communities: Case Studies from Meso America." *Global Environmental Change* 17 (3–4): 365–80. http://dx.doi.org/10.1016/j.gloenvcha.2006.12.005.

da Fonseca, Gustave A. B., Carlos Manuel Rodriguez, Guy Midgley, Jonah Busch, Lee Hannah and Russell A. Mittermeier. 2007. "No Forest Left Behind." *PLoS Biology* 5 (8): 1645–46. http://dx.doi.org/10.1371/journal.pbio.0050216.

De Beer, Frik. 2013. "Community-Based Natural Resource Management: Living with Alice in Wonderland?" *Community Development Journal* 48 (4): 555–70. doi:10.1093/cdj/bss058.

Depledge, Joanna. 2006. "The Opposite of Learning: Ossification in the Climate Change Regime." *Global Environmental Politics* 6 (1): 1–22. doi:10.1162/glep.2006.6.1.1.

DFID (Department for International Development). 1999. *Sustainable Livelihoods Guidance Sheets*. http://www.eldis.org/vfile/upload/1/document/0901/section2.pdf.

Dietz, Thomas, and Paul C. Stern. 1995. "Towards a Theory of Choice: Socially Embedded Preference Construction." *Journal of Socio-Economics* 24 (2): 261–79. http://dx.doi.org/10.1016/1053–5357(95)90022–5.

Di Gessa, Stefano. 2008. *Participatory Mapping as a Tool for Empowerment: Experiences and Lessons Learned from the ILC Network*. Rome, Italy: ILC. http://www.landcoalition.org/pdf/08_ILC_Participatory_Mapping_Low.pdf.

Docherty, Jayne Seminare. 2001. *Learning Lessons from Waco: When the Parties Bring Their Gods to the Negotiation Table*. Syracuse, NY: Syracuse University Press.

Dodman, David, and Diana Mitlin. 2013. "Challenges for Community-Based Adaptation: Discovering the Potential for Transformation." *Journal of International Development* 25 (5): 640–59. doi:10.1002/jid.1772.

Edmunds, David, and Eva Wollenberg. 2001. "A Strategic Approach to Multistakeholder Negotiations." *Development and Change* 32 (2): 231–53. doi:10.1111/1467–7660.00204.

Erni, Christian. 2011. *Understanding Community-Based REDD+: A Manual for Indigenous Communities*. Chiang Mai, Thailand: AIPP Printing Press Co. http://www.iwgia.org/iwgia_files_publications_files/0565_CB-REDD-Trainers_small-20120117172426.pdf.

Fals-Borda, Orlando. 1987. "The Application of Participatory Action-Research in Latin America." *International Sociology* 2 (4): 329–47. doi:10.1177/026858098700200401.

———. 2006. "Participatory (Action) Research in Social Theory." In *Handbook of Action Research*, edited by Peter Reason and Hilary Bradury, 27–37. London: Sage.

Fals-Borda, Orlando, and Md. Anisur Rahman, eds. 1991. *Action and Knowledge. Breaking the Monopoly with Participatory Action Research*. London: Intermediate Technology Publications.

Fisher, Roger, and William Ury. 1991. *Getting to Yes: Negotiating Agreement Without Giving In*. New York: Penguin Books.

Fogel, Cathleen Ann. 2002. "Greening the Earth with Trees: Science, Storylines and the Construction of International Climate Change Institutions." PhD diss., University of California, Santa Cruz. Proquest (UMI No. 3078493).

Foley, Tony. 2007. "Environmental Conflict Resolution: Relational and Environmental Attentiveness as Measures of Success." *Conflict Resolution Quarterly* 24 (4): 485–504. doi:10.1002/crq.186.

Folger, Joseph P., Marshall Scott Poole and Randall K. Stutman. 2005. *Working Through Conflict: Strategies for Relationships, Groups and Organizations.* 5th ed. New York: Pearson.

Ford, James D., Barry Smit and Johanna Wandel. 2006. "Vulnerability to Climate Change in the Arctic: A Case Study from Arctic Bay Canada." *Global Environmental Change* 16 (2): 145–60. http://dx.doi.org/10.1016/j.gloenvcha.2005.11.007.

Frank, Elisa., Hallie Eakin and David López-Carr. 2011. "Social Identity, Perception and Motivation in Adaptation to Climate Rrisk in the Coffee Sector of Chiapas, Mexico." *Global Environmental Change* 21 (1): 66–76. http://dx.doi.org/10.1016/j.gloenvcha.2010.11.001.

Fraser Institute. 2012. "Mining Facts: Resources on Mining and Mining Policy." http://www.miningfacts.org/.

Frediani, Alexandre A. 2007. "Amartya Sen, the World Bank and the Redress of Urban Poverty: A Brazilian Case Study." *Journal of Human Development* 8 (1): 133–52. doi:10.1080/14649880601101473.

———. 2010. "Sen's Capability Approach as Framework to the Practice of Development." *Development in Practice* 20 (2): 173–87. http://www.jstor.org/stable/27806685.

Freire, Paulo. 1970. *Pedagogy of the Oppressed.* New York: Herder and Herder.

FUNDAMINGA (Fundación La Minga). 2002. "Diagnóstico Participativo: El Uso de la Cartografía Social: Cómo se Hacen los Mapas." *Cartilla.* Bogotá, Colombia: Comisión Europea.

———. 2012. "Poligrafia Social." http://FUNDAMINGA.blogspot.com/p/poligrafia-social.html.

Furlong, Gary T. 2005. *The Conflict Resolution Toolbox: Models and Maps for Analyzing, Diagnosing and Resolving Conflict.* Mississauga, ON: Wiley.

Galtung, Johan. 1996. *Peace by Peaceful Means: Peace and Conflict, Development and Civilizations.* Thousand Oaks, CA: Sage.

Giddens, Anthony. 1984. *The Constitution of Society: Outline of the Theory of Structuration.* Cambridge, UK: Polity Press.

Gogus, Sırça S. 2014. *Understanding Impasse in Climate Change Negotiations: The North-South Conflict and Beyond.* https://climate-exchange.org/2014/02/06/understanding-impasse-in-climate-change-negotiations-the-north-south-conflict-and-beyond.

Habegger, Sabina, and Iulia Mancila. 2006. *"El Poder de la Cartografía Social en las Prácticas Contrahegemónicas: La Cartografía Social Como Estrategia para Diagnosticar Nuestro Territorio."* *Revista Arciniega,* last modified April 14, 2006, http://www2.fct.unesp.br/docentes/geo/girardi/Cartografia%20PPGG%202015/TEXTO%2027.pdf

Habermas, Jürgen. n.d. *The Structural Transformation of the Public Sphere.* http://courses.ischool.berkeley.edu/i218/s10/JH-STPS.pdf.

———. 1971. *Knowledge and Human Interest.* Boston: Beacon Press.

Hajek, Frank, Mark J. Ventresca, Joel Scriven and Augusto Castro. 2011. "Regime-Building for REDD+: Evidence from a Cluster of Local Initiatives in South-Eastern Peru." *Environmental Science and Policy* 14 (2): 201–15. http://dx.doi.org/10.1016/j.envsci.2010.12.007.

Hall, Anthony L. 2012. *Forests and Climate Change: The Social Dimensions of REDD in Latin America.* Cheltenham, UK: Edward Elgar Publishing.

Healy, Christopher, Beverly De Vries, Minu Parahoe and Hera Van Ommeren. 2003. *Kwamalasamutu: An Analysis of Governance, Resource Management and Development Issues.* Paramaribo, Suriname: Amazon Conservation Team Suriname.

Heemskerk, Marieke, and Katia Delvoye. 2007. *Trio Baseline Study: A Sustainable Livelihoods Perspective on the Trio Indigenous Peoples of South Suriname.* Paramaribo, Suriname: Amazon Conservation Team. http://mariekeheemskerk.org/data/images/trio.

Herlihy, Peter H., and Gregory Knapp. 2003. "Maps of, by, and for the Peoples of Latin America." *Human Organization* 62 (4): 303–14. doi:0018-7259/03/040303-12$1.70/1.

Hulme, Mike. 2010. "Problems with Making and Governing Global Kinds of Knowledge." *Global Environmental Change* 20 (4): 550–64. http://dx.doi.org/10.1016/j.gloenvcha.2010.07.005.

Hulme, Mike, and David Viner. 1998. "A Climate Scenario for the Tropics." *Climatic Change* 39 (2–3): 145–76. doi:10.1023/A:1005376007729.

Hulse, Joseph H. 2007. *Sustainable Development at Risk: Ignoring the Past.* New Delhi, India: Cambridge University Press. http://www.idrc.ca/EN/Resources/Publications/openebooks/368-3/index.html.

Humphreys, Macartan. 2005. "Natural Resources, Conflict, and Conflict Resolution: Uncovering the Mechanisms." *Journal of Conflict Resolution* 49 (4): 508–37. doi:10.1177/0022002705277545.

Huntington, Henry P. 2000. "Using Traditional Ecological Knowledge in Science: Methods and Applications." *Ecological Applications* 10 (5): 1270–74. http://www.jstor.org/stable/2641282.

Hutyra, L. R., J. W. Munger, C. A. Nobre, S. R. Salesta, S. A. Vieira and S. C. Wofsy. 2005. "Climate Variability and Vegetation Vulnerability in Amazonia." *Geographical Research Letters* 32 (24): 1–4. doi:1029/2005GL024981.

IFAD (International Fund for Agricultural Development). 2011. *Rural Poverty Report 2011: New Realities, New Challenges: New Opportunities for Tomorrow's Generation.* http://www.ifad.org/rpr2011/report/e/rpr2011.pdf.

Ife, Jim. 2013. *Community Development in an Uncertain World: Vision, Analysis and Practice.* New York: Cambridge University Press.

Ikeme, Jekwu. 2003. "Equity, Environmental Justice and Sustainability: Incomplete Approaches in Climate Change Politics." *Global Environmental Change* 13 (3): 195–206. http://dx.doi.org/10.1016/S0959-3780(03)00047-5.

Inglehart, Ronald, and Wayne E. Baker. 2000. "Modernization, Cultural Change and the Persistence of Traditional Values." *American Sociological Review* 65 (1): 19–51. http://www.jstor.org/stable/2657288.

IPCC (International Panel on Climate Change). n.d. "Organization." http://www.ipcc.ch/organization/organization.shtml.

———. 2001. *Climate Change 2001: Synthesis Report. A Contribution of Working Groups I, II, and III to the Third Assessment Report of the Intergovernmental Panel on Climate Change.* Edited by Robert T. Watson and Core Writing Team. Cambridge, UK: Cambridge University Press. http://www.ipcc.ch/pdf/climate-changes-2001/synthesis-syr/english/front.pdf.

———. 2013. *Climate Change 2013: The Physical Science Basis: Summary for Policymakers.* Working Group 1 Contribution to the Fifth Assessment Report. Edited by Thomas F. Stocker, Dahe Qin, Gian-Kasper Plattner, Melinda M. B. Tignor, Simon K. Allen, Judith Boschung, Alexander Nauels, Yu Xia, Vincent Bex and Pauline M. Midgley. https://www.ipcc.ch/pdf/assessment-report/ar5/wg1/WGIAR5_SPM_brochure_en.pdf.

Jantzi, Terrence L., and Vernon E. Jantzi. 2009. "Development Paradigms and Peace Building Theories of Change: Analyzing Embedded Assumptions in Development and Peacebuilding." *Journal of Peacebuilding and Development* 5 (1): 65–80. doi:10.1080/15423166.2009.128586577324.

Johnson, Kris A., Dana Genya, Nicholas R. Jordan, Kathy J. Draeger, Anne Kapuscinski, Laura K. Schmitt Olabisi and Peter B. Reich. 2012. "Using Participatory Scenarios to Stimulate Social Learning for Collaborative Sustainable Development." *Ecology and Society* 17 (2): 9. http://dx.doi.org/10.5751/ES-04780-170209.

Katz, Neal H., John W. Lawyer and Marcia Sweedler. 2011. *Communication and Conflict Resolution Skills*. 2nd ed. Iowa City: Kendall/Hunt Publishing Company.

Kemmis, Stephen, and Robin McTaggart. 2000. "Participatory Action Research." In *Handbook of Qualitative Research*, 2nd ed., edited by Norman K. Denzin and Yyonnna S. Lincoln, 567–606. Thousand Oaks, CA: Sage Publications.

Kluckhohn, Florence R., and Fred L. Strodtbeck. 1961. *Variations in Value Orientations*. Evanston, IL: Row, Peterson.

Koelewijn, Cees. 2003. *Testament van Tamenta: 90 Verhalen en een Autobiografie van de Surinaamse Trio indiaan, ex Sjamaan en Meesterverteller Tamenta Wetaru*. Katwijk, The Netherlands: Van den Berg.

Komarraju, Meera, Stephen J. Dollinger and Jennifer L. Lovell. 2008. "Individualism-Collectivism in Horizontal and Vertical Directions as Predictors of Conflict Management Styles." *International Journal of Conflict Management* 19 (1): 20–35. http://dx.doi.org/10.1108/10444060810849164.

Kriesberg, Louise. 2003. *Constructive Conflicts: From Escalation to Resolution*. 2nd ed. Oxford, UK: Rowman & Littlefield.

Kritsanaphan, Amorn, and Edsel E. Sajor. 2011. "Intermediaries and Informal Interactions in Decentralized Environmental Management in Peri-Urban Bangkok." *International Development Planning Review* 33 (3): 247–71. doi:10.3828/idpr.2011.11.

Laidler, Gita J. 2006. "Inuit and Scientific Perspectives on the Relationship Between Sea Ice and Climate Change: The Ideal Complement?" *Climate Change* 78 (2–4): 407–44. doi:10.1007/s10584-006-9064-z.

Larson, Anne M. 2011. "Forest Tenure Reform in the Age of Climate Change: Lessons for REDD+." *Global Environmental Change* 21 (2): 540–49. http://dx.doi.org/10.1016/j.gloenvcha.2010.11.008.

Laszlo, Alexander, and Stanley Krippner. 1998. "Systems Theories: Their Origins, Foundations and Development." In *Systems Theories and A Priori Aspects of Perception*, edited by J. Scott Jordan, 47–74. Amsterdam: Elsevier Science.

Laukkonen, Julia, Paula Kim Blanco, Jennifer Lenhart, Marco Keiner, Marco, Branko Cavric and Cecilia Kinuthia-Njenga. 2009. "Combining Climtate Change Adaptation and Mitigation Measures." *Habitat International* 33 (3): 287–92. http://dx.doi.org/10.1016/j.habitatint.2008.10.003.

Lederach, John Paul. 1995. *Preparing for Peace: Conflict Transformation Across Cultures*. Syracuse, NY: Syracuse University Press.

———. 2003. *The Little Book of Conflict Transformation*. Intercourse, PA: Good Books.

Leiserowitz, Anthony. 2006. "Climate Change Risk Perception and Policy Preferences: The Role of Affect, Imagery and Values." *Climatic Change* 77 (1–2): 45–72. doi:10.1007/s10584-006-9059-9.

Lejano, Raul P., Joana Tavares and Fikret Berkes. 2011. "Climate Narratives: What Is Modern about Traditional Ecological Knowledge?" Unpublished manuscript. Portable Document File. http://socialecology.uci.edu/sites/socialecology.uci.edu/files/users/pdevoe/climatenarratives.pdf.

Leonard, Sonia, Meg Parsons, Knut Olawsky and Frances Kofod. 2013. "The Role of Culture and Traditional Knowledge in Climate Change Adaptation: Insights from East Kimberley, Australia." *Global Environmental Change* 23 (3): 623–32. http://dx.doi.org/10.1016/j.gloenvcha.2013.02.012.

Lewicky, Roy J., Bruce Barry and David M. Saunders. 2007. *Essentials of Negotiation.* 4th ed. New York: McGraw-Hill/Irwin.

Li, Ya, Zhichang Zhu and Catherine M. Gerard. 2012. "Learning from Conflict Resolution: An Opportunity to Systems Thinking." *Systems Research and Behavioral Science* 29 (2): 209–20. doi:10.1002/sres.2107.

Little, Paul E. 2005. "Indigenous Peoples and Sustainable Development Subprojects in Brazilian Amazonia: The Challenges of Interculturality." *Law and Policy* 27 (3): 450–96. http://ssrn.com/abstract=740678.

Locatelli, Bruno, Vanessa Evans, Andrew Wardell, Angela Andrade and Raffaele Vignola. 2011. "Forest and Climate Change in Latin America: Linking Adaptation and Mitigation." *Forests* 2 (1): 431–50. http://dx.doi.org/10.3390/f2010431.

Loomis, Terrence M. 2000. "Indigenous Populations and Sustainable Development: Building on Indigenous Approaches to Holistic, Self-Determined Development." *World Development* 28 (5): 893–910. http://dx.doi.org/10.1016/S0305-750X(99)00162-X.

Lu Holt, Flora. 2005. "The Catch-22 of Conservation: Indigenous Peoples, Biologist, and Cultural Change." *Human Ecology* 33 (2): 199–215. doi:10.1007/s10745-005-2432-X.

Mansuri, Ghazala, and Vijayendra Roa. 2004. "Community-Based and -Driven Development: A Critical Review." *World Bank Research Observer* 19 (1): 1–39. doi:10.1093/wbro/lkh012.

Martin, Adrienne, and John Sherington. 1997. "Participatory Research Methods— Implementation, Effectiveness and Institutional Context." *Agricultural Systems* 55 (2): 195–216. http://dx.doi.org/10.1016/S0308-521X(97)00007-3.

Marx, Sabine M., Elke U. Weber, Benjamin S. Orlove, Anthony Leiserowitz, David H. Krantz, Carla Roncoli and Jennifer Phillips. 2007. "Communication and Mental Processes: Experiential and Analytic Processing of Uncertain Climate Information." *Global Environmental Change* 17 (1): 47–58. http://dx.doi.org/10.1016/j.gloenvcha.2006.10.004.

Maslow, Abraham. 1943. "A Theory of Human Motivation." *Psychological Review* 50 (4): 370–96. doi: 10.1037/h0054346.

Mayer, Bernard S. 2004. *Beyond Neutrality: Confronting the Crisis in Conflict Resolution.* San Francisco: Jossey-Bass.

Mazzocchi, Fulvio. 2008. "Analyzing Knowledge as Part of a Cultural Framework: The Case of Traditional Ecological Knowledge." *Environments* 138 (2): 39–57.

Meckling, Jonas. 2011. "The Globalization of Carbon Trading: Transational Business Coalitions in Climate Politics." *Global Environmental Politics* 11 (2): 26–50. doi:10.1162/GLEP_a_00052.

Mejía, Daniel Abreu. 2010. "The Evolution of the Climate Change Regime: Beyond the North-South Divide?" Institut Catalá international per la Pau (ISIP) Working Paper 2010/6. http://dx.doi.org/10.2139/ssrn.1884192.

[CE: *Merriam-Webster Dictionary, s. v.* " territory", accessed September 15, 2016, http://www.merriam-webster.com/dictionary/territory.]

Metz, Bert, Ogunlade Davidson, Peter Bosch, Rutu Dave and Leo Meyer, eds. 2007. *Contribution of Working Group III to the Fourth Assessment Report of the Intergovernmental Panel on*

Climate Change. Cambridge, UK: IPCC. http://www.ipcc.ch/publications_and_data/ar4/wg3/en/contents.html.

Miller, Elmer S., ed. 1999. *Peoples of the Gran Chaco.* Westport, CT: Bergin and Garvey.

Mitchell, Christopher R. 1981. *The Structure of International Conflict.* London: Palgrave Macmillan.

Mitchell, Tom, and Simon Maxwell. 2010. "Defining Climate Compatible Development." Climate & Development Knowledge Network Policy Brief (November). http://cdkn.org/wp-content/uploads/2012/10/CDKN-CCD-Planning_english.pdf.

Moore, Christopher W. 2003. *The Mediation Process: Practical Strategies for Resolving Conflict.* 3rd ed. San Francisco: Jossey-Bass.

Moran, Emilio F. 1993. *Through Amazonian Eyes.* Iowa City: University of Iowa Press.

Nakashima, Douglas, Kirsty Galloway McLean, Hans Thulstrup, Ameyali Ramos Castillo and Jennifer Rubis, J. 2012. *Weathering Uncertainty: Traditional Knowledge for Climate Change Assessment and Adaptation.* Paris: UNESCO and Darwin. http://unesdoc.unesco.org/images/0021/002166/216613E.pdf.

Nelson, Kristen C., and Ben H. J. De Jong. 2003. "Making Global Initiatives Local Realities: Carbon Mitigation Projects in Chiapas, Mexico." *Global Environmental Change* 13 (1): 19–30. http://dx.doi.org/10.1016/S0959-3780(02)00088-2.

Nudler, Oscar. 1993. "In Search of a Theory of Conflict Resolution: Taking a New Look at World View Analysis." *Institute for Conflict Analysis and Resolution Newsletter* 5 (Summer): 1–5.

Nurmohamed, Riad. 2008. "The Impact of Climate Change and Climate Variability on the Water Resources in Suriname: A Case Study in the Upper-Suriname River Basin." PhD diss., Anton de Kom University of Suriname, Paramaribo.

O'Brien, Karen L., and Johanna Wolf. 2010. "A Values-Based Approach to Vulnerability and Adaptation to Climate Change." *WIREs Climate Change* 1 (2): 232–42. doi:10.1002/wcc.30.

O'Brien, Karen, Robin Leichenko, Ulka Kelkar, Henry Venema, Guro Aandahl, Heather Tompkins, Akram Javed, Suruchi Bhadwal, Stephan Barg, Lynn Nygaard and Jennifer West. 2004. "Mapping Vulnerability to Multiple Stressors: Climate Change and Globalization in India." *Global Environmental Change* 14 (4): 303–13. http://dx.doi.org/10.1016/j.gloenvcha.2004.01.001.

Ocklenburg, Sebastian, and Onur Güntürkün. 2012. "Hemispheric Asymmetries: The Comparative View." *Frontiers in Psychology* 3 (5). http://dx.doi.org/10.3389/fpsyg.2012.00005.

ODI (Overseas Development Institute). 1998. "The State of the International Humanatarian System" (news brief). Retrieved from http://www.odi.org/sites/odi.org.uk/files/odi-assets/publications-opinion-files/2624.pdf.

Oishi, Mikio. 1995. "Conflict Resolution and Development: A Case Study of Domestic Development and Related Conflicts in Malaysia." Master's thesis, University of Bradford.

O'Riordan, Timothy, and Andrew Jordan. 1999. "Institutions, Climate Change and Cultural Theory: Towards a Common Analytical Framework." *Global Environmental Change* 9 (2): 81–93. http://dx.doi.org/10.1016/S0959-3780(98)00030-2.

Oyama, Marcos D., and Carlos A. Nobre. 2003. "A New Climate-Vegetation Equilibrum State for Tropical South America." *Geophysical Research Letters* 30 (23). doi:10.1029/2003GI018600.

Özesmi, Uygar, and Stacy L. Özesmi. 2004. "Ecological Models Based on Peoples Knowledge: A Multi-step Fuzzy Cognitive Mapping Approach." *Ecological Modelling* 176 (1–2): 43–64. http://dx.doi.org/10.1016/j.ecolmodel.2003.10.027.

Parker, Charlie, Andrew W. Mitchell, Mandar Trevidi and Niki Mardas. 2009. *The Little REDD+ Book: An Updated Guide to Governmental and Non-Governmental Proposals for Reducing*

Emission from Deforestation and Degradation. http://theredddesk.org/sites/default/files/lrb_en.pdf.

Parlee, Brenda, and Fikret Berkes. 2006. "Indigenous Knowledge of Ecological Variability and Commons Management: A Case Study on Berry Harvesting from Northern Canada." *Human Ecology: An Interdisciplinary Journal* 34 (4): 515–29. http://www.jstor.org/stable/27654137.

Parry, Martin L., Osvaldo Canziani, Jean Palutikof, Paul Van der Linden and Clair Hansen, eds. 2007. *Climate Change 2007: Impacts, Adaptation and Vulnerability. Contribution of Working Group II to the Fourth Assessment Report of the IPCC.* Cambridge, UK: IPCC. http://www.ipcc.ch/publications_and_data/ar4/wg2/en/.

Parsons, Talbot. 2003. "The Functional Prerequisites of Social Systems." In *Social Theory: Roots and Branches: Readings,* 2nd ed., edited by Peter Kivisto, 188–93. Belmont, CA: Roxbury Publishing Company.

Pennesi, Karen Elizabeth. 2007. "The Predicament of Prediction: Rain Prophets and Meteorologist in Northeast Brazil." PhD diss., University of Arizona. http://anthropology.uwv.ca/pennesi/predicament.pdf.

Petheram, Lisa, Natasha Stacey, Bruce M. Campbell and Christ High. 2012. "Using Visual Products Derived from Community Research to Inform Natural Resource Management Policy." *Land Use Policy* 29 (1): 1–10. http://dx.doi.org/10.1016/j.landusepol.2011.04.002.

Petheram, Lisa, Kerstin Zander, Bruce Campbell, C. High and Natasha Stacey. 2010. "'Strange Changes': Indigenous Perspectives of Climate Change and Adaptation in NE Arnhem Land (Australia)." *Global Environmental Change* 20 (4): 681–92. http://dx.doi.org/10.1016/j.gloenvcha.2010.05.002.

Pickerill, Jenny. 2009. "Finding Common Ground? Spaces of Dialogue and the Negotiation of Indigenous Interests in Environmental Campaigns in Australia." *Geoforum* 40 (1): 66–79. http://dx.doi.org/10.1016/j.geoforum.2008.06.009.

Pierotti, Raymond. 2011. *Indigenous Knowledge, Ecology, and Evolutionary Biology.* London: Routledge.

Pierotti, Raymond, and Daniel Wildcat. 2000. "Traditional Ecological Knowledge: The Third Alternative." *Ecological Applications* 10 (5): 1333–40. http://dx.doi.org/10.1890/1051-0761(2000)010%5B1333:TEKTTA%5D2.0.CO;2.

Probst, Kirsten, Jürgen Hagmann, Thomas Becker and Maria Fernandez. 2000. "Developing a Framework for Participatory Research Approaches in Risk Prone Diverse Environments." *Proceedings of Deutscher Tropentag,* University of Hohenheim, Stuttgart, Germany, 2000.

Pruitt, Dean G., and Sung Hee Kim. 2004. *Social Conflict: Escalation, Stalemate, and Settlement.* New York: McGraw-Hill.

Putnam, Robert D. 1993. *Making Democracy Work: Civic Traditions in Modern Italy.* Princeton, NJ: Princeton University Press.

Rahim, Hardy Loh, Zanariah Zainel Abidin, Selina Dang Siew Ping, Mohamed Khaidir Alias and Azim Izzuddin Muhamad. 2014. "Globalization and Its Effects on World Poverty and Inequality." *Global Journal of Management and Business* 1 (2): 9–13.

RAISG (Cartographer). 2012. "Amazononia Under Pressure." Amazonia Network of Georeferenced Socio-Environmental Information. http://issuu.com/instituto-socioambiental/docs/amazonia_under_pressure/3?e=3045194/2467865.

Ramirez-Gomez, Sara O. I., Gregory G. Brown and Annette Tjon Sie Fat. 2013. "Participatory Mapping with Indigenous Communities for Conservation: Challenges and Lessons from Suriname." *Electronic Journal of Information Systems in Developing Countries* 58 (2): 1–22. http://www.ejisdc.org/ojs2/index.php/ejisdc/article/view/1164.

Restrepo, Gloria. 2005. "Una Aproximación Cultural al Concepto de Territorio." *Biblioteca Virtual Banco de la República.* http://www.lablaa.org/blaavirtual/letra-a/aprox/1.htm.

Restrepo, Gloria, and Alvaro César Velasco. 1998. *Cartografía Social.* Santafé de Bogotá: Instituto Geográfico Agustín Codazzi.

Restrepo, Gloria, Alvaro César Velasco and J. C. Preciado. 1999. "Cartografía Social." In *Tierra Nostra: Especialización en Gestión de Proyectos,* no. 5. Tunja, Colombia: Universidad Pedagógica y Tecnológica de Colombia.

Ricketts, Taylor H., Britaldo Soares-Filho, Gustavo A. G. da Fonseca, Daniel Nepstad, Alexander Pfaff, Annie Petsonk, Anthony Anderson, Doug Boucher, Andrea Cattaneo, Marc Conte, Ken Creighton, Lawrence Linden, Claudio Maretti, Paulo Moutinho, Roger Ullman and Ray Victurine. 2010. "Indigenous Lands, Protected Areas, and Slowing Climate Change." *PLoS Biology* 8 (3). doi:10.1371/journal.pbio.1000331.

Ring, Irene., Martin Drechsler, Astrid J. A. Van Teeffelen, Silvia Irawan and Oscar Venter. 2010. "Biodiversity Conservation and Climate Mitigation: What Role Can Economic Instruments Play?" *Current Opinion in Environmental Sustainability* 2 (1–2): 50–58. http://dx.doi.org/10.1016/j.cosust.2010.02.004.

Ritzer, George. 2008. *Sociological Theory.* 7th ed. New York: McGraw-Hill.

Robards, Martin D., Michael L. Schoon, Chanda L. Meek and Nathan L. Engle. 2011. "The Importance of Social Drivers in the Resilient Provision of Ecosystem Services." *Global Environmental Change* 21 (2): 522–29. http://dx.doi.org/10.1016/j.gloenvcha.2010.12.004.

Roberts, J. Timmons, and Bradley C. Parks. 2007. *A Climate of Injustice: Global Inequality, North-South Politics, Climate Policy.* Cambridge, MA: MIT Press.

Roncoli, Carla. 2006. "Ethnographic and Participatory Approaches to Research on Farmers' Responses to Climate Predictions." *Climate Research* 33 (1): 81–99. doi:10.3354/cr033081.

Root, Terry L., Jeff T. Price, Kimberly R. Hall, Stephen H. Schneider, Cynthia Rosenzweig and J. Allan Pounds. 2003. "Fingerprints of Global Warming on Animals and Plants." *Nature* 421, 57–60. doi:10.1038/nature01333.

Rubin, Olivier. 2010. "Social Perspective on the Symbiotic Relationship between Climate Change and Conflict." *Social Development Issues* 32 (2): 29–41.

Salomon, Frank, and Stuart B. Schwartz. 1999. *The Cambridge History of Native Peoples of the Americas* (vol. 3, part 2). http://dx.doi.org/10.1017/CHOL9780521630764.001.

Schmink, Marianne, Susan Paulson and Elena Bastidas, eds. 2002. *Learning to MERGE.* Unpublished book. Gainesville: University of Florida. http://www.tcd.ufl.edu/Data/Sites/44/media/documents/merge%20program/LearningtoMERGE8-2011.pdf.

Sen, Amartya. 1999. *Development as Freedom.* New York: Anchor Books.

Sharoni, Simona. 1996, August. "Rethinking Conflict Resolution: Historical Overview, Contemporary Trends and New Directions." Paper presented at the Fourth Annual Seminar of the International University of People's Institutions for Peace, Rovereto, Italy.

Sheppard, Stephen R. J., Alison Shaw, David Flanders, Sarah Burch, Arnim Wiek, Jeff Carmicheal, John Robinson and Stewart Cohen. 2011. "Future Visioning of Local Climate Change: A Framework for Community Engagement and Planning with Scenarios and Visualisation." *Futures* 43 (4): 400–12. http://dx.doi.org/10.1016/j.futures.2011.01.009.

Sikor, Thomas, Johannes Stahl, Thomas Enters, Jesse C. Ribot, Nerra Singh, William D. Sunderlin and Lini Wollenberg. 2010. "REDD-Plus, Forest People's Rights and Nested Climate Governance." *Global Environmental Change* 20 (3): 423–25. http://dx.doi.org/10.1016/j.gloenvcha.2010.04.007.

Sletto, Bjørn, Joe Bryan, Marla Torrado, Charles Hale and Deborah Barry. 2013. "Territorialidad, Mapeo Participativo y Política Sobre los Recursos Naturales: La Experiencia de América Latina." *Cuadernos de Geografía: Revista Colombiana de Geografía* 22 (2): 193–209. http://www.scielo.org.co/scielo.php?script=sci_arttext&pid=S0121-215X2013000200011&lng=en&tlng=.

Slimak, Michael W., and Thomas Dietz. 2006. "Personal Values, Beliefs and Ecological Risk Perception." *Risk Analysis* 26 (6): 1689–705. doi:10.1111/j.1539-6924.2006.00832.x.

Smit, Barry, and Johanna Wandel. 2006. "Adaptation, Adaptive Capacity and Vulnerability." *Global Environmental Change* 16 (3): 282–92. http://dx.doi.org/10.1016/j.gloenvcha.2006.03.008.

Smith, Gwendolyn. 2006. *Indigenous Workshop on Environmental and Social Impact Assessment.* Kwamalasamutu, Suriname: Amazon Conservation Team Suriname.

———. 2010a. "Carbon-Based Conservation Projects in Ecuador and Suriname: An Analysis of Vulnerability and Conflict Potential." *Peace and Conflict Review* 5 (1): 1–10. http://www.review.upeace.org/pdf.cfm?articulo=109&ejemplar=20.

———. 2010b. "Planet or Profit: Remodeling the Climate Change Negotiations." *Journal of Alternative Perspectives in Social Sciences* 2 (1): 28–45. http://www.japss.org/upload/2._Gwendolyn%5B1%5D.pdf.

———. 2013. "Participation of the Trio Indigenous Community in Climate Change Mitigation Projects in Suriname: A Worldview Conflict Analysis." PhD diss., Nova Southeastern University.

Smith, Gwendolyn, and Karin Lachmising. 2012. *Summary Report of the Stakeholder Engagement Process for the R-PP Formulation Project.* Paramaribo, Suriname: Attune.

———. 2013. *Final Report of the Facilitation Team Assignment for the R-PP Formulation Project.* Paramaribo, Suriname: Attune.

Smith, Gwendolyn, Karin Lachmising, Rachelle Bong A Jan and Dan Fullerton. 2012. *The Indigenous Park Ranger Program 2008–2012.* Paramaribo, Suriname: Amazon Conservation Team Suriname.

Smith, Gwendolyn, Gina Marie Michaud, Susana Bertuna Reynoso and Pamela Kay Struss. 2014. "MAPCID: A Model for the Analysis of Potential Conflict in Development." *Journal of Conflict Management* 2 (1): 7–32. http://jocm.net/v2/no.1/2014v2n1_smith.pdf.

Smith, Gwendolyn, and Melvin Uiterloo. 2007. *The Story of the Indigenous Medicine Clinics in Suriname: A Model for Complementing Conventional Healthcare in Remote Areas.* Paramaribo, Suriname: Amazon Conservation Team Suriname.

Smith, Linda Tuhiwai. 1999. *Decolonizing Methodologies: Research and Indigenous Peoples.* New York: Zed Books and University of Tago Press.

Sperry, R.W. 1961. "Cerebral Organization and Behavior." *Science* 133 (3466): 1749–57. doi:10.1126/science.133.3466.1749

Stephan, Benjamin. 2012. "Bringing Discourse to the Market: The Commodification of Avoided Deforestation." *Environmental Politics* 21 (4): 621–39. doi:10.1080/09644016.2012.688357.

Stern, Nicholas H. 2007. *The Economics of Climate Change.* http://webarchive.nationalarchives.gov.uk/+/http://www.hm-treasury.gov.uk/stern_review_report.htm.

Stone, Susan, and Mario Chacón León, M. 2010. *Climate Change and the Role of Forests: A Community Manual.* Washington, DC: Conservation International and Iwokrama. http://www.conservation.org/publications/Documents/redd/CI_Climate_Change_and_the_Role_of_Forests_Community_Manual.pdf.

Sutton, Stephen G., and Renae C. Tobin. 2011. "Constraints in Community Engagement with Great Barrier Reef Climate Change Reduction and Mitigation." *Global Environmental Change* 21(3): 894–905. http://dx.doi.org/10.1016/j.gloenvcha.2011.05.006.

Tannen, Deborah. 1986. *That's Not What I Meant! How Conversational Style Makes or Breaks Relationships.* New York: Random House.

Tebtebba. 2012. *Indigenous Peoples Release Rio +20 Declaration.* http://www.tebtebba.org/index.php/content/220-indigenous-peoples-release-rio-20-declaration.

Teunissen, Peter, Dirk Noordam and Fritz Van Troon. 2003. *Ecological Survey of the Lands Inhabited/Used by the Trio People of Suriname: Physical and Biological Resources, Their Current Use, and Recommendations for a Development Plan.* Paramaribo, Suriname: Amazon Conservation Team Suriname.

Thomas, David S. G., and Chasca Twyman. 2005. "Equity and Justice in Climate Change Adaptation amongst Natural-Resource-Dependent Societies." *Climate Change* 15 (2): 115–24. http://dx.doi.org/10.1016/j.gloenvcha.2004.10.001.

Ting-Toomey, Stella. 2001. "Toward a Theory of Conflict and Culture." In *The Conflict and Culture Reader*, edited by Pat K. Chew, 46–51. New York: New York University Press.

Triandis, Harry C., Christopher McCusker and C. Harry Hui. 2001. "Multimethod Probes of Individualism and Collectivism. In *The Conflict and Culture Reader*, edited by Pat K. Chew, 52–56. New York: New York University Press.

Tucker, Catherine M., Hallie Eatin and Edwin J. Castellanos. 2010. "Perceptions of Risk and Adaptation: Coffee Producers, Market Shocks and Extreme Weather in Central America and Mexico." *Global Environmental Change* 20 (1): 23–32. http://dx.doi.org/10.1016/j.gloenvcha.2009.07.006.

Turner, Nancy J., and Helen Clifton. 2009. " 'It's So Different Today': Climate Change and Indigenous Lifeways in British Columbia, Canada." *Global Environmental Change* 19 (2): 180–90. http://dx.doi.org/10.1016/j.gloenvcha.2009.01.005.

Uiterloo, Melvin. (Cartographer). 2011. *Kwamalasamutu Deforestation Map 1987–2009.* Paramaribo, Suriname: Amazon Conservation Team Suriname.

UNESCO (United Nations Educational, Scientific and Cultural Organization). 2008. *United Nations Declaration on the Rights of Indigenous Peoples.* http://www.un.org/esa/socdev/unpfii/documents/DRIPS_en.pdf.

United Nations. 2004. "The Concept of Indigenous Peoples." Background Paper prepared for United Nations Workshop on Data Collection and Disaggregation for Indigenous Peoples. United Nations Department of Economic and Social Affairs, January 19–21, New York.

———. 2009. "State of the World's Indigenous Peoples." http://www.un.org/esa/socdev/unpfii/documents/SOWIP/en/SOWIP_web.pdf.

———. 2011. "Kari-Oca2 Declaration: The World Conference of Indigenous Peoples on Territory, Environment and Development." http://www.uncsd2012.org/index.php?page=view&nr=892&type=230&menu=38.

UN-REDD Programme (United Nations Programme on Reducing Emissions from Deforestation and Forest Degradation). 2009. "About the UN-REDD Programme." http://www.un-redd.org/AboutUN-REDDProgramme/tabid/102613/Default.aspx.

UNU (United Nations University). 2012. "Climate Change Mitigation with Local Communities and Indigenous Peoples: Practices, Lessons Learned and Prospects." *Workshop Meeting Report Institute of Advanced Studies: Traditional Knowledge Initiative.* Cairns, Australia: United Nations University. http://www.unutki.org/default.php?doc_id=226.

Ury, William. 2000. *The Third Side: Why We Fight and How We Can Stop*. New York: Penguin Books.

van Aalst, Maartin K., Terry Cannon and Ian Burton. 2008. "Community Level Adaptation to Climate Change: The Potential Role of Participating Community Risk Assessment." *Global Environmental Change* 18 (1): 165–79.

Velasco, Alvaro César. 2012. *El Resurgimiento de las Culturas Raizales: Territorialidades y Lenguajes Emergentes*. Bogotá: FUNDAMINGA. https://docs.google.com/file/d/0B9ovZIH4Tt2 vVWVYNzNfVGNUdnVLc11OYWhqVWNuZw/edit?pli=1

Von Stein, Jana. 2008. "The International Law and Politics of Climate Change: Ratification of the United Nations Framework Convention and the Kyoto Protocol." *Journal of Conflict Resolution* 52 (2): 243–68. doi: 10.1177/0022002707313692.

Walker, Gordan. 2011. "The Role of Community in Forest Governance." *Wiley Interdisciplinary Reviews: Climate Change* 2 (5): 777–82.

Weber, Elke U. 2006. "Experience-Based and Description-Based Perceptions of Long-Term Risk: Why Global Warning Does Not Scare Us (Yet)." *Climate Change* 77 (1–2): 103–20. doi:10.1007/s10584-006-9060-3.

Weeks, Dudley. 1992. *The Eight Essential Steps to Conflict Resolution: Preserving Relationships at Work, at Home, and in the Community*. New York: Putnam's Sons, Inc.

Wehr, Paul. 1979. *Conflict Regulation*. Boulder, CO: Westview Press.

Wilshusen, Peter R., Steven R. Brechin, Crystal L. Fortwangler and Patrick C. West. 2002. "Reinventing a Square Wheel: Critique of a Resurgent 'Protection Paradigm' in International Biodiversity Conservation." *Society and Natural Resources* 15 (1): 17–40. doi:10.1080/089419202317174002.

Winslade, John, and Gerald Monk. 2001. *Narrative Mediation: A New Approach to Conflict Resolution*. New York: Jossey-Bass.

Wolf, Johanna, Ilana Allice and Trevor Bell. 2013. "Values, Climate Change, and Implications from Adaptation: Evidence from Two Communities in Labrador, Canada." *Global Environmental Change* 23 (2): 548–62. http://dx.doi.org/10.1016/j.gloenvcha.2012.11.007.

Wolf, Johanna, and Susanne C. Moser. 2011. "Individual Understandings, Perceptions and Engagement with Climate Change: Insights from In-Depth Studies Across the World." *Wiley Interdisciplinary Reviews: Climate Change* 2 (4): 547–69. doi:10.1002/wcc.120.

World Bank. 2013. *Building Resilience: Integrating Climate and Disaster Risk into Development*. Washington, DC: International Bank for Reconstruction and Development/The World Bank.

Yeganeh, Hamid. 2011. "The 'Great Satan' talks with the 'Evil'": A Cross Cultural Analysis of the American-Iranian Communication/Negotiation Styles. *International Journal of Conflict Management* 22 (3): 219–38.

Yin, Robert K. 2009. *Case Study Research: Design and Methods*. 4th ed. Thousand Oaks, CA: Sage.

INDEX

accountability
  researchers and 162–64
  for sustainable development 3
acultural projects 15–16
adaptation
  climate change, adaptation strategies for 21, 157
  meaning-making by Trio peoples, adaptation strategies 126–27
  researchers and 164
  vulnerability and adaptation framework 30–32
Agrawal, Arun 81
Akanopatoro (tree) as seasonal indicator 116–17
anthropological background of Trio peoples 85–87
attitudes 141–42
avoidance among Trio peoples 93–94
Avruch, Kevin 154–55

BASIC countries 19–20
basic human needs of Trio peoples 157
Bastidas, Elena 25, 61
"being" ethic 141
Berkes, Fikret 5, 6, 11, 15–16, 32, 54, 116, 125–26, 129, 136
Black, Peter W 154–55
Branch Davidians 44
Brundtland Commission 2, 149
Byg, Anja 32

capability framework 36–37
Carpenter, Susan L 51–52, 110, 135, 141, 152
Chambers, Robert 6–7
Christianity, Trio peoples and 90–91

climate change
  adaptation strategies 21, 157
  bad behavior and 128–29
  BASIC countries and 19–20
  construction of community views, effect on 49–50
  Copenhagen negotiations 19–20
  deforestation and 21
  effects of 20
  emissions trading and 21–22
  Framework Convention on Climate Change 2, 19
  Intergovernmental Panel on Climate Change 21, 23
  least developed countries (LDC) and 19–20
  meaning-making by Trio peoples and 126–27, 128–29, 131–32
  mitigation strategies 20–21, 157
  "Northern view" 19, 20
  overview 18–19
  Paris negotiations 19–20
  punishment and 128–29
  REDD+ and 66
  "Southern view," 19, 20
  Trio peoples, views of 150
  VIEW framework and 61–62, 65, 66
comanagement 6
common consciousness 129
communication
  alternative forms of 81–82
  community views and 154
  researchers and 165–66
community-based conservation 5
community views
  awareness and 154–55
  bridging differences in views 152–53

community views (*cont.*)
  communication and 154
  cooperation, establishing 154–55
  holism 153
  model for working with 157–59
  narrative and 157–59
  negotiation and 157–59
  overview 26, 149
  participation 155–57
  policymakers, recommendations for
    168–69
  promoting sustainability under
    uncertainty 149–50
  shared goals 153–54, 157
  social learning and 155
  trust 154–55
  VIEW framework and 151
Conference on the Human
  Environment (UN) 1
conflict resolution framework
  characteristics of 40
  context-specific nature of 41
  differences versus similarities in 42
  hidden values 42–43
  holistic nature of 40–41
  MAPCID model and 41
  narrative analysis and 44
  Nudler model of 44–45, 61
  overview 37–40, 43–45
  power disparities 41
  "pro-poor" participation and 39
  systems approach of 40
cooperation 154–55
cultural and social relations map 74
cultural background of Trio peoples 87–88

Declaration of the Rights of Indigenous
  Peoples (UN) 161
deforestation 21
development organizations
  assistance from 157
  attitudes, conflicts with Trio
    peoples 141–42
  feedback from 157
  interests, conflicts with Trio peoples 138
  participation with 6–8
  scientific capacity 11
  social capital and 7–8

  strategies, conflicts with Trio peoples
    141–40
  sustainable development, view of 6–11
  technical capacity 9–10
  values, conflicts with Trio peoples
    138–39
development paradigm 62–66
Development Program (UN) 1
development-related values of Trio
  peoples 99–104
"development with conservation" model 4
Dietz, Thomas 88
discourse in VIEW framework 57, 59–60
Docherty, Jane Seminare 44
"doing" ethic 141
dominant projects 16–17
Durkheim, Émile 1, 129

economic growth paradigm
  overview 149
  sustainable development in 3
ecosystem services map 13
education of Trio peoples 102, 157
Ëkui aki (insect) as seasonal
  indicator 115–16
emissions trading 21–22
environmentalists, perspective of 29–30
environment-related values of Trio
  peoples 95–99
equality, researchers and 161–62
esteem needs 138
ethics, researchers and 160–61

Fals-Borda, Orlando 69–70, 84
Federal Bureau of Investigation (US) 44
feedback from development
  organizations 157
"feminine" culture 141
food security 15
forest health as seasonal indicator 119–20
Framework Convention on Climate
  Change (UN) 2, 19
Free and Prior Informed Consent 17–18
Freire, Paulo 73
frogs
  as seasonal indicator 117–18
FUNDAMINGA Foundation
  67–68, 77–78

future maps 76
fuzzy, projects seen as overly 17–18

Gitga'at peoples 32
goals for sustainable development 55

Habermas, Jürgen 3, 110
historical background of Trio peoples 87
historical maps 75–76
holism
    community views and 153
    conflict resolution framework 40–41
    REDD+ and 153

income of Trio peoples 102, 157
indigenous peoples
    acultural projects 15–16
    comanagement 6
    community-based conservation 5
    conservation versus development and 5
    construction of community views 47–48
    destruction of environment 5
    "development with conservation" model 4
    forest nuts 10
    fuzzy projects 17–18
    local reality of 54
    narrow projects 14–15
    pepper products and 165
    photography and 162
    radios and 7
    REDD+ and 24–25
    short projects 12–13
    souvenirs and 28
    sustainable development, view of 11–18
    tourism projects and 14
    Trio peoples (*See* Trio peoples)
    water and 63
information selection in VIEW framework
    57, 58–59
interests, conflicts affecting sustainable
    decision making 136–38
Intergovernmental Panel on Climate Change
    21, 23
International Development Department
    (UK) 35

judgment against values in VIEW framework
    57–58

Karau Alawata (plant) as seasonal
    indicator 119
Kennedy, William J. D 51–52, 110, 135,
    141, 152
Kriesberg, Louis 153
Kuweimë (snail) as seasonal indicator 120–21

language, Trio peoples and 103
least developed countries (LDC) 19–20
leaves, shedding of as temporal
    indicator 122–23
Lederach, John Paul 41
life stories 50–51
livelihood among Trio peoples 96–97
local reality of indigenous peoples 54

MAPCID model 41
mapping phase of social polygraphy 72–77
    cultural and social relations map 74
    future maps 76
    historical maps 75–76
    infrastructure maps 74
    people and nature maps 73–74
    present maps 75–76
"Masculine" culture 141
Maslow, Abraham 138
meaning-making
    overview 52–54
    in VIEW framework 52–54
meaning-making by Trio peoples
    adaptation strategies 126–27
    agricultural plots and 123
    Akanopatoro and 116–17
    bad behavior and 128–29
    climate change and 126–27,
        128–29, 131–32
    Ëkui aki and 115–16
    forest health and 119–20
    frogs and 117–18
    Karau Alawata and 119
    Kuweimë and 120–21
    leaves, shedding of 122–23
    microclimate and 120–21
    overview 26, 109–10
    Poko Poko and 115
    punishment and 128–29
    rainy season and 116–18
    scorpions and 118

meaning-making by Trio peoples (*cont.*)
  seasonal indicators 111–21, 112t6.2
  soil health and 119
  stars and 123
  survival, rules for 125–26
  sustainable development and 133–34
  Tamo and 119–20
  temporal indicators 122–24
  VIEW framework, application of 129–33
  water levels and 123–24
Miriwoong peoples 32–33, 128
mitigation strategies for climate change
      20–21, 157
Moken peoples 30
Monk, Gerald 158
multidisciplinary teams 82–83
rutual learning 81

narrative, community views and 157–59
narrative analysis 44
narrow projects 14–15
needs assessments 62–63
negative identity of Trio peoples 103
negotiation 157–59
"Northern view," 19, 20
Nudler, Oscar 44–45, 61

Organization for Economic Cooperation
      and Development 20

participation
  community views and 155–57
  with development organizations 6–8
participatory action research (PAR) 69–70
past maps 75–76
people and nature maps 73–74
physiological needs 138
Pierotti, Raymond 4–5, 11, 24, 53, 122,
      124, 125
Poko Poko (insect) as seasonal indicator 115
policymakers, recommendations for 168–69
present maps 75–76
"projectism," 9–10
"pro-poor" participation 39, 159

rainy season as seasonal indicator 116–18
REDD+
  attitudes, conflicting 141–42

awareness and 154–55
bridging differences in views and 152–53
climate change and 66
dominant projects 16–17
facilitation 65
holism 153
indigenous peoples and 24–25
participation 155–57
policymakers, recommendations
      for 168–69
rigidity of 65
social learning and 155
strategies, conflicting 140
Surui peoples and 51
sustainable decision making by Trio
      peoples and 135, 146–47
uncertainty, sustainable decision making
      under 142–45
values, conflicting 138–39
REDD Programme (UN) 23
reducing emissions from deforestation and
      forest degradation (REDD) 23
religion among Trio peoples 90–91
researchers
  accountability and 162–64
  adaptation and 164
  communication and 165–66
  equality and 161–62
  ethics and 160–61
  meaning-making 61
  self-transformation of 159
  social learning and 166
  sustainable decision making 61
  time sensitivity and 166–68
  values 61
  VIEW framework 60–61, 62t3.1
Restrepo, Gloria 68, 72
Robles, social polygraphy in 79–80

Salick, Jan 32
"saving face" among Trio peoples 92
scientific capacity 11
scorpions as seasonal indicator 118
seasonal indicators of Trio peoples 111–21
  Akanopatoro as 116–17
  Ëkui aki as 115–16
  forest health as 119–20
  frogs as 117–18

Karau Alawata as 119
Kuweimë as 120–21
Poko Poko as 115
rainy season as 116–18
scorpions as 118
soil health as 119
Tamo as 119–20
security needs 138
self-transformation of researchers 159
Sen, Amartya 36–37
Shamans 48, 90–91, 101–02
shared goals, creating 153–54, 157
short projects 12–13
Slimak, Michael W 88
Smith, Gwendolyn 3, 5, 35–36, 39–40,
        41, 42, 56, 90–91, 95, 98, 101–02,
        103, 111, 115–16, 117–18, 119,
        120–21, 124, 127, 128, 129, 139,
        143–44, 154–57
social behavior-related values of Trio
        peoples 92–95
social capital 7–8
social cartography (*See* social polygraphy)
social learning
    community views and 155
    REDD+ and 155
    researchers and 166
social needs 138
social organization 8–9
social polygraphy
    alternative forms of communication 81–82
    conceptual basis of 68–71
    cultural and social relations map 74
    data interpretation phase 77–78
    defined 67–68, 70
    diagnosis phase 71–72
    enhancing partnerships in 83–84
    future maps 76
    historical maps 75–76
    infrastructure maps 74
    limitations of 80–81
    mapping phase 72–77
    methodological basis of 68–71
    multidisciplinary teams and 82–83
    mutual learning and 81
    overview 25, 61, 67
    participatory action research (PAR)
        and 69–70

people and nature maps 73–74
present maps 75–76
theoretical basis of 68–71
soil health as seasonal indicator 119
"Southern view," 19, 20
stars as temporal indicator 123
Stern, Nicholas 22–23
Stern Review 23
strategies, conflicts affecting sustainable
        decision making 141–40
Surui peoples 51
sustainable decision making
    overview 54–56
    researchers 61
    in VIEW framework 54–56
sustainable decision making by Trio peoples
    attitudes 141–42
    conflicting views 135–42, 137t7.1
    discourse 142–45, 146
    interests 136–38
    overview 26, 135
    REDD+ and 135, 146–47
    strategies 141–40
    uncertainty, under 142–45
    values 136–38
    VIEW framework 145–47
sustainable development
    accountability for 3
    community views and
        (*See* Community views)
    defined 2
    development organizations, view of 6–11
    discourse toward 59–60
    in economic growth paradigm 3
    global level 3
    goals, defining 55
    historical background 1–2
    indigenous peoples, view of 11–18
    local level 3
    meaning-making by Trio peoples
        and 133–34
    values of Trio peoples and 107–08
sustainable livelihood framework 35–36, 37

Tamo (tree) as seasonal indicator 119–20
temporal indicators of Trio peoples 122–24
    agricultural plots as 123
    leaves, shedding of as 122–23

temporal indicators of Trio peoples (*cont.*)
  stars as 123
  water levels as 123–24
Thailand tsunami (2004) 30
theoretical frameworks of research
  capability framework 36–37
  conflict resolution framework
    (*See* Conflict resolution framework)
  development specialists, perspective
    of 33–35
  environmentalists, perspective of 29–30
  overview 25, 27–29
  sustainable livelihood framework
    35–36, 37
  traditional ecological knowledge
    framework 32–33
  VIEW framework (*See* VIEW
    framework)
  vulnerability and adaptation
    framework 30–32
threats to land, Trio peoples and 97–99
time sensitivity, researchers and 166–68
Tjafel, Henri 103
togetherness among Trio peoples 89–90
traditional ecological knowledge
  framework 32–33
Trio peoples
  anthropological background 85–87
  apocalypse and 128
  basic human needs of 157
  Christianity and 90–91
  climate change, views of 150
  cultural background 87–88
  frogs and 167
  historical background 87
  language and 103
  lightning and 105–06
  luxuries and 101
  meaning-making by (*See* Meaning-
    making by Trio peoples)
  rangers and 168
  sustainable decision making by
    (*See* Sustainable decision making by
    Trio peoples)
  tourism projects and 104
  values of (*See* Values of Trio peoples)
trust, establishing 154–55
Turner, John 103

United Kingdom, International
  Development Department 35
United Nations
  Conference on the Human
    Environment 1
  conflict resolution framework and 38
  Declaration of the Rights of Indigenous
    Peoples 161
  Framework Convention on Climate
    Change 2, 19
  REDD Programme 23
United States
  emissions trading and 21–22
  Federal Bureau of Investigation 44

values
  conflicts affecting sustainable decision
    making 136–38
  judgment against 57–58
  overview 51–52
  researchers 61
  in VIEW framework 51–52
values of Trio peoples
  accommodation 103
  avoidance 93–94
  collective-related values 88–91
  development-related values 99–104
  education 102, 157
  environment-related values 95–99
  income 102, 157
  livelihood 96–97
  mining as threat to 98
  negative identity 103
  overview 26, 85, 150
  religion 90–91
  "saving face," 92
  social behavior-related values 92–95
  sustainable development and 107–08
  threats to land and 97–99
  togetherness 89–90
  VIEW framework, application of 104–07
Velasco, Alvaro César 77–78
VIEW framework
  climate change-related development
    and 61–62
  community views and 151
  conflicting views in climate change
    and 65, 66

development paradigm 62–66
discourse in 57, 59–60
information selection in 57, 58–59
judgment against values in 57–58
life stories and 50–51
meaning-making by Trio peoples,
    application to 129–33
meaning-making in 52–54
overview 25, 47, 57
policymakers, recommendations
    for 168–69
researchers 60–61, 62t3.1

sustainable decision making by Trio
    peoples, application to 145–47
sustainable decision making in 54–56
values in 51–52
values of Trio peoples, application to 104–07
vulnerability and adaptation
    framework 30–32

water levels as temporal indicator 123–24
Winslade, John 158
Wolf, Johanna 31–32
World Bank 1, 20, 38, 65, 143–44

www.ingramcontent.com/pod-product-compliance
Lightning Source LLC
Chambersburg PA
CBHW030836300326
41935CB00036B/230